Essentials of Marketing Management

Essentials of Marketing Management

Dr. Mithun Nandy

CRESCENT
PUBLISHING CORPORATION

Essentials of Marketing Management

Edition : 2026

ISBN 978-81-949754-5-8

Published by:

CRESCENT PUBLISHING CORPORATION

4806/24, Mathur Lane,
Ansari Road, Darya Ganj,
New Delhi - 110 002
Ph.: 011 - 23244131
Mob.: + 91 - 9711991838, 9999021668
E-mail: crescentbook@gmail.com
Website: www.crescentpublishingcorp.weebly.com

Printed at:

Roshan Offset Printers

Delhi

PRINTED IN INDIA

MEMORABLE MOMENT

Dr. Mithun Nandy during receiving his Degree of Doctor of Philosophy (Ph.D.) in Management from Shri Jagdeep Dhankhar, Hon'ble Governor of West Bengal State in Twenty First (21st) Convocation Ceremony of Vidyasagar University, Midnapore, West Bengal, India dated 29th September 2019 (Sunday).

Dedicated to
My respected Maa (Mother) Smt. Ila Nandy
and
Baba (Father) Shri Swapan Kumar Nandy
who have sacrificed their whole life in my upbringing and provided me enormous freedom to chase my colourful dreams.

Preface

Marketing management facilitates the important activities and functions which are connected in the distribution of different goods and services to the end users. According to Philip Kotler, "Marketing management is the analysis, planning, implementation and control of programmes designed to bring about desired exchanges with target markets for the purpose of achieving organisational objectives. It relies heavily on designing the organisations offering in terms of the target markets needs and desires and using effective pricing, communication and distribution to inform, motivate and service the market." Marketing management is concerned with the chalking out of a definite programme, after careful analysis and forecasting of the market situations and the ultimate execution of these plans to achieve the objectives of the organisation. Further, the business plans of the corporate organizations to a greater extent rest upon the requirements and motives of the consumers in the market. To achieve this objective, the organisation has to pay attention to the right pricing, effective advertising and sales promotion, distribution and stimulating the consumers through the best services. To sum up, marketing management may be defined as the process of management of marketing programmes for accomplishing organisational goals and objectives. It involves planning, implementation and control of marketing programmes or campaigns.

Purpose of this book

This book will serve the purpose of a guide book to the students of under graduate (UG) and post graduate (PG) courses such as:

- Bachelor's Degree in Business Administration (BBA)
- Master's Degree in Business Administration (MBA)
- Post Graduate Diploma in Business Administration (PGDBA)

The above academic as well as professional courses which are offered by reputed universities world-wide, up-to-date syllabus/curriculum have been considered while designing the contents in this book and hence the academic fraternities can refer this book to serve the purpose of a fundamental subject paper. All the up-to-date topics have been incorporated to make the book more versatile and hence will be of considerable value to the students as well.

Dr. Mithun Nandy

Acknowledgements

First of all I would like to extend my deep sense of gratitude and heartfelt thanks to my Ph.D. Supervisor Dr.Brajaballav Pal, Associate Professor, Department of Commerce, Vidyasagar University without whose assistance and guidance it would not have been possible for me to complete my doctoral study. I would also like to express my sincere thanks and warm regards to Dr.Debasish Biswas, Assistant Professor, Department of Business Administration, Vidyasagar University for providing his motivational support and encouragement in all my academic endeavours. I would also like to express my deep sense of regards and warm gratitude to Dr.B.V.Hegde (Designated Partner- Hon'ble Chairman) and Dr.Hemanth Hegde (Designated Partner- Hon'ble Managing Director), Hegde & Hegde Pharmaceutica LLP, Mumbai for their immense support and encouragement for having excellence in the academics. I express deep sense of gratitude to my respected mother Mrs.Ila Nandy and father Mr.Swapan Kumar Nandy who are the inspirational force for my higher studies. My wife, Mrs. Anindita Maiti Nandy, M.Sc. (Chemistry), MBA (Human Resource Management) deserves a heartfelt thank from the core of my heart whose tremendous sacrifices enabled me to complete this book writing. The exceptional help and cooperation of Master Archisman Nandy, my sweet son and record holder in the India Book of Records (IBR) with the record title "*Most Academic Tests Qualified*" is really commendable. I would also like to extend my sincere thanks and warm gratitude to my mother-in-law Mrs.Lakshmi Maiti and father-in-law Mr.Bankim Behari Maiti, an alumnus of Indian Institute of Technology (IIT), Kharagpur for their constant motivational support and encouragement for my higher studies and excellence. I would also like to extend my sincere thanks to the entire Hegde & Hegde Pharmaceutica LLP family members for providing their immense support and encouragement during my professional journey in Hegde & Hegde.

I am highly indebted to my learned colleagues for providing the necessary stimulus, motivation and encouragement for writing this book. I am grateful to all those persons whose writing and works have helped me in preparation of this book. I am equally grateful to the senior academicians who made extremely valuable suggestions and thus contributed in enhancing the standard of the book. I thankfully acknowledge their assistance. A note of acknowledgement to all those who have been directly or indirectly associated with the book. I would also like to extend my sincere thanks to my reputed publisher for their keen interest in the publication of this book in such a record time and format.

I would like to extend my sincere thanks to Mr.Shammi Kumar Bhutani, founder of M/s *Crescent Publishing Corporation*, New Delhi, India, for rendering his unmatched efforts for publishing the book after completing all editorial work by incorporating zero defect approach.

I sincerely hope that the book will immensely benefit the readers. Despite the best efforts there may be some errors. I will however, be obliged if these errors are brought to my notice so that in the subsequent editions the errors are eliminated. Any suggestions from the readers for the improvement of the book will be gratefully acknowledged.

Dr. Mithun Nandy

“Marketing management is the art and science of choosing target markets and getting, keeping and growing customers through creating, delivering, and communicating superior customer value.”

Philip Kotler, Father of Modern Marketing

“Make your marketing so useful, people would pay for it”.
Jay Baer

“People don’t buy what you do; they buy why you do it”.
Simon Sinek

“You cann’t sell anything if you can’t tell anything”.
Beth Comstock

“Marketing is no longer about the stuff that you make, but about the stories you tell.”

Seth Godin

“Speak to your audience in their language about what’s in their heart.”

Abbreviations

AIDA: Attention/Awareness, Interest, Desire, Action

The AIDA Model, which stands for Attention, Interest, Desire, and Action model, is an advertising effect model that identifies the stages that an individual goes through during the process of purchasing a product. The AIDA model is commonly used in digital marketing, sales strategies.

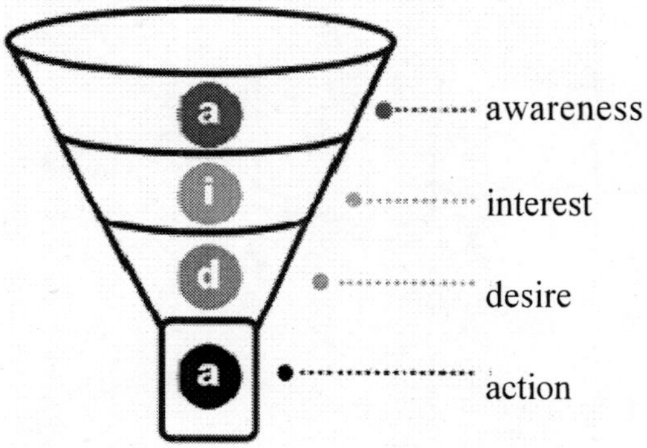

ATM: Automated Teller Machine

A machine that dispenses cash or performs other banking services when an account holder inserts a bank card.

AMA: American Marketing Association

The American Marketing Association is a professional association for marketing professionals with 30,000 members as of 2012. It has 76 professional chapters and 250 collegiate chapters across the United States.

B2B: Business-to-Business

Business-to-business (B2B), also called B-to-B, is a form of transaction between businesses, such as one involving a manufacturer and wholesaler, or a wholesaler and a retailer. Business-to-business refers to business that is conducted between companies, rather than between a company and individual consumer. Business-to-business is a situation where one business makes a commercial transaction with another. This typically occurs when: A business is sourcing materials for their production process for output.

Example:

- Providing raw material to the other company that will produce output.
- Companies that sell to technological solutions other businesses like Slack, Google.

B2C: Business-to-Consumer

Business-to-consumer refers to the process of businesses selling products and services directly to consumers, with no middleman. B2C is typically used to refer to online retailers who sell products and services to consumers through the Internet.

CRM: Customer Relationship Management

Customer relationship management (CRM) is an approach to manage a company's interaction with current and potential customers. It uses data analysis about customers' history with a company to improve business relationships with customers or end users, specifically focusing on customer retention as well as ensures customer loyalty and ultimately driving sales growth.

DSA: Direct Selling Agents

Direct Selling Agents are the one who connects an individual to the loan provider, take care of the needed documentation for Loan Application forms, do fundamental check for application and ensure that the submitted documents are in accordance with the guidelines of the loan provider.

KOL: Key Opinion Leaders

Opinion leadership is leadership by an active media user who interprets the meaning of media messages or content for lower-end media users. Typically the opinion leader is held in high esteem by those who accept their opinions. Key opinion leaders (KOLs) are people or organizations that have such a strong social status that their recommendations and opinions are listened to when making important decisions.

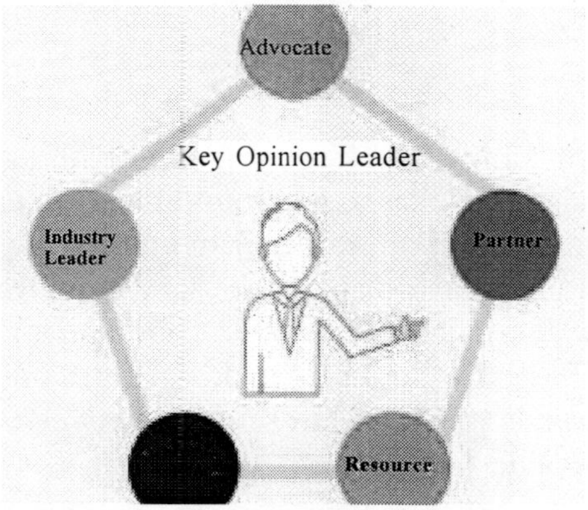

Good examples of key opinion leaders are:

- Political figures
- Columnists
- Health care providers (HCPs) and
- Social media celebrities

MLM: Multi-level marketing (MLM)

Multi-level marketing (MLM) also called as pyramid selling, network marketing, and referral marketing, is a marketing strategy for the sale of products or services where the revenue of the MLM company is derived from a non-salaried workforce selling the company's products/services, while the earnings of the participants are derived from a pyramid-shaped or binary compensation commission system.

PR: Public Relations

PR is all about getting a company in front of the right audiences at the right time with messages that make its spokespeople sound like human beings, not robots. The idea is to earn media attention, rather than buy it. The goal? To inform the public, prospective customers, investors, partners, and employees, and prompt them to adopt a certain view about the company, its leadership and employees, and its products or services. Basically Public relations are the practice of deliberately managing the release and spread of information between an individual or an organization and the public.

SEO: Search Engine Optimization

Search engine optimization is the process of increasing the quality and quantity of website traffic by increasing the visibility of a website or a web page to users of a web search engine. SEO refers to the improvement of unpaid results and excludes direct traffic/visitors and the purchase of paid placement. SEO is backed by a technique that help company's website rank higher in organic search results, making company's website more visible to people who are looking for its brand, product, or service via search engines like Google, Bing, and Yahoo. There are a ton of components to improve the SEO of company's site pages. Search engines look for elements including title tags, keywords, image tags, internal link structure, and inbound links and that's just to name a few. Search engines also look at site structure and design, visitor behaviour, and other external, off-site factors to determine how highly ranked company's site should be in the search engine results pages.

SCM: Supply Chain Management

In marketing supply chain management is the management of the flow of goods and services, involves the movement and storage of raw materials, work-in-process inventory and of finished goods from point of origin to the point of consumption.

SKU: Stock Keeping Unit

A Stock Keeping Unit or SKU is a number that is generally assigned to a product for the purpose of inventory management. An inventory audit is considered a generally accepted auditing procedure and ease of tracking. In other words, a stock keeping unit is a unique identifier assigned to each product for easy identification. In the field of marketing management, a stock keeping unit is a distinct type of item for sale, such as a product or service and all attributes associated with the item type that distinguish it from other item types.

WOM: Word-of-Mouth

The passing of information from person to person. Technically, the term refers to oral communication, but today it refers to online communication, as well. WOM marketing is inexpensive, but it takes work and involves leveraging many components of inbound marketing like product marketing, content marketing, and social media marketing. Word-of-mouth marketing differs from naturally occurring word of mouth, in that it is actively influenced or encouraged by organizations. While it is difficult to truly control WOM, different researchers have shown that there are three generic avenues to 'manage' WOM for the purpose of WOMM:

- Build a strong WOM foundation (e.g. sufficient levels of satisfaction, trust and commitment),
- Indirect WOM management which implies that managers only have a moderate amount of control (e.g. controversial advertising, teaser campaigns, customer membership clubs),
- Direct WOM management, which has higher levels of control (e.g. paid WOM 'agents', "friend get friend" schemes). Pro-consumer WOM has been suggested as a counterweight to commercially motivated word of mouth.

ROI: Return on Investment

A performance measure used to evaluate the efficiency and profitability of an investment. The formula for ROI is: Gain from Investment minus Cost of Investment, divided by Cost of Investment. The result is expressed as a percentage or ratio. If ROI is negative, then that initiative is losing money. The calculation can vary depending on what you input for gains and costs. Marketers should measure the ROI on every tactic and channel they use. Many facets of marketing have fairly straightforward ROI calculations (like PPC), but others are more difficult.

The basic formula for ROI is:

*ROI = Net Profit / Total Investment * 100*

We need to keep in mind that if we have a net loss on our investment, then ROI will be negative. Shareholders can evaluate the ROI of their stock holding by using the following formula:

*ROI = {Net Income + (Current Value - Original Value)} / Original Value * 100*

SWOT: Strengths, Weaknesses, Opportunities, Threats

A SWOT analysis is when a company conducts a study to pinpoint its internal strengths and weaknesses and its external opportunities and threats. It gives a strategic view of the main opportunities and challenges that exist within their particular market. The outcome of the analysis is to have a high-level action plan containing the most important tasks that will impact the success of a given department or the organization as a whole.

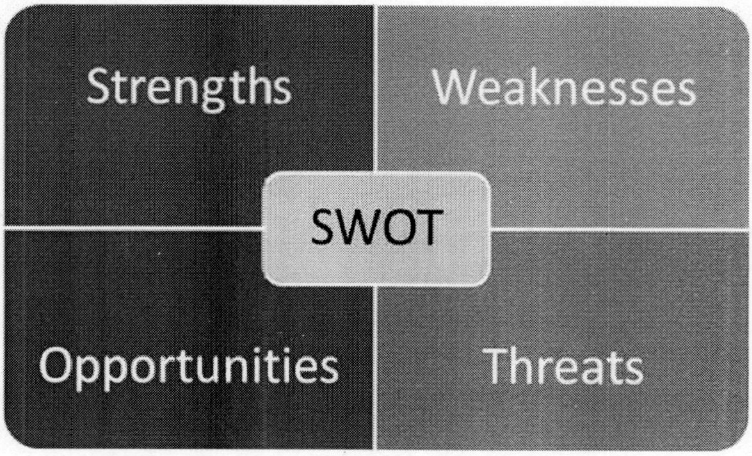

PLC: Product Life Cycle

The product life cycle is the process a product goes through from when it is first introduced into the market until it declines or is removed from the market. The life

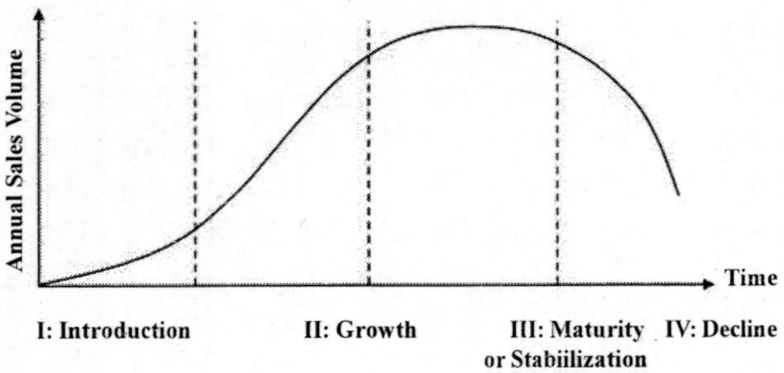

cycle has four stages - introduction, growth, maturity and decline. Product life-cycle management is the succession of strategies by business management as a product goes through its life-cycle. The conditions in which a product is sold changes over time and must be managed as it moves through its succession of stage.

USP: Unique Selling Propositions

The unique selling proposition or unique selling point is a marketing strategy of making a unique proposition to customers that convinced them to switch brands. It was used in successful advertising campaigns of the early 1940s. A unique selling proposition (USP) refers to the unique benefit exhibited by a company, service, product or brand that enables it to stand out from competitors. It must be unique either in the brand or a claim the rest of that particular advertising area does not make.

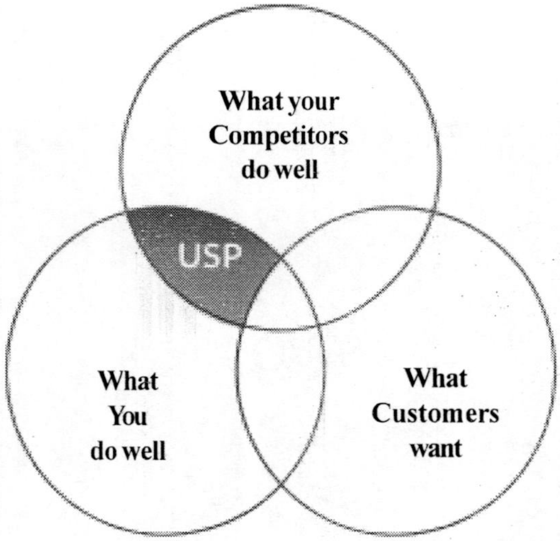

CONTENTS

Preface ix
Acknowledgments xi
Quotations xiii
Abbreviations xv

Chapter 1: Introduction 1
1.1. Market – Meaning and Definition 1
1.2. Importance of Markets 1
1.3. Classification of Markets 3
1.4. Marketing : Conceptual Framework 8
1.5. Definitions of Marketing Management 10
1.6. Features of Marketing 11
1.7. Evolution of Marketing Concept 13
1.8. Difference Between Traditional and Modern Concept 17
1.9. Marketing and Selling 18
1.10. Scope of Marketing 18
1.11. Significance of Marketing 20
1.12. Functions of Marketing 20
1.13. Role of Marketing in Developing Economy 24
1.14. Objectives of Marketing Management 25
1.15. Modern Marketing – Recent Developments 26

Chapter 2: Marketing Environment and Marketing Mix 30
2.1. Marketing Environment – Meaning and Definition 30
2.2. Marketing Mix 34
2.3. Place 35
2.4. Price 37
2.5. Promotion 39
2.6. Product 40

Chapter 3: Market Segmentation **44**
3.1. Market Segmentation – Meaning and Definition 44
3.2. Mass Marketing 45
3.3. Market Segmentation 46
3.4. Benefits of Market Segmentation 46
3.5. Basis of Market Segmentation 47
3.6. Market Segmentation for Organizational Markets 48
3.7. Target Marketing 48

Chapter 4: Consumer Behaviour **49**
4.1. Consumer Behaviour – Meaning and Definition 49
4.2. Consumer Behaviour Versus Buyer Behaviour 52
4.3. Buyer and User 53
4.4. Consumer Behaviour Versus Consumption Behaviour 53
4.5. Signification of Consumer Behaviour 54
4.6. Factors Influencing Consumer Behaviour 56
4.7. Types of Consumer Behaviour 62
4.8. Theories of Buying Behaviour 63
4.9. Buying Motives 64
4.10. Types of Buying Motives 65

Chapter 5: Marketing Organisation and Planning **68**
5.1. Marketing Organization – Meaning and Definition 68
5.2. Need for Marketing Organization 68
5.3. Factors Influencing Size of Marketing Organization 69
5.4. Marketing Organization Structure 71
5.5. Functional Organization 71
5.6. Product Based Organization 72
5.7. Customer Based Organization 72
5.8. Geographic Organization 73
5.9. Essentials of a Good Marketing Organization Structure 74
5.10. Marketing Planning 75
5.11. What is Marketing Planning? 76
5.12. Types of Marketing Planning 76
5.13. Process of Marketing Planning 77
5.14. Factors Affecting Marketing Planning 79
5.15. Importance of Marketing Planning 80
5.16. Difficulties in Marketing Planning 80

Chapter 6: Marketing Information System **81**
6.1. Marketing Information – Meaning and Definitions 81
6.2. Need for Marketing Information 81
6.3. Significance of Marketing Information 82

6.4. Characteristics of Good Marketing Information System 83
6.5. Components of Marketing Information System 83

Chapter 7: Marketing Research 87
7.1. Marketing Research – Meaning and Definition 87
7.2. Features of Marketing Research 87
7.3. Objectives of Marketing Research 88
7.4. Scope of Marketing Research 89
7.5. Significance of Marketing Research 90
7.6. Limitations of Marketing Research 92
7.7. Marketing Research Process / Steps Involved in Marketing Research 93
7.8. Characteristics of Good Marketing Research 96
7.9. Methods of Conducting Marketing Research 96
7.10. Marketing Research Vs. Market Research 108
7.11. Need and importance of Marketing Research 109
7.12. Advantages of Marketing Research 110
7.13. Essential stages of Marketing Research Process 113

Chapter 8: Product Decision 115
8.1. Product – Meaning and Definition 115
8.2. Elements of Product 116
8.3. Significance of Product 117
8.4. Product Classification 118
8.5. Product item, Product line and Product mix 120
8.6. Product Line Policies and Strategies 123
8.7. Factors Influencing Product Decision 124
8.8. Product Life Cycle (PLC) 127
8.9. Marketing Strategies adopted during PLC 129
8.10. Product Planning and Development 134
8.11. New Product Development (NPD) and Planning 135
8.12. New Product Failure 138
8.13. Organization for New Product Development (NPD) 141
8.14. Pricing Strategy for New Product 142

Chapter 9: Product Related Decision and Strategies 146
9.1. Brand – Meaning and Definition 146
9.2. Need for Branding 148
9.3. Purpose of Branding 150
9.4. Essentials of Good Branding 151
9.5. Merits and Demerits of Branding 152
9.6. Classification of Brands 153

9.7. Brand Testing 157
9.8. Trademark 159
9.9. Packaging 159
9.10. Merits and Demerits of Packaging 159
9.11. Packaging Strategies 159
9.12. Labeling 160
9.13. Purpose of Labeling 161
9.14. After Sale Services 161

Chapter 10: Pricing Decisions **166**
10.1. Price and Pricing – Meaning and Definition 166
10.2. Importance of Pricing 167
10.3. Factors Influencing Pricing Decisions 168
10.4. Pricing Objectives 173
10.5. Methods of Pricing Determination 177

Chapter 11: Channels of Distribution Decisions **180**
11.1. Channels of Distribution – Meaning and Definition 180
11.2. Channel Objectives 180
11.3. Role of Distribution Channels 181
11.4. Factors Influencing Distribution Channels 182
11.5. Functions of Distribution Channels 188
11.6. Types of Distribution Channels 188
11.7. Role of Intermediaries 190
11.8. Wholesalers 191
11.9. Functions of Wholesalers 191
11.10. Services of Wholesalers 192
11.11. Classification of Wholesalers 193
11.12. Services Rendered by Retailers 194
11.13. Physical Distribution 195
11.14. Objectives of Physical Distribution 196
11.15. Importance of Physical Distribution System 196

Chapter 12: Marketing Communication **197**
12.1. Marketing Communication – Meaning and Definition 197
12.2. Communication Process 197
12.3. Objectives of Communication 200
12.4. Importance of Communication in Marketing 201
12.5. Barriers to Communication 202
12.6. Marketing Communication and Four Ps 202
12.7. Product 203
12.8. Place 203
12.9. Price 203

12.10. Promotion 203

Chapter 13: Promotion Decision-I **204**
13.1. Promotion – Meaning and Definition 204
13.2. Objectives of Promotion 205
13.3. Methods of Promotion 206
13.4. Factors Determining of Promotion – Mix 207
13.5. Personal Selling 209
13.6. Features of Personal Selling 209
13.7. Importance of Personal Selling 209
13.8. Merits of Personal Selling 211
13.9. Demerits Personal Selling 211
13.10. Salesmanship : Meaning and Definition 211
13.11. Features of Salesmanship 211
13.12. Qualities of Successful Salesman 212
13.13. Kinds of Salesman 214
13.14. Selling Process 214

Chapter 14: Promotion Decision–II **216**
14.1. Advertising – Meaning and Definition 216
14.2. Objectives of Advertising 216
14.3. Functions of Advertising 217
14.4. Role of Advertising 218
14.5. Advertising vs. Personal Selling 222
14.6. Types of Advertising 225
14.7. Institutional Advertising 226
14.8. Advertisement Media 226
14.9. Different Advertisement Media 226
14.10. Factors Determining Choice of Advertisement Media 227
14.11. Limitation of Advertising 228
14.12. Advertising Budget 228
14.13. Factor Governing Size of Advertising Budget 229
14.14. Methods of Framing Advertising Budget 230
14.15. Advertising Agency 237
14.16. Function of an Advertising Agency 237
14.17. Factors Affecting Selection of Advertising Agency 237
14.18. Advertising Appeal 239
14.19. Classification of Advertising Appeals 239
14.20. Advertising Copy 242
14.21. Essentials of a Good Advertising Copy 242
14.22. Types of Advertising Copy 243
14.23. Structure of Advertising Copy 244
14.24. Copy Testing 246

14.25. Types of Copy Testing 237
14.26. Sales Promotion – Meaning and Definition 238
14.27. Advertising Effectiveness 238
14.28. Methods to Measure Advertising Effectiveness 238

1

INTRODUCTION

1.1. Market – Meaning and Definition

The word 'marketing' encompasses such a broad scope of activities and ideas that settling on one definition is often difficult. Ask three people to define marketing, and three different definitions are likely to follow. We are exposed to so much advertising and personal selling that most people link marketing only to those activities. But marketing begins long before a product hits the shelf. It involves analyzing customer needs, obtaining the information necessary to design and produce goods or services that match buyer expectations, satisfying customer preferences, and creating and maintaining relationships with customers and suppliers. Marketing activities apply to profit oriented businesses such as Apple Computer and Zappos.com as well as not-for-profit organizations such as Save the Children and the Red Cross. Even government agencies such as the U.S. Postal Service engage in marketing activities. Today's definition takes all these factors into account. Marketing is an organizational function and a set of processes for creating, communicating, and delivering value to customers and for managing customer relationships in ways that benefit the organization and its stakeholders. The expanded concept of marketing activities permeates all functions in businesses and not-for-profit organizations. It assumes that organizations conduct their marketing efforts ethically and that these efforts serve the best interests of both society and the organization. The concept also identifies the marketing variables product, price, promotion, and distribution that combine to provide customer satisfaction. In addition, it assumes that the organization begins by identifying and analyzing who its potential customers are and what they need. At all points, the concept emphasizes creating and maintaining long-term relationships with customers and suppliers.

1.2. Importance of Markets

Before going into the details of Market and its due importance, it has to be understood first the perspective of the market? Basically a market is one of the many varieties of systems, institutions, procedures, social and infrastructures whereby parties engage in exchange process. While parties may exchange goods and services by barter, most markets rely on sellers offering their goods or services (including labour) in exchange for money from buyers. It can be said that a market is the process by which the prices of goods and services are established. Markets facilitate trade and enables the distribution and allocation of resources in a society. Markets allow any trade-able item to be evaluated and priced. A market emerges more or less spontaneously or may be constructed deliberately by human interaction in order to enable the exchange of rights (cf. ownership) of services and goods. The geographic boundaries of a market may vary considerably, for example the food market in a single building, the real estate market in a local city, the consumer market in an entire country, or the economy of an international trade bloc where the same rules apply throughout. Markets can also be worldwide, for example the global diamond trade. National economies can be classified, for example as developed markets or developing markets. In mainstream economics, the concept of a market is any structure that allows buyers and sellers to exchange any type of goods, services and information.

Some Images of the different types of Indian Markets are displayed in the following.

Indian Rural Market
Source: www.flickr.com

In the above mentioned image the connectivity between Indian Rural Buyer and Supplier has been shown. This physical market place basically caters the consumers are lying in the Bottom-of-the pyramid (BoP) level.

Image: Indian Urban Market
Source: http://www.thehindubusinessline.com

The decorum of the Indian Urban Market place has been shown in the above mentioned image. The products are being displayed in a very systematic manner to attract the urban areas of different parts of India.

Image: Indian Metropolitan Market
Source: http:// www.metro.co.in

The above mentioned market place basically caters to the consumers living in the top of the pyramid (ToP). This market is highly sophisticated in nature where consumers are mostly encouraged into cash less transactions by obtaining a membership / loyalty card. Depending on the volume of the purchase the customers are rewarded bonus points which they can redeem later on while the next time purchase is made followed by applicable terms and conditions (T&C) as prescribed during the application of the membership card / loyalty program. From the above mentioned 'market' discussion, the importance of the market can be drawn and discussed. The very basic level of discussion pertain to the importance of market is in the following.

In brief the importance of the markets is discussed in the following.

a. Connect Buyer & Seller: Through the presence of the market connectivity is being made between the buyers and sellers.

b. Fulfillment of Need, Want and Demand: The fulfillment of need (basic needs of a human being / consumer like food, shelter, clothing), want (when need becomes specific, like in the category of food any consumer would like to have Domino's Pizza) and Demand (when the need is being backed by the purchasing power, for example when a customer can afford to buy the Domino's Pizza) take place with the presence of market.

c. Financial Transactions: With the help of the market, different kinds financial transactions (Cash, Debit Card Payment, Credit Card Payment, Mobile Money, Paytm) is being performed.

d. Analyzing Consumer Behavior: A market also provides a sense of direction to the supplier / producer to analyze the purchasing pattern and analyzing the consumer behavior.

e. Economic Development: The economic development of a country solely depends on the presence and functions of the market.

f. Wide Range of Service: A wide range of service can be delivered by utilizing market and its powerful forces.

g. Execution of 4 Ps: The basic fundamental of marketing is the 4 Ps' viz. Product, Price, Place and Promotion. The 4 Ps' can be connected and executed well with the presence of market.

h. Sustainable Development: The different corporate houses can achieve the sustainable development in their business model by utilizing and exploiting its target market.

i. Volatility Prediction: Volatility can well be predicted by analyzing the different market related factors.

j. Setting benchmarks: A market only enables an enterprise to set its future benchmarks.

k. Income, Revenue and Profit Generation: By using the market force corporate generate income, revenue and profit.

l. Standard of living of the community : Different products and services are being catered or served with the help of market to the wide range of customers or consumers which enable them to satisfy their various kinds of needs, wants and demands through which they can attain the standard of living in the place where they are living and residing.

1.3. Classification of Markets

Classification of Markets—Traditional

Markets can be classified on different bases of which most common bases are: area, time, transactions, regulation, and volume of business, nature of goods, and nature of competition, demand and supply conditions. This classification is off-shoot of traditional approach. Traditionally, a market was a physical place where buyers and sellers gathered to buy and sell the goods. Economists describe a market as a collection buyers and sellers who transact over a particular product or product class.

A. On the Basis of Area

Using area, there can be local, regional, national and international markets. Local markets confine to locality mostly dealing in perishable and semi-perishable goods like fish, flowers, vegetables, eggs, milk, and others. Regional market covers a wider area may be a district, a state or inter-state dealing in durables both consumer and non durables and industrial products, including agricultural produce. In case of national markets the area covered are national boundaries dealing in durable and non-durable consumer goods, industrial goods, metals, forest products, agricultural produce. In case of world or international market, the movement of goods is widespread throughout the world, making it as a single market. It should be noted that due to the latest technologies in transport, storage and packaging, even the most perishable goods are sold all over the world, not that only durables.

B. On the basis of Time

The time duration is the factor. Accordingly, there can be short period and long period markets. Short-period markets are for highly perishable goods of all kinds and long-period markets are for durable goods of different varieties may be produced or manufactured.

C. On the basis of Transactions

Taking the nature of transactions, these can be 'spot' and 'future' markets. In 'spot' market, once the transaction takes place, the delivery takes place, while in case of future markets, transactions are finalized pending delivery and payment for future dates.

D. On the basis of Regulation

Taking regulation, markets can be regulated and non-regulated. A 'regulated market' is one in which business dealings take place as per set rules and regulations regarding, quality, price, source changes and so on. These can be in agricultural products or produce and securities. On the other hand, unregulated market is a free market where there are no rules and regulations; even if they are there, they are amended as per the requirements of parties of exchange.

E. On the Basis of Volume of Business

Taking volume of business as a basis, there can be two types of markets namely, "Wholesale" and "Retail". Wholesale markets are featured by large volume business and wholesalers. On the other hand, 'Retail' markets are those where quantity bought and sold is on small-scale. The dealers are retailers who buy from wholesalers and sell back to consumers.

F. On the basis of Nature of Goods

Taking the nature of goods, there can be commodity markets, capital markets. 'Commodity' markets deal in favour of material, produce, manufactured goods may be consumer and industrial and bullion market dealing precious metals. 'Capital' market is a market for finance. These markets can be subdivided into 'money' market dealing in lending, and borrowing of money; 'Securities' market or 'stock' market dealing in buying and selling of shares and debentures and 'foreign exchange' market where it is a forex market dealing buying and selling of foreign currencies may be hard or soft.

G. On the basis of Nature of Competition

Based on competition or competitive forces, there can be variety of markets for a product or service. However, only two are the most important namely, perfect and imperfect.

A 'perfect' market is one which is characterized by:

(a) Large number of buyers and sellers

(b) Prevalence of single lowest price for products those are 'homogeneous'

(c) The perfect knowledge on the part of buyers and sellers

(d) Free entry and exit of firms in market. These types for markets exist hardly.

The other one is 'imperfect' which is featured by:

(a) Products may be similar but not identical

(b) Different prices for a class of goods

(c) Existence of physical and psychological barriers on movement of good

(d) No perfect knowledge of products and other dimensions on the part of buyers and sellers.

H. On the basis of Demand and Supply

Based on demand and supply conditions or hold of buyers and sellers, there can be seller's and buyer's markets. A seller's market is one where sellers are in driver's seat and the buyers are at the receiving end. In other words, it is a situation where demand for goods exceeds supply. On the other hand, buyer's market is one where buyers are in commanding position. That is, supply is exceeding the demand for the goods.

Classification of Markets—Modern

The modern classification is based on the consumer orientation because in modern economic system consumer is the king-pin and a decisive driving force.

Accordingly, the marketing experts have identified markets based on such broad-based classification namely, consumer, business, global and, non--profit and government markets.

Consumer Markets

These markets specialize in selling mass consumer durable and non-durable products and services devote good deal of time in an attempt to establish a superior brand image. These items may be shoes, apparels, clothing, household items like television, sound system, washing machines, fans, on one hand and tea, coffee, tea powder, coffee powder, biscuits, bread spreads, dental cream, personal care beauty-aids, rice, wheat, oat, gourmet mixes and so on the other. Much of the brand's strength rests on developing a superior product and packaging, ensuring its availability and backing with engaging communications and reliable service. This task of image building is really ticklish as consumer market goes on changing its colour over the period of time.

Business Markets

This is a market of business buyers and sellers. Business buyers buy goods with a view to make or resell a product to others at a profit. Therefore, business marketeers are to effectively demonstrate as to how their products will help the buyers in getting higher revenue or lower costs. Therefore, companies selling business goods and services often face well-trained and well informed professional buyers who are skills in evaluating competitive offerings. These markets deal in raw-materials, fabricated-parts, appliances, equipments, supplies and services that become the part of end products of the business consumers. Advertising plays its due role. However, personal selling has the upper hand. Product price, quality and business suppliers' reputation have significant role.

Global Markets

Global markets consist of buyers and sellers all over the world. The companies selling goods and services in the global market place play global gain involving decisions and challenges. To be successful, they must decide as to which country to enter? How to enter each country? That is, as an exporter, license partner of a joint venture, contract manufacturer or only manufacturer, how to adapt their product and source features to each country? How to price their products in different countries? And how to adapt their communications to differing cultures of various countries? These decisions are to be made in the face of differing requirements for buying, negotiating, owning, and disposing of property under different culture, language, and legal and political systems; and the foreign currency that is subject to fluctuations having its own implications. It is needless to say that these goods and services both consumer and industrial or business.

Non-profit and Government Markets

Companies do sell their products and services to non-profit organizations like temples, churches, universities, charitable institutions and to governmental departments at local, state and central level. The companies that market their products and services have to consider the price aspect because these buyers have limited purchasing power. Again, lower prices badly affect the features and quality of products and services if an attempt is made to design such an offering. Hence, these buyers buy through bidding where lowest bid is favored as there is no alternative. They also need longer period of credit.

1.4. Marketing: Conceptual Framework

The conceptual framework of Marketing Management is provided in the following.

Customers

- **Consider their decision making values, processes & factors**
- **What are their needs? How can those be satisfied?**

Company

- **What are our capabilities & weaknesses?**
- **Do customer needs fit with our corporate objectives?**

Competition

- **Create a response profile for competitors**
- **Who else can satisfy uncovered needs?**

Segmentation

- **Primary bases (e.g. needs)**
- **Secondary bases (e.g. age)**

Targetting

- **Fit (including with company)**
- **Potential (size, growth, etc)**
- **Defensibility (against competiton, etc.)**

Positioning

- **Place product relation to alternative in customer's mind**
- **Core benefit proposition**
- **Unique selling proposition**
- **Positioning statement**
- **Identify product**
- **Category selection**
- **Primary benefits, points of differentiation**

Figure: Analysis & Strategy (3 Cs)

Create Value	Capture Value	Communicate Value	Deliver Value
Product	**Price**	**Promotion**	**Place (Distribution)**
• New product development • Product line management	• Setting • Adapting	• Awareness • Loyalty	• Channel design • Channel management

Figure: Planning & Implementation (The 4 Ps)

Any business venture that any corporate plans to embark upon should go through the "3Cs and 4Ps" exercise. While at first the corporate may think that it is wasting their valuable time, the corporate soon realize how incredibly valuable and insightful this exercise is. It may seem simple, but the "3Cs and 4Ps" exercise really allows corporate to think about a business venture in a structured way. Once corporate force really go through this exercise, corporate will realize how much corporate didn't know about the business idea corporate had in mind. Let's review what the 3 Cs and the 4 Ps are.

The 3 Cs are: Company, Customer and Competition.

The 4 Ps are: Product, Price, Promotion and Place (distribution).

Here is a little more detail about each part of this exercise.

First, the 3 Cs

Company: Corporate first need to think about what type of company corporate plans to operate. What will it look like? What values will corporate aspire to? What is Its mission? Will it be a Private Limited Company (Pvt. Ltd.), Partnership, Limited Liability Partnership (LLP) or a sole proprietorship? Where will it be located? What will be its name? Basically, corporate needs to think about anything that defines the type of company corporate plans to run.

Customer: Next, Its needs to think its target audience. What type of customer will most likely be interested in Its product or service? What are the demographics? Where will they live? To what income brackets will they belong?

Competition: Last but not least, corporate really needs to consider its competition. If corporate leaves this part out, it will get eaten alive. Corporate needs to know its competition very well. Corporate needs to learn how they operate, what marketing tactics they use, who their supplier's are, what financial position they are in and anything else corporate can dig up.

Now the 4 Ps

Product: This is where corporate defines its product or service. If corporate are selling something, then define exactly what it will do. But equally important, corporate needs to define exactly what it won't do. What will it look like? How will it be packaged? Will it need special certifications such as ISO (International Organization for Standardization).

If corporate is offering a service, then the same applies. Its service needs to be really well defined. Corporate needs to clearly articulate what corporate does offer and what corporate does not offer. If this is not clear, then corporate may fall victim to "scope creep" where customers will keep expanding the scope of what corporate had originally promised them.

Price: How will corporate price its product or service? If corporate is selling a product, what price can its target market pay? Do corporate have any pricing power? That is, if corporate is a famous coffee house, then corporate may be able to sell coffee at higher prices than a local coffee shop. If corporate is offering a service, how will corporate charge for its work? Will it be hourly, fixed bid or some other combination? Corporate will look much more professional if corporate can clearly define its services and its prices to a customer. Corporate doesn't want to look like corporate winging it during a sales call.

Promotion: How will corporate market its product? What advertising channels will it use? What social marketing strategies will it deploy? Will corporate consider pay-per-click advertising? Will corporate attend any trade shows? What is its marketing budget? What return on investment (ROI) do corporate wants to achieve from the money corporate plans to invest in marketing?

Place (Distribution): How will corporate store and distribute its product? Basically, corporate need to figure out how it's going to get its product from its supplier to its warehouse and then to its customer. What logistics (transportation / shipping) methods will these steps require? Will corporate have a warehouse or will corporate use a public warehouse? Perhaps corporate plans to have everything drop-shipped for corporate so corporate does not have to carry any inventory. What distribution channels will it use? Will corporate sell through distributors or are corporate planning on sell direct to its customers?

If corporate is offering a service, then where will this service be offered? Will it be out of its office or in a coffee shop? Will it require corporate to go to its clients or will they come to corporate? What are the travelling costs associated with its service? I can't stress enough how important the 3 Cs and 4 Ps are in the business planning process. In fact, corporate should start its business planning with this exercise. It should always be remembered that the 3Cs and 4Ps will continually need updating as its business grows and changes. It is what we call a "living exercise" so corporate needs to come back to it often to refine its strategy and approach. The exercise may seem obvious, but once corporate starts thinking about each step in the process, corporate will be amazed at how much more organized its business planning will become.

1.5. Definitions of Marketing Management

Some of the definition of Marketing Management is given in the following.

Definition 1: Marketing Management is the organizational discipline which focuses on the practical application of marketing orientation, techniques and methods inside enterprises and organizations and on the management of a firm's marketing resources and activities.

Definition II: Marketing management may be defined as the process of management of marketing programmes for accomplishing organizational goals and objectives. It involves planning, implementation and control of marketing programmes or campaigns.

Definition III: Marketing management is "the art and science of choosing target markets and getting, keeping, and growing customers through creating, delivering, and communicating superior customer value" (Kotler and Keller, 2008: 5).

Definition IV: Marketing is the activity, set of institutions, and processes for creating, communicating, delivering, and exchanging offerings that have value for customers, clients, partners, and society at large. (Definition Approved By: American Marketing Association Board of Directors, July 2013).

1.6. Features of Marketing

Some of the most important features of marketing are as follows:

- Customer focus
- Customer satisfaction
- Objective-oriented
- Marketing is both art and science
- Continuous and regular activity
- Exchange process
- Marketing environment
- Marketing mix
- Integrated approach
- Commercial and non-commercial organizations
- Precedes and follows production.

A brief discussion of the above mentioned marketing features are discussed in the following.

Customer focus

The marketing function of a business is customer-centred. It makes an attempt to study the customer needs, and goods are produced accordingly. The business existence depends on human needs. In a competitive market, the goods that are best suited to the customer are the ones that are well-accepted. Hence, every activity of a business is customer-oriented.

Customer satisfaction

A customer expects some services or benefits from the product for which payment is made. If this benefit is more than the amount paid, then the customer is satisfied. In the long run, customer satisfaction helps to retain market demand. It helps achieve organizational objectives. Customer satisfaction can be enhanced by providing value-added services, which includes providing additional facilities at little or no extra cost.

Objective-oriented

All marketing activities are objective-oriented. Different objectives are fixed at different levels, but the main objective is to earn profit from business along with the satisfac-tion of human wants. Marketing activities undertaken by sellers make an attempt to find out the weaknesses in the existing system, and measures are taken to improve the shortfalls so that the objectives are achieved.

Marketing is both art and science

Art refers to a specific skill that is required in marketing activities of any type of business. Science refers to a systematic body of knowledge, based on facts and principles. The concept of marketing includes a bunch of social sciences such as economics, sociology, psychology and law. It indicates market operations based on some principles. Hence, marketing is an art as well as a science.

Continuous and regular activity

Marketing is an activity designed to plan, price, promote and distribute products. At the same time, it also addresses both the current and future consumers. Thus, it is a continuous process. A marketer has to consistently monitor environment. This helps in coming up with new products.

Exchange process

Marketing involves exchange of goods, services and ideas with the medium of money. Exchange takes place between sellers and buyers. Most of marketing activities are concerned with the exchange of goods. Functions such as distribution, after-sale services and packaging help in the exchange process. Channels of distribution and physical distribution play an important role in the exchange process by creating place utility.

Marketing environment

Economic policies, market conditions, and environmental factors, such as political, technological, demographic and international, influence marketing activities. Marketing activities are inseparable from such environmental factors. A successful marketer needs to adapt to these changing factors and adjust marketing strategies to suit new market developments.

Marketing mix

A combination of four inputs constitutes the core of a company's marketing system product, price, place, and promotion. Marketing mix is a flexible combination of variables. They are influenced by consumer behaviour, trade factors, competition and government regulatory measures.

Integrated approach

The marketing activities must be co-ordinated with other functional areas of an organization. Functions such as production, finance, research, purchasing, storekeeping and public relations (PR) are to be integrated with marketing. This will help in achieving organiza-tional objectives. Otherwise, it will result in organizational conflicts.

Commercial and non-commercial organizations

With the societal marketing concept gaining importance, social marketers are finding useful new ways of applying marketing principles. Commercial organizations are also adopting cause-related marketing to strike long-term relations with consumers.

Business organizations such as educational institutions, hospitals, religious institutions and charitable trusts have also found meaningful applications of marketing. Thus, marketing is applicable to both business and non-business organizations.

Precedes and follows production

Identifying consumer needs and wants is the primary task of a marketing manager. Production activities are adapted to these consumer needs. Thus, marketing precedes production. Marketing helps in the distribution of the goods which follows production. Hence, production and marketing activities are closely related to each other.

1.7. Evolution of Marketing Concept

A correct understanding of marketing concept is fundamental to the study of modern marketing and marketing management. In any walk of life, thinking precedes doing; the way of thinking that determines the very course of action. A 'concept' is a philosophy, an attitude, a course of thinking, an idea or a notion relating to any aspect of divine and human creations. The philosophy of an organization in the dynamic realm of marketing is referred to as a 'marketing concept.' A concept is an orientation or a philosophy. Thus, marketing concept is the way of life in which all the resources of an organization are mobilized to create, stimulate and satisfy the consumer at a profit. It represents a distinct philosophy of business and considers marketing more than a physical process. Wherever this concept prevails, that marketing organization is future oriented, customer oriented, value oriented, profit oriented and applies modern management practices to all sales, distribution and other marketing functions. It is a managerial philosophy and organizational structure that centres on the desires of the consumers. It calls on the company, in essence, to make only "what it can sell. It, therefore, reserves the right of reversing the logic of the past that the task of marketing is to sell what the firm makes. This marketing philosophy has undergone a thorough and gradual change since the great Industrial Revolution that took place during the latter-half of the 18th and first-half of the 19th centuries. This gradual change can be traced under four periods and captions namely, production orientation period, sales-orientation period, customer-orientation period and social orientation period. Following is the brief explanation of each philosophy and corresponding period:

Production Orientation Philosophy

Till 1930s, there prevailed a strong feeling that whenever a firm has a good product, it results in automatic consumer response and that needed little or no promotional efforts. This production-oriented marketing concept was built on "Good wine needs no push." That is, if the product is really good and the price is reasonable, there is no need for special marketing efforts.

The assumptions of this concept are:

(i) Anything that can be produced can be sold,

(ii) The most important task of management is to keep the cost of production down.

(iii) A firm should produce only certain basic products.

This concept can be illustrated as under:

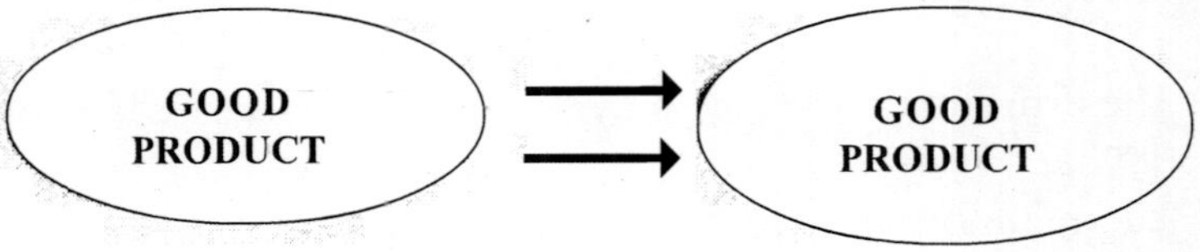

Under this concept, production is the starting point. The product acceptability occurs after the product is produced.

Sales Orientation Philosophy

The failures of the production orientation philosophy of 1930s paved the way for change in the outlook that was possible during 1940s. This reshaped philosophy was sales-orientation that holds good to a certain extent even today. It states that mere making available the best product is not enough; it is futile unless the firm resorts to aggressive salesmanship. Effective sales-promotion, advertising and public relations are of top importance. High pressure salesmanship and heavy doses of advertising are a must to move the products of the firm. The essence of sales orientation philosophy is "Goods are not bought but sold." The maker of product must say that his product is best and he fails if he keeps mum. The assumptions of this philosophy are:

(i) Producing the best possible product.
(ii) Finding the buyer for the product,
(iii) The management's main task is to convince the buyers through high pressure tactics, if necessary.

It can be illustrated as under:

The philosophy has been prevailing since 1940. It is more prevalent in selling all kinds of insurance policies, consumer non-durables and consumer durable products, particularly the status-symbols.

Customer Orientation Philosophy

This philosophy was brought into play during 1950s and points out that the fundamental task of business undertaking is to study and understand the needs, wants, desires and values of potential consumers and produce the goods in the light of these findings so that consumer specifications are met totally. Here, the starting point is the customer rather than the product. The enterprise is to commence with the consumer and end with the requisite product. It emphasizes the role of marketing research well before the product is made available in the market place. The assumptions are:

a. The firm should produce only that product as desired by the consumer.

b. The management is to integrate all its activities in order to develop programmes to satisfy the consumer wants.

c. The management is to be guided by 'long-range profit goals' rather than 'quick sales.'

It can be illustrated as under:

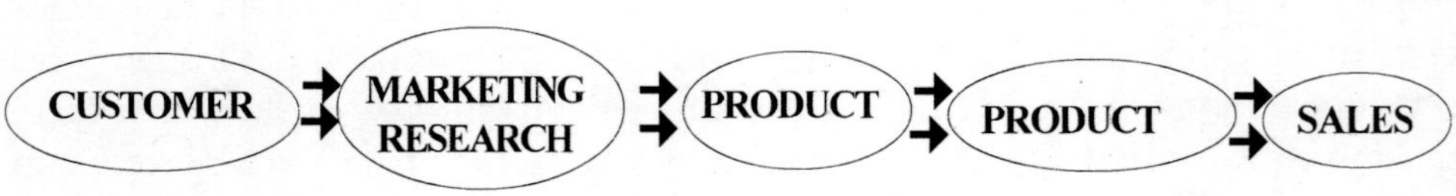

This means a radical change in the philosophy.

It meant two basic changes namely:

(i) Move from production to market-orientation,

(ii) Gradual shift from age old "Caveat emptor" to "Caveat vendor".

Since 1950, this philosophy is in vogue and will continue so long as consumer is the King of the market.

Social Orientation Philosophy:

There has been a further refinement in the marketing concept particularly during 1970s and 1980s. Accordingly, the new concept goes beyond understanding the consumer needs and matching the products accordingly. This philosophy cares for not only consumer satisfaction but for consumer welfare or social welfare. Such social welfare speaks of pollution-free environment and quality of human life. Thus, a firm manufacturing a pack of cigarettes for consumer must not only produce the best cigarettes but pollution-free cigarettes; an automobile not only fuel efficient but less pollutant one. In other words, the firm is to discharge its social responsibilities. Thus, social welfare becomes the added dimension.

The assumptions of social-orientation philosophy are:

(i) The firm is to produce only those products as are wanted by the consumers,

(ii) The firm is to be guided by long-term profit goals rather than quick sales.

(iii) The firm should discharge its social responsibilities.

(iv) The management is to integrate the firm's resources and activities to develop programme to meet these individual consumer and social needs.

This concept can be illustrated as under:

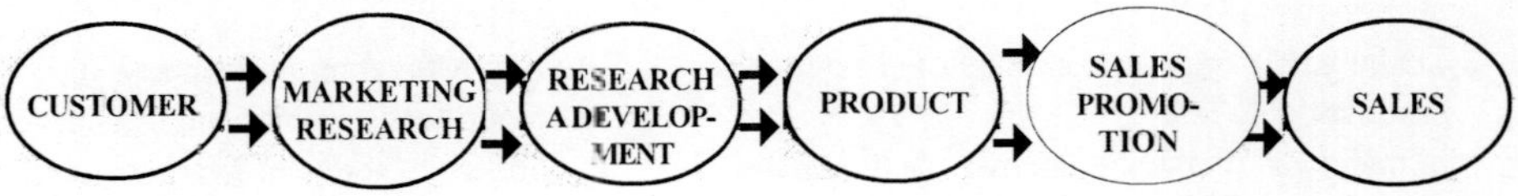

This social oriented philosophy is the latest and is considered as an integrated concept. This philosophy, as it covers earlier long-standing concepts, is bound to rule the marketing world for pretty long time. However, we are to wait and see as to what changes are likely in the coming years and decades that will shape the new marketing concept.

1.8. Difference between Traditional and Modern Concept

The difference between Traditional and Modern Concept of Marketing Management is shown in a tabular form as per the following.

Sl. No.	Traditional Marketing	Modern Marketing
i	In traditional marketing, more importance is given on selling the product. They start with production and marketing is done while selling and promoting the product to attain sales at profit. In this technique, the existing products are imposed on the market through aggressive selling and promotional pressures.	Its main motive is customer satisfaction that is building a relationship with Marketing Information System (MIS) customer and is achieved through an integrated, corporate wide set of marketing activities. This technique understands the needs and desires of the customer and product is designed accordingly.
ii	Traditional marketing concentrate on favorable products.	Modern Marketing concentrate on customer needs, wants and satisfaction.
iii	In traditional marketing the manufacturer sells only thoseproducts which he produces & not focuses on consumerpreference.	In Modern Marketing, Manufacturer analyses the consumerpreferences.
iv	Here the target or traditional concept is to earn maximum profit by maximizing the sales.	In modern concept, the profits are earned through satisfaction of consumer needs.
v	Traditional marketing is not consumer focused it is basically production and product focused.	Modern marketing is service driven and customer oriented. Marketing focus is increasing day by day. Utilizing resources to optimum level and giving best product for lesser price is new mantra of modern marketing.
vi	Traditional marketing is old concept market.	But modern marketing is very critical market. It involves : · Planning· Controlling· Promotion· Price· Environment etc.
vii	The principle of traditional market:The basic principal followed is " caveat emptor " let buyer beware.	The principle of modern market:The principal followed is " caveat vendor" let the seller beware.
viii	Traditional marketing concentrate on favorable products.	Modern Marketing concentrate on customer needs, wants and satisfaction.
ix	In traditional marketing the manufacturer sells only thoseproducts which he produces & not focuses on consumerpreference.	In Modern Marketing, Manufacturer analyses the consumerpreferences.
x	Here the target or traditional concept is to earn maximum profit by maximizing the sales.	In modern concept, the profits are earned through satisfaction of consumer needs.
xi	Traditional marketing is not consumer focused it is basically production and product focused.	Modern marketing is service driven and customer oriented. Marketing focus is increasing day by day. Utilizing resources to optimum level and giving best product for lesser price is new mantra of modern marketing.
xii	The principle of traditional market: The basic principal followed is "caveat emptor" let buyer beware.	The principle of modern market: The principal followed is "caveat vendor" let the seller beware.

1.9. Marketing and Selling

In general we use 'marketing' and 'selling' as synonyms but there is a substantial difference between both the concepts. It is necessary to understand the differences between marketing vs selling for a successful marketing manager. Selling has a product focus and mostly producer driven. It is the action part of marketing only and has short-term goal of achieving market share. The emphasis is on price variation for closing the sale where the objective can be stated, as "I must somehow sell the product". This short-term focus does not consider a prudential planning for building up the brand in the market place and winning competitive advantage through a high loyal set of customers. The end means of any sales activity is maximizing profits through sales maximization.

When the focus is on selling, the businessman thinks that after production has been completed the task of the sales force starts. It is also the task of the sales department to sell whatever the production department has manufactured. Aggressive sales methods are justified to meet this goal and customer's actual needs and satisfaction are taken for granted. Selling converts the product in to cash for the company in the short run. Marketing as a concept and approach is much wider than selling and is also dynamic as the focus is on the customer rather than the product. While selling revolves around the needs and interest of the manufacturer or marketer, marketing revolves around that of consumer. It is the whole process of meeting and satisfying the needs of the consumer.

1.10. Scope of Marketing

Some of the most important scope of marketing are as follows:

1. Goods 2. Services 3. Events 4. Experiences 5. Persons 6. Places 7. Properties 8. Organizations 9. Information 10. Idea. The scope of marketing deals with the question, 'what is marketed?' According to Kotler, marketing people are involved with ten types of entities.

Goods

Physical goods constitute the major part of a country's production and marketing effort. Companies market billions of food products, and millions of cars, refrigerators, television and machines.

Services

As economies advance, a large proportion of their activities is focused on the pro-duction of services. Services include the work of airlines, hotels, car rental firms, beauticians, software programmers, management consultants, and so on. Many market offerings consist of a mix of goods and services. For example, a restaurant offers both goods and services.

Events

Marketers promote events. Events can be trade shows, company anniversaries, entertainment award shows, local festivals, health camps, and so on. For example, global sporting events such as the Olympics or Common Wealth Games are promoted aggressively to both companies and fans.

Experiences

Marketers create experiences by offering a mix of both goods and services. A product is promoted not only by communicating features but also by giving unique and interesting experiences to customers. For example, Maruti Sx4 comes with Bluetooth technology to ensure connectivity while driving; similarly residential townships offer landscaped gardens and gaming zones.

Persons

Due to a rise in testimonial advertising, celebrity marketing has become a business. All popular personalities such as film stars, TV artists, and sportspersons have agents and personal managers. They also tie up with PR agencies for better marketing of oneself

Places

Cities, states, regions, and countries compete to attract tourists. Today, states and coun-tries are also marketing places to factories, companies, new residents, real estate agents, banks and business associations. Place marketers are largely real estate agents and builders. They are using mega events and exhibitions to market places. The tourism ministry is also aggressively promoting tourist spots locally and globally.

Properties

Properties can be categorized as real properties or financial properties. Real property is the ownership of real estates, whereas financial property relates to stocks and bonds. Properties are bought and sold through marketing. Marketing enhances the need of ownership and creates possession utility. With improving income levels in the economy, people are seeking better ways of saving money. Financial and real property marketing need to build trust and confidence at higher levels.

Organizations

Organizations actively work to build image in the minds of their target public. The PR department plays an active role in marketing an organization's image. Marketers of the services need to build the corporate image, as exchange of services does not result in the owner-ship of anything. The organization's goodwill promotes trust and reliability. The organization's image also helps the companies in the smooth introduction of new products.

Information

Information can be produced and marketed as a product. Educational institutions, encyclopedias, non-fiction books, specialized magazines and newspapers market information. The production, packaging, and distribution of information is a major industry. Media revolution and increased literacy levels have widened the scope of informa-tion marketing.

Idea

Every market offering includes a basic idea. Products and services are used as platforms for delivering some idea or benefit. Social marketers widely promote ideas. Maruti Udyog Limited promoted safe driving habits, need to wear seat belts, need to prohibit children from sitting near the driver's seat, and so on.

1.11. Significance of Marketing

Marketing management has gained importance to meet increasing competition and the need for improved methods of distribution to reduce cost and to increase profits. Marketing management today is the most important function in a commercial and business enterprise. The following are the other factors showing significance of the marketing management:

(i) Introduction of new products in the market.

(ii) Increasing the production of existing products.

(iii) Reducing cost of sales and distribution.

(iv) Export market.

(v) Development in the means of communication and modes of transportation within and outside the country.

(vi) Rise in per capita income and demand for more goods by the consumers.

1.12. Functions of Marketing

Marketing is related to the exchange of goods and services. Through its medium the goods and services are brought to the place of consumption. This satisfies the needs of the customers. The following activities are undertaken in respect of the exchange of goods and services:

Gathering and Analyzing Market Information

Gathering and analyzing market information is an important function of marketing. Under it, an effort is made to understand the consumer thoroughly in the following ways:

Marketing Planning

In order to achieve the objectives of an organization with regard to its marketing, the marketer chalks out his marketing plan. For example, a company has a 25% market share of a particular product. The company wants to raise it to 40%. In order to achieve this objective the marketer has to prepare a plan in respect of the level of production and promotion efforts. It will also be decided as to who will do what, when and how. To do this is known as marketing planning.

Product Designing and Development

Product designing plays an important role in product selling. The company whose product is better and attractively designed sells more than the product of a company whose design happens to be weak and unattractive. In this way, it can be said that the possession of a special design affords a company to a competitive advantage. It is important to remember that it is not sufficient to prepare a design in respect of a product, but it is more important to develop it continuously.

Standardization and Grading

Standardization refers to determining of standard regarding size, quality, design, weight, colour, raw material to be used, etc., in respect of a particular product. By doing so, it is ascertained that the given product will have some peculiarities. This way, sale is made possible on the basis of samples. Mostly, it is the practice that the traders look at the samples and place purchase order for a large quantity of the product concerned. The basis of it is that goods supplied conform to the same standard as shown in the sample. Products having the same characteristics (or standard) are placed in a given category or grade. This placing is called grading. For example, a company produces commodity – X, having three grades, namely A'. 'B' and 'C', representing three levels of quality; best, medium and ordinary respectively. Customers who want best quality will be shown 'A' grade product. This way, the customer will have no doubt in his mind that a low grade product has been palmed off to him. Grading, therefore, makes sale-purchase easy. Grading process is mostly used in case of agricultural products like food grains, cotton, tobacco, apples, mangoes, etc.

Packaging and Labeling

Packaging aims at avoiding breakage, damage, destruction, etc., of the goods during transit and storage. Packaging facilitates handling, lifting, conveying of the goods. Many a time, customers demand goods in different quantities. It necessitates special packaging. Packing material includes bottles, canister, plastic bags, tin or wooden boxes, jute bags etc. Label is a slip which is found on the product itself or on the package providing all the information regarding the product and its producer. This can either be in the form of a cover or a seal. For example, the name of the medicine on its bottle along with the manufacturer's name, the formula used for making the medicine, date of manufacturing, expiry date, batch no., price etc., are printed on the slip thereby giving all the information regarding the medicine to the consumer. The slip carrying all these is details called Label and the process of preparing it as Labelling.

Branding

Every producer/seller wants that his product should have special identity in the market. In order to realize his wish he has to give a name to his product which has to be distinct from other competitors.

Giving of distinct name to one's product is called branding. Thus, the objective of branding is to show that the products of a given company are different from that of the competitors, so that it has its own identity. For instance, if a company wants to popularise its commodity – X under the name of "777" (triple seven) then its brand will be called "777". It is possible that another company is selling a similar commodity under AAA (Triple 'A') brand name. Under these circumstances, both the companies will succeed in establishing a distinct identity of their products in the market. When a brand is not registered under the trade Mark Act, 1999, it becomes a Trade Mark.

Customer Support Service

Customer is the king of market. Therefore, it is one of the chief functions of marketer to offer every possible help to the customers. A marketer offers primarily the following services to the customers:

(i) After-sales-services

(ii) Handling customers' complaints

(iii) Technical services

(iv) Credit facilities

(v) Maintenance services

Helping the customer in this way offers him satisfaction and in today's competitive age customer's satisfaction happens to be the top-most priority. This encourages a customer's attachment to a particular product and he starts buying that product time and again.

Pricing of Products

It is the most important function of a marketing manager to fix price of a product. The price of a product is affected by its cost, rate of profit, price of competing product, policy of the government, etc. The price of a product should be fixed in a manner that it should not appear to be too high and at the same time it should earn enough profit for the organization.

Promotion

Promotion means informing the consumers about the products of the company and encouraging them to buy these products. There are four methods of promotion: (i) Advertising, (ii) Personal selling, (iii) Sales promotion and (iv) Publicity. Every decision taken by the marketer in this respect affects the sales. These decisions are taken keeping in view the budget of the company.

Physical Distribution

Under this function of marketing the decision about carrying things from the place of production to the place of consumption is taken into account. To accomplish this task, decision about four factors are taken. They are: (i) Transportation, (ii) Inventory, (iii) Warehousing and (iv) Order Processing. Physical distribution, by taking things, at the right place and at the right time creates time and place utility.

Transportation

Production, sale and consumption-all the three activities need not be at one place. Had it been so, transportation of goods for physical distribution would have become irrelevant. But generally it is not possible. Production is carried out at one place, sale at another place and consumption at yet another place. Transport facility is needed for the produced goods to reach the hands of consumers. So the enterprise must have an easy access to means of transportation. Mostly we see on the road side's private vehicles belonging to Pepsi, Coca Cola, LML, Britannia, etc. These private carriers are the living examples of transportation function of marketing. Place utility is thus created by transportation activity.

Storage or Warehousing

There is a time-lag between the purchase or production of goods and their sale. It is very essential to store the goods at a safe place during this time-interval. Godowns are used for this purpose. Keeping of goods in godowns till the same are sold is called storage. For the marketing manager storage is an important function. Any negligence on his part may damage the entire stock. Time utility is thus created by storage activity.

1.13. Role of Marketing in Developing Economy

Marketing plays a vital role in economic growth in the present global world. It ensures the planned economic growth in the developing economy where the scarcity of goods, services, ideas and excessive unemployment, thereby marketing efforts are needed for mobilization of economic resources for additional production of ideas, goods and services resulting in greater employment. Marketing stimulates the aggregate demand thereby enlarges the size of market. Marketing in basic industries, agriculture, mining and plantation industries helps in distribution of output without which there is no possibility of mobilization of goods and services which is the key point for economic growth. These industries are the back bone of economic growth. It also accelerates the process of monetizing the economy which in turn facilitates the transfer of investible resources. It helps in discovery of entrepreneurial talent. Intermediate industrial goods and Semi-industrial products etc. essentially marketed for industrial purpose in order to develop the industrial sector with a view to economic growth. In Export trade and services like tourism and baking marketing plays eminent role in order to growth economy. Now days economic and social changes are necessary for bring about the development of a nation.Social changes are brought about in a planned manner through social marketing technology. Social marketing can be defined as the design, implementation and control of programmers calculated to influences the acceptability of social ideas and involving consideration of product planning, pricing, communication, distribution and marketing research. With the rapid growing marketing business, technology is playing a more important role in the demands of analyzing and utilizing the large scale information gathered from customers. To predict the consequent business strategy by using technology, it is required to evaluate the customerperformance, discover the trends or patterns in customer behavior. For this purpose the in modern world using the technology at a maximum level by e-commerce, Internet marketing and services etc.Even though in several developing countries, Government involves in marketing efforts in order to provide equitable distribution at minimum social costs by setting ceiling and floor prices of foods grains and industrial raw materials, setting maximum whole sale and retail prices of scarce consumer products etc. which ensures the smooth flow of essential goods and even influencing the decisions pertaining to distribution and advertising. Even though the economic recession affects the market at larger extent, it plays major role in economic growth. The end result will be the maximization of growth of the economy in order to provide higher standard of living for all and the development of a economic levels of the people that fosters entrepreneurial-ism.

1.14. Objectives of Marketing Management

Some of the major objectives of marketing management are as follows:

a. Creation of Demand

b. Customer Satisfaction

c. Market Share

d. Generation of Profits

e. Creation of Goodwill and Public Image.

The basic purpose of marketing management is to achieve the objectives of the business. A business aims at earning reasonable profits by satisfying the needs of customers. In the light of this statement, we can highlight the objectives of marketing management as follows:

Creation of Demand

The marketing management's first objective is to create demand through various means. A conscious attempt is made to find out the preferences and tastes of the consumers. Goods and services are produced to satisfy the needs of the customers. Demand is also created by informing the customers the utility of various goods and services.

Customer Satisfaction

The marketing manager must study the demands of customers before offering them any goods or services. Selling the goods or services is not that important as the satisfaction of the customers' needs. Modern marketing is customer- oriented. It begins and ends with the customer.

Market Share

Every business aims at increasing its market share, i.e., the ratio of its sales to the total sales in the economy. For instance, both Pepsi and Coke compete with each other to increase their market share. For this, they have adopted innovative advertising, innovative packaging, sales promotion activities, etc.

Generation of Profits

The marketing department is the only department which generates revenue for the business. Sufficient profits must be earned as a result of sale of want-satisfying products. If the firm is not earning profits, it will not be able to survive in the market. Moreover, profits are also needed for the growth and diversification of the firm.

Creation of Goodwill and Public Image

To build up the public image of a firm over a period is another objective of marketing. The marketing department provides quality products to customers at reasonable prices and thus creates its impact on the customers. The marketing manager attempts to raise the goodwill of the business by initiating image-building activities such a sales promotion, publicity and advertisement, high quality, reasonable price, convenient distribution outlets, etc.

1.15. Modern Marketing – Recent Developments

More Emphasis on Quality, Value, and Customer Satisfaction

Today's customers place a greater weight to direct motivations (convenience, status, style, features, services and qualities) to buy product. Today's marketers give more emphasis on the notion, "offer more for less."

More Emphasis on Relationship Building and Customer Retention

Today's marketers are focusing on lifelong customers. They are shifting from transaction thinking to relationship building. Large companies create, maintain and update large customer database containing demographic, life-style, past experience, buying habits, degree of responsiveness to different stimuli, etc., and design their offerings to create, please, or delight customers who remain loyal to them. Similarly more emphasis is given to retain them throughout life. Marketers strongly believe: "Customer retention is easier than customer creation."

More Emphasis on Managing Business Processes and Integrated Business Functions

Today's companies are shifting their thinking from managing a set of semi independent departments, each with its own logic, to managing a set of fundamental business processes, each of which impact customer service and satisfaction. Companies are assigning cross-disciplinary personnel to manage each process. Marketing personnel are increasingly working on cross- disciplinary terms rather than only in the marketing department. This is the positive development, which broadens marketers' perspectives on business and also leads to broaden perspective of employees from other department.

More Emphasis on Global Thinking and Local Market Planning

As stated earlier, today's customers are global, or cosmopolitan. They exhibit international characteristics. This is due to information technology, rapid means of transportation, liberalization, and mobility of people across the world. Companies are pursuing markets beyond their borders. They have to drop their traditions, customs, and assumptions regarding customers. They have to adapt to their offering as per the cultural prerequisites. Decisions are taken by local representatives, who are much aware of the global economic, political, legal, and social realities. Companies must think globally, but act locally. Today's marketers believe: "Act locally, but think globally."

More Emphasis on Strategic Alliances and Networks

A company cannot satisfy customers without help of others. It lacks adequate resources and requirements to succeed. Company needs to involve in partnering with other organizations, local as well as global partners who supply different requirements for success. Senior manager at top-level management spends an increasing amount of time for designing strategic alliance and network that create competitive advantages for the partnering firms. Merger, acquisition, and partnering are result of a strong thirst for strategic alliance and networks.

More Emphasis on Direct and Online Marketing

Information technology and communication revolution promise to change the nature of buying and selling. Companies follow direct channel in term hiring salesmen, setting own distribution network, designing network marketing, applying online marketing, and contracting with giant shopping/retailing malls. People anywhere in the world can access the Internet and companies' home pages to scan offers and order goods. Via online service, they can give and get advice on products and services by chatting with other users, determine the best values, place orders, and get next-day delivery. As a result of advances in database technology, companies can do more direct marketing and rely less on wholesale and retail intermediaries. Beyond this, much company buying is now done automatically through electronic data interchange link among companies. All these trends portend a greater buying and selling efficiency.

More Emphasis on Services Marketing

As per general survey, about 70% people are, either directly or indirectly, involved in service marketing. Because services are intangible and perishable, variable and inseparable, they pose additional challenges compared to tangible good marketing. Marketers are increasingly developing strategies for service firms that sell insurance, software, consulting services, banking, insurance, and other services.

More Emphasis on High-tech Industries

Due to rapid economic growth, high-tech firms emerged, which differ from traditional firms. High-tech firms face higher risk, slower product acceptance, shorter product life cycles, and faster technological obsolescence. High-tech firms must master the art of marketing their venture to the financial community and convincing enough customers to adopt their new products.

More Emphasis on Ethical Marketing Behaviour

The market place is highly susceptible to abuse by those who lack scruples and are willing to prosper at the expense of others. Marketers must practice their craft with high standards. Even, governments have imposed a number of restrictions to refrain them from malpractices. Marketers are trying to sell their products by obeying and observing moral standards or business ethics.

Other issues

i. Craze for international standards and emphasis on quality, value and customer satisfaction. Application of TQM (even, Six Sigma) in every aspect of marketing management.

ii. Changed attitude toward competition. They compete not for maximum gains but for maximum offers to customers.

iii. Relationship marketing at both levels at internal functions of organisation and at outside with service providers, to satisfy customers.

iv. Concept of global and complex customers.

v. Marketing department is placed in the center of management. It enjoys unique and dominant status in organization.

vi. Use of latest technology for survey and research.

vii. More emphasis on after-sales services.

viii. Entertaining value in advertising, etc.

2

MARKETING ENVIRONMENT AND MARKETING-MIX

2.1. Marketing Environment – Meaning and Definition

The market environment is a marketing term and refers to factors and forces that affect a firm's ability to build and maintain successful relationships with customers. Three levels of the environment are 3:

- Micro (internal) environment - small forces within the company that affect its ability to serve its customers.
- Meso environment – the industry in which a company operates and the industry's market(s).
- Macro (national) environment - larger societal forces that affect the microenvironment.

Micro-Environment

Company aspect of micro-environment refers to the internal environment of the company. This includes all departments, such as management, finance, research and development, purchasing, operations and accounting. Each of these departments influences marketing decisions. For example, research and development have input as to the features a product can perform and accounting approves the financial side of marketing plans and budget in customer dissatisfaction. Marketing managers must watch supply availability and other trends dealing with suppliers to ensure that product will be delivered to customers in the time frame required in order to maintain a strong customer relationship. Marketing intermediaries refers to resellers, physical distribution firms, marketing services agencies, and financial intermediaries. These are the people that help the company promote, sell, and distribute its products to final buyers. Resellers are those that hold and sell the company's product. They match the distribution to the customers and include places such as Wal-Mart, Target, and Best Buy. Physical distribution firms are places such as warehouses that store and transport the company's product from its origin to its destination. Marketing services agencies are companies that offer services such as conducting marketing research, advertising, and consulting. Financial intermediaries are institutions such as banks, credit companies and insurance companies. Another aspect of micro-environment is the customer market. There are different types of customer markets including consumer markets, business markets, government markets, international markets, and reseller markets. The consumer market is made up of individuals who buy goods and services for their own personal use or use in their household. Business markets include those that buy goods and services for use in producing their own products to sell. This is different from the reseller market which includes businesses that purchase goods to resell as is for a profit. These are the same companies mentioned as market intermediaries. The government market consists of government agencies that buy goods to produce public services or transfer goods to others who need them. International markets include buyers in other countries and includes customers from the previous categories. Competitors are also a factor in the micro-environment and include companies with similar offerings for goods and services. To remain competitive a company must consider who their biggest competitors are while considering its own size and position in the industry. The company should develop a strategic advantage over their competitors. The final aspect of the micro environment is publics, which is any group that has an interest in or effect on the organization's ability to meet its goals. For example, financial publics can hinder a company's ability to obtain funds affecting the level of credit a company has. Media public include newspapers and magazines that can publish articles of interest regarding the company and editorials that may influence customers' opinions. Government public can affect the company by passing legislation and laws that put restrictions on the company's actions. Citizen-action publics include environmental groups and minority groups and can question the actions of a company and put them in the public spotlight. Local publics are neighbourhood and community organizations and will also question a company's effect on the local area and the level of responsibility of their actions. The general public can affect the company as any change in their attitude, whether positive or negative, can cause sales to go up or down because the general public is often the company's customer base. And finally those who are employed within the company and deal with the organization and construction of the company's product.

Meso Environment

The meso environment is the setting between the macro and micro opportunities. It shapes the framework of a business or organisation and can be considered as its infrastructure: policies, standard operating procedures, rules and guidelines. The meso concept is a difficult one to understand, there is very little research relating to the idea. From a practitioner's point of view, it is fair to say that the meso environment is rarely considered. In reality however, most companies are actually using it. Quality systems or staff hand-books are good examples of the meso. The big question is, "how many companies have considered the impact to the strategic processes when writing these documents"? A good example of where most businesses fail is with their IT policies. Technology has changed so much, yet most corporate organisations have failed to capitalise on the opportunities: social networking can bring a new perspective to the marketing plan but the team is unable to exploit it because of IT restrictions! The Meso environment relates to the factors with which the business cannot respond to the environment whether directly or indirectly. This is the industry where it is active. Research primary factors of the market wherein it is active. A simple example. A business can not directly influence whether a market is easy or difficult to penetrate for newcomers (External Analysis - ABCD Analysis - Industry Analysis - Porter's Five Forces Model) . The company can try as it might to make it difficult but the case is ultimately the same. From the meso-environment, come opportunities and threats. Research on the Meso-environment can be conducted using an External Analysis. You can find more information about this by clicking on the following link: External Analysis. The specific component of the External Analysis to research the Meso-environment is the ABCD Analysis. You can find more information about this by clicking on the following link: ABCD Analysis. Researching meso-environment is an important component of the research phase of the marketing plan. Also, more information on this by clicking on the following link: Research Phase of the Marketing Plan. The Meso-environment consists of factors of the market wherein the business is active: Distribution, Competition, Competitors, and General industrial factors

Macro-Environment

The macro-environment refers to all forces that are part of the larger society and affect the micro-environment. It includes concepts such as demography, economy, natural forces, technology, politics, and culture. Factors affecting organization in Macro environment are known as PESTEL, that is: Political, Economical, Social, Technological, Environmental and Legal. Demography refers to studying human populations in terms of size, density, location, age, gender, race, and occupation. This is a very important factor to study for marketers and helps to divide the population into market segments and target markets. An example of demography is classifying groups of people according to the year they were born. These classifications can be referred to as baby boomers, who are born between 1946 and 1964, generation X, who are born between 1965 and 1976, and generation Y, who are born between 1977 and 1994. Each classification has different characteristics and causes they find important. This can be beneficial to a marketer as they can decide who their product would benefit most and tailor their marketing plan to attract that segment. Demography covers many aspects that are important to marketers including family dynamics, geographic shifts, work force changes, and levels of diversity in any given area. Another aspect of the macro-environment is the economic environment. This refers to the purchasing power of potential customers and the ways in which people spend their money. Within this area are two different economies, subsistence and industrialized. Subsistence economies are based more in agriculture and consume their own industrial output. Industrial economies have markets that are diverse and carry many different types of goods. Each is important to the marketer because each has a highly different spending pattern as well as different distribution of wealth. The natural environment is another important factor of the macro-environment. This includes the natural resources that a company uses as inputs that affects their marketing activities. The concern in this area is the increased pollution, shortages of raw materials and increased governmental intervention. As raw materials become increasingly scarcer, the ability to create a company's product gets much harder. Also, pollution can go as far as negatively affecting a company's reputation if they are known for damaging the environment. The last concern, government intervention can make it increasingly harder for a company to fulfil their goals as requirements get more stringent. The technological environment is perhaps one of the fastest changing factors in the macro-environment. This includes all developments from antibiotics and surgery to nuclear missiles and chemical weapons to automobiles and credit cards. As these markets develop it can create new markets and new uses for products. It also requires a company to stay ahead of others and update their own technology as it becomes outdated. They must stay informed of trends so they can be part of the next big thing, rather than becoming outdated and suffering the consequences financially. The political environment includes all laws, government agencies, and groups that influence or limit other organizations and individuals within a society. It is important for marketers to be aware of these restrictions as they can be complex. Some products are regulated by both state and federal laws. There are even restrictions for some products as to who the target market may be, for example, cigarettes should not be marketed to younger children. There are also many restrictions on subliminal messages and monopolies. As laws and regulations change often, this is a very important aspect for a marketer to monitor.

The final aspect of the macro-environment is the cultural environment, which consists of institutions and basic values and beliefs of a group of people. The values can also be further categorized into core beliefs, which passed on from generation to generation and very difficult to change, and secondary beliefs, which tend to be easier to influence. As a marketer, it is important to know the difference between the two and to focus your marketing campaign to reflect the values of a target audience. When dealing with the marketing environment it is important for a company to become proactive. By doing so, they can create the kind of environment that they will prosper in and can become more efficient by marketing in areas with the greatest customer potential. It is important to place equal emphasis on both the macro and micro environment and to react accordingly to changes within them.

2.2. Marketing Mix

Marketing involves a number of activities. To begin with, an Organization may decide on its target group of customers to be served. Once the target group is decided, the product is to be placed in the market by providing the appropriate product, price, distribution and promotional efforts. These are to be combined or mixed in an appropriate proportion so as to achieve the marketing goal. Such mix of product, price, distribution and promotional efforts is known as 'Marketing Mix'. According to Philip Kotler "Marketing Mix is the set of controllable variables that the firm can use to influence the buyer's response". The controllable variables in this context refer to the 4 'P's [product, price, place (distribution) and promotion]. Each firm strives to build up such a composition of 4'P's, which can create highest level of consumer satisfaction and at the same time meet its Organizational objectives. Thus, this mix is assembled keeping in mind the needs of target customers, and it varies from one Organization to another depending upon its available resources and marketing objectives. Let us now have a brief idea about the four components of marketing mix.

- **Product**: Product refers to the goods and services offered by the Organization. A pair of shoes, a plate of dahi-vada, a lipstick, all are products. All these are purchased because they satisfy one or more of our needs. We are paying not for the tangible product but for the benefit it will provide. So, in simple words, product can be described as a bundle of benefits which a marketer offers to the consumer for a price. While buying a pair of shoes, we are actually buying comfort for our feet, while buying a lipstick we are actually paying for beauty because lipstick is likely to make us look good. Product can also take the form of a service like an air travel, telecommunication, etc. Thus, the term product refers to goods and services offered by the Organization for sale.

- **Price**: Price is the amount charged for a product or service. It is the second most important element in the marketing mix. Fixing the price of the product is a tricky job. Many factors like demand for a product, cost involved, consumer's ability to pay, prices charged by competitors for similar products, government restrictions etc. have to be kept in mind while fixing the price. In fact, pricing is a very crucial decision area as it has its effect on demand for the product and also on the profitability of the firm.

- **Place**: Goods are produced to be sold to the consumers. They must be made available to the consumers at a place where they can conveniently make purchase. Woolens are manufactured on a large scale in Ludhiana and you purchase them at a store from the nearby market in your town. So, it is necessary that the product is available at shops in your town. This involves a chain of individuals and institutions like distributors, wholesalers and retailers who constitute firm's distribution network (also called a channel of distribution). The Organization has to decide whether to sell directly to the retailer or through the distributors/wholesaler etc. It can even plan to sell it directly to consumers.

- **Promotion:** If the product is manufactured keeping the consumer needs in mind, is rightly priced and made available at outlets convenient to them but the consumer is not made aware about its price, features, availability etc, its marketing effort may not be successful. Therefore promotion is an important ingredient of marketing mix as it refers to a process of informing, persuading and influencing a consumer to make choice of the product to be bought. Promotion is done through means of personal selling, advertising, publicity and sales promotion. It is done mainly with a view to provide information to prospective consumers about the availability, characteristics and uses of a product. It arouses potential consumer's interest in the product, compare it with competitors' product and make his choice. The proliferation of print and electronic media has immensely helped the process of promotion.

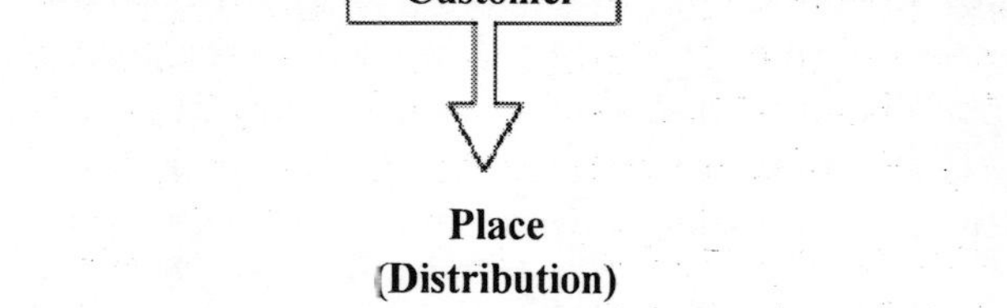

Figure: Marketing mix: A bird's eye view

2.3. Place

A channel of distribution thus, refers to the pathway used by the manufacturer for transfer of the ownership of goods and its physical transfer to the consumers and the user/buyers (industrial buyers).Stanton has also defined it as "A distribution channel consists of the set of people and firms involved in the transfer of title to a product as the product moves from producer to ultimate consumer or business user". Basically it refers to the vital links connecting the manufacturers and producers and the ultimate consumers/users. It includes both the producer and the end user and also the middlemen/agents engaged in the process of transfer of title of goods. Primarily a channel of distribution performs the following functions:

a. It helps in establishing a regular contact with the customers and provides them the necessary information relating to the goods.

b. It provides the facility for inspection of goods by the consumers at convenient points to make their choice.

c. It facilitates the transfer of ownership as well as the delivery of goods.

d. It helps in financing by giving credit facility.

e. It assists the provision of after sales services, if necessary.

f. It assumes all risks connected with the carrying out the distribution function.

Types of channels of distribution

Generally we do not buy goods directly from the producers. The producers/ manufacturers usually use services of one or more middlemen to supply their goods to the consumers. But sometimes; they do have direct contact with the customers with no middlemen in between them. This is true more for industrial goods where the customers are highly knowledgeable and their individual purchases are large. The various channels used for distribution of consumer goods can be described as follows:

(a) Zero stage channel of distribution

Zero stage distribution channels exists where there is direct sale of goods by the producer to the consumer. This direct contact with the consumer can be made through door-todoor salesmen, own retail outlets or even through direct mail. Also in case of perishable products and certain technical household products, door-to-door sale is an easier way of convincing consumer to make a purchase. Eureka Forbes, for example, sells its water purifiers directly through their own sales staff.

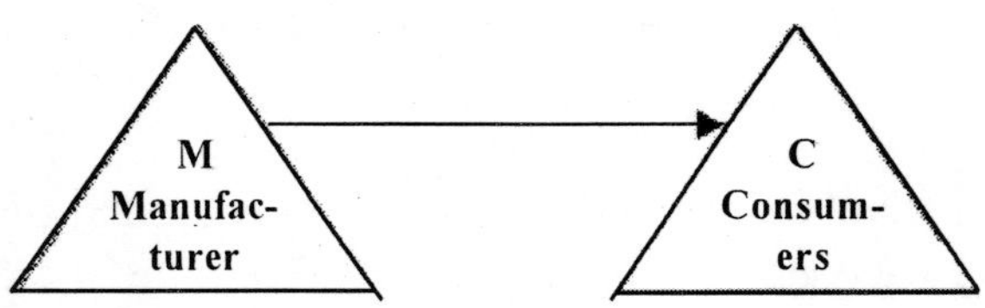

(b) One stage channel of distribution

In this case, there is one middleman i.e., the retailer. The manufacturers sell their goods to retailers who in turn sell it to the consumers. This type of distribution channel is preferred by manufacturers of consumer durables like refrigerator, air conditioner, machine, etc. where individual purchase involves large amount. It is also used for distribution through large scale retailers such as departmental stores (Big Bazaar, Spencer and super markets).

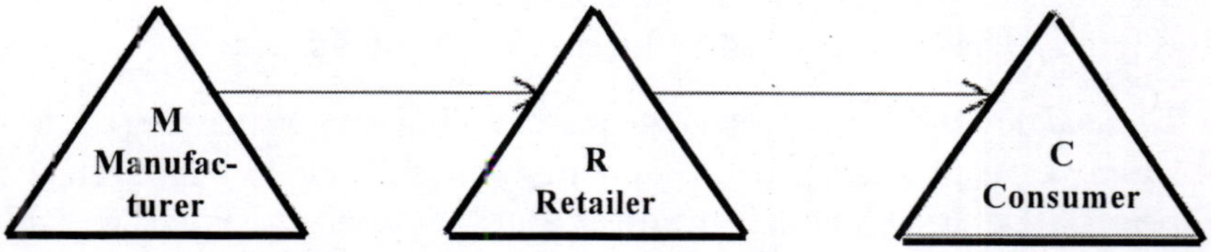

(c) Two stage channel of distribution

This is the most commonly used channel of distribution for the sale of consumer goods. In this case, there are two middlemen used, namely, wholesaler and retailer. This is applicable to products where markets are spread over a large area, value of individual purchase is small and the frequency of purchase is high.

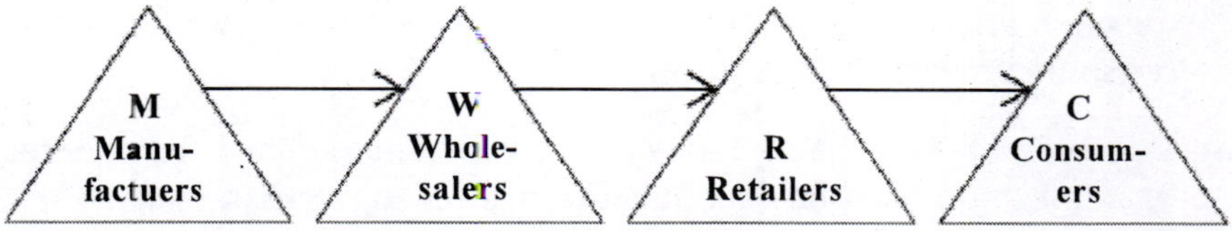

(d) Three stage channel of distribution

When the number of wholesalers used is large and they are scattered throughout the country, the manufacturers often use the services of mercantile agents who act as a link between the producer and the wholesaler. They are also known as distributors.

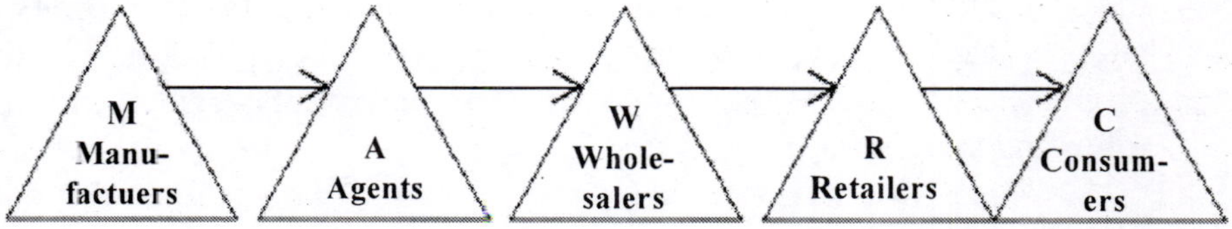

2.4. Price

In simple terms, it is the exchange value of goods and services in terms of money. Pricing (determination of price to be charged) is another important element of marketing mix and it plays a crucial role in the success of a product in the market. If the price fixed is high, it is likely to have an adverse effect on the sales volume. If, on the other hand, it is too low, it will adversely affect the profitability. Hence, it has to be fixed after taking various aspects into consideration. The factors usually taken into account while determining the price of a product can be broadly described as follows:

(a) *Cost*: No business can survive unless it covers its cost of production and distribution. In large number of products, the retail prices are determined by adding a reasonable profit margin to the cost. Higher the cost, higher is likely to be the price, lower the cost lower the price.

(b) *Demand*: Demand also affects the price in a big way. When there is limited supply of a product and the demand is high, people buy even if high prices are charged by the producer. But how high the price would be is dependent upon prospective buyers' capacity and willingness to pay and their preference for the product. In this context, price elasticity, i.e. responsiveness of demand to changes in price should also be kept in view.

(c) *Competition*: The price charged by the competitor for similar product is an important determinant of price. A marketer would not like to charge a price higher than the competitor for fear of losing customers. Also, he may avoid charging a price lower than the competitor. Because it may result in price war which we have recently seen in the case of soft drinks, washing powder, mobile phone etc.

(d) *Marketing Objectives*: A firm may have different marketing objectives such as maximization of profit, maximization of sales, bigger market share, survival in the market and so on. The prices have to be determined accordingly. For example, if the objective is to maximize sales or have a bigger market share, a low price will be fixed. Recently one brand of washing powder slashed its prices to half, to grab a bigger share of the market.

(e) *Government Regulation*: Prices of some essential products are regulated by the government under the Essential Commodities Act. For example, prior to liberalization of the economy, cement and steel prices were decided by the government. Hence, it is essential that the existing statutory limits, if any, are also kept in view while determining the prices of products by the producers. Methods of fixing the price can be broadly divided into the following categories.

a) Cost based pricing

b) Competition based pricing

c) Demand based pricing

d) Objective based pricing

a. *Cost Based Pricing*

Under this method, price of the product is fixed by adding the amount of desired profit margin to the cost of the product. If a particular soap costs the marketeer Rs. 8 and he desires a profit of 25%, the price of the soap is fixed at Rs 8 + (8x25/100) =Rs. 10. While calculating the price in this way, all costs (variable as well as fixed) incurred in manufacturing the product are taken into consideration.

b. *Competition Based Pricing*

In case of products where market is highly competitive and there is negligible difference in quality of competing brands, price is usually fixed closer to the price of the competing brands. It is called 'young rate pricing' and is a very convenient method because the marketers do not have to worry much about demand and cost and effect the change as per the changes by the industry leaders.

c. *Demand Based Pricing*

At times, prices are determined by the demand for the product. Under this method, without paying much attention to cost and competitors' prices, the marketers try to ascertain the demand for the product. If the demand is high they decide to take advantage and fix a high price. If the demand is low, they fix low prices for their product. At times they resort to differential prices and charge different prices from different groups of customers depending upon their perceived values and capacity to pay. Take the case of cinema halls where the rates of tickets differ for the different sets of rows in the hall.

d. *Objective Based Pricing*

This method is applicable to introduction of new (innovative) products. If, at the introductory stage of the products, the organization wishes to penetrate the market i.e., to capture large parts of the market and discourage the prospective competitors to enter into the fray, it fixes a low price. Alternatively, the organization may decide to skim the market i.e., to earn high profit by taking advantage of a group of customers give more importance to their status or distinction and are willing to pay even a higher price for it. In such a situation they fix quite high price at the introductory stage of their product and market it to only those customers who can afford it.

2.5. Promotion

Promotion refers to the process of informing and persuading the consumers to buy certain product. By using this process, the marketers convey persuasive message and information to its potential customers. The main objective of promotion is to seek buyers' attention towards the product with a view to:

- Arouse his interest in the product
- Inform him about its availability and

- Inform him as to how is it different from others.

It is thus a persuasive communication and also serves as a reminder. A firm uses different tools for its promotional activities which are as follows:

a. Advertising

b. Publicity

c. Personal selling

d. Sales promotion

These are also termed as four elements of a promotion mix. Let us have a brief idea about these promotion tools.

a. *Advertising*: Advertising is the most commonly used tool for informing the present and prospective consumers about the product, its quality, features, availability, etc. It is a paid form of non-personal communication through different media about a product, idea, a service or an Organization by an identified sponsor. It can be done through print media like newspaper, magazines, billboards, electronic media like radio, television, etc. It is a very flexible and comparatively low cost tool of promotion.

b. *Publicity*: This is a non-paid process of generating wide range of communication to contribute a favorable attitude towards the product and the organization. You may have seen articles in newspapers about an organization, its products and policies. The other tools of publicity are press conference, publication and news in the electronic media etc. It is published or broadcasted without charging any money from the firm. Marketers often spend a lot of time and effort in getting news items placed in the media for creation of a favorable image of the company and its products.

c. *Personal selling*: You must have come across representatives of different companies knocking at your door and persuading you to buy their product. It is a direct presentation of the product to the consumers or prospective buyers. It refers to the use of salespersons to persuade the buyers to act favorably and buy the product. It is most effective promotional tool in case of industrial goods.

d. *Sales promotion*: This refers to short-term and temporary incentives to purchase or induce trials of new goods. The tool includes contests, games, gifts, trade shows, discounts, etc. Sales promotional activities are often carried out at retail levels.

2.6. Product

Product refers to the goods and services offered by the organization for sale. Here the marketers have to recognize that consumers are not simply interested in the physical features of a product but a set of tangible and intangible attributes that satisfy their wants. For example, when a consumer buys a washing machine he is not buying simply a machine but a gadget that helps him in washing clothes. It also needs to be noted that the term product refers to anything that can be offered to a market for attention, acquisition, or use. Thus, the term product is defined as "anything that can be offered to a market to satisfy a want". It normally includes physical objects and services. In a broader sense, however, it not only includes physical objects and services but also the supporting services like brand name, packaging accessories, installation, after sales service etc.

Classification of Products

Product can be broadly classified on the basis of (A) use, (B) durability, and (C) tangibility.

Let us have a brief idea about the various categories and their exact nature under each head, noting at the same time that in marketing the terms 'product' and 'goods' are often used interchangeably.

A. Based on use, the product can be classified as:

(a) Consumer Goods and

(b) Industrial Goods

(a) *Consumer goods*: Goods meant for personal consumption by the households or ultimate consumers are called consumer goods. This includes items like toiletries, groceries, clothes etc. Based on consumers' buying behavior the consumer goods can be further classified as:

(i) Convenience Goods

(ii) Shopping Goods and

(iii) Specialty Goods

(i) Convenience Goods: Do you remember, the last time when did you buy a packet of butter or a soft drink or a grocery item? Perhaps you don't remember, or you will say last week or yesterday. Reason is, these goods belong to the categories of convenience goods which are bought frequently without much planning or shopping effort and are also consumed quickly. Buying decision in case of these goods does not involve much pre-planning. Such goods are usually sold at convenient retail outlets.

(ii) Shopping Goods: These are goods which are purchased less frequently and are used very slowly like clothes, shoes, household appliances. In case of these goods, consumers make choice of a product considering its suitability, price, style, quality and products of competitors and substitutes, if any. In other words, the consumers usually spend a considerable amount of time and effort to finalize their purchase decision as they lack complete information prior to their shopping trip. It may be noted that shopping goods involve much more expenses than convenience goods.

(iii) Specialty Goods: Because of some special characteristics of certain categories of goods people generally put special efforts to buy them. They are ready to buy these goods at prices at which they are offered and also put in extra time to locate the seller to make the purchase. The nearest car dealer may be ten kilometers away but the buyer will go there to inspect and purchase it. In fact, prior to making a trip to buy the product he/she will collect complete information about the various brands. Examples of speciality goods are cameras, TV sets, new automobiles etc.

(b) *Industrial Goods*: Goods meant for consumption or use as inputs in production of other products or provision of some service is termed as 'industrial goods'. These are meant for non-personal and commercial use and include (i) raw materials, (ii) machinery, (iii) components, and (iv) operating supplies (such as lubricants, stationery etc). The buyers of industrial goods are supposed to be knowledgeable, cost conscious and rational in their purchase and therefore, the marketers follow different pricing, distribution and promotional strategies for their sale. It may be noted that the same product may be classified as consumer goods as well as industrial goods depending upon its end use. Take for example the case of coconut oil. When it is used as hair oil or cooking oil, it is treated as consumer goods and when used for manufacturing bath soap it is termed as industrial goods. However, the way these products are marketed to these two groups are very different because purchase by industrial buyer is usually large in quantity and bought either directly from the manufacturer or the local distributor.

B. Based on Durability

The products can be classified as:

(a) Durable Goods and

(b) Non-durable Goods

(a) *Durable Goods*: Durable goods are products which are used for a long period i.e., for months or years together. Examples of such goods are refrigerator, car, washing machine etc. Such goods generally require more of personal selling effortsand have high profit margins. In case of these goods, seller's reputation and presale and after-sale service are important determinants of purchase decision.

(b) *Non-durable Goods*: Non-durable goods are products that are normallyconsumed in one go or last for a few uses. Examples of such products are soap, salt, pickles, sauce etc. These items are consumed quickly and we purchase these goods more often. Such items are generally made available by the producer through large number of convenient retail outlets. Profit margins on such items are usually kept low and heavy advertising is done to attract people towards their trial and use.

C. Based on tangibility

The products can be classified as:

(a) Tangible Goods and

(b) Intangible Goods

(a) ***Tangible Goods*****:** Most goods, whether these are consumer goods or industrial goods and whether these are durable or non-durable, fall in this category as they have a physical form, that can be touched and seen. Thus, all items like groceries, cars, raw-materials, machinery etc. fall in the category of tangible goods.

(b) ***Intangible Goods*****:** Intangible goods refer to services provided to the individual consumers or to the Organizational buyers (industrial, commercial, institutional, government etc.). Services are essentially intangible activities which provide want or need satisfaction. Medical treatment, postal, banking and insurance services etc., all fall in this category.

3

MARKET SEGMENTATION

3.1. Market Segmentation – Meaning and Definition

Marketers have recognized that the target audience of a certain product is not all alike. They differ in terms of demographics, attitudes, needs, location and social affiliations. Most markets are made up of different individual customers, sub-markets or segments. Segmentation and targeting of customers allows the marketer to deliver a product within the target audience needs and wants. It is a necessity to establish the needs and values of the target customers within each segment, in order for companies to promote their products, brands or services appropriately. The landline telephones have during the past ten-fifteen years met a hard competition from the mobile telephones and therefore it can be argued that the landline telephones have to be marketed in a different way than the mobile telephone. In order for marketers to design the right marketing strategy it is necessary for the marketer to have a great knowledge about the needs and wants. By following the segmentation process the marketer will achieve the necessary knowledge and thereby be able to design a persuasive and appropriate marketing strategy. This thesis will provide a framework for exemplifying how market segmentation can determine the right target audience. This will be done by using the landline telephone and mobile telephone as examples in an analysis according to two models. The aim of this thesis is to understand the segmentation process and the concepts regarding the segmentation process. Furthermore by gaining knowledge of these concepts it should be possible to determine the right target customers of respectively the landline telephone and the mobile telephone by analyzing. The analysis will be entirely fictional and will not have further relevance in other connections besides this thesis. This thesis will focus on the segmentation process and defining a target audience which will be studied according to the leading researchers. Furthermore since this thesis is based upon mobile phones and landline phones it is not one singular brand that will be taken into consideration but the landline telephone and the mobile telephone in general. Due to the fact that a questionnaire has been conducted with Danish participants, the analysis in the last part of the thesis will not provide a picture of the English market, but the Danish. Therefore the theoretical part of the thesis is to provide knowledge of the technical terms used during the thesis. In addition to that, the results from the questionnaire are entirely fictional and have no relevance in other aspects beside this thesis. Furthermore, the structure and content of the thesis is build on a business-to-customer approach within the telephone industry and business-to-business approaches will not be examined. In connection with the analysis, the Minerva model and the Mosaic model will be the only models used. In the field of segmentation, the VALS, PRIZM and ACORN models etc. are of certain relevance. However, these will not be explained and/or used in this thesis.

3.2. Mass Marketing

Throughout the history of the world, businesses have traditionally served very small geographic markets. The size of a business's target markets was generally limited to the range of the entrepreneur's personal mode of travel. In the late 1800s and early 1900s, advances in transportation such as railways and automobiles opened up the door for mass distribution. In the 1920s, radio broadcasts made it possible for companies to send advertising messages to large, undifferentiated audiences at once, giving birth to the mass market concept and the first mass marketing techniques. The term mass market refers to a large, undifferentiated market of consumers with widely varied backgrounds. Products and services needed by almost every member of society are suited for the mass market. Such items as electric and gas utilities, soap, paper towels and gasoline, for example, can be advertised and sold to almost anyone, making them mass market goods.

3.3. Market Segmentation

The market segmentation is mentioned as being one of the key elements of modern marketing and is, as mentioned, the process of dividing the market into several groups and/or segment(s) based on factors such as demographic, geographic, psychological and behavioral factors. By doing so the marketers will have a better understanding of their target audience and thereby make their marketing more effective. This is due to the fact that by using the analytical process that puts customers first, the marketer will get more satisfied customers and thereby gain a great advantage over competitors. Market segments can be characterized in different ways on way is to characterize the preferences of the target customers; homogeneous preferences, referring to customers that roughly have the same preferences. Secondly there are diffused preferences which mean that the customers vary in their preferences and finally clustered preferences which mean that the natural market segments emerge from groups of consumers with shared preferences. When talking about market segmentation it is necessary to briefly mention the three areas of marketing which is to be taken into consideration when market a product. The first area is mass marketing. It covers the area of mass producing, mass distributes and mass promotes on product to all buyers. However, marketers have realized the great variety in each individual customer and therefore the market segmentation is a helpful tool for the marketers to customize their marketing programmes for each individual customer. The second area is product differentiated marketing. The marketer produces two or more products that display different features, styles, quality, sizes etc. The third, and dominating, area is target marketing. The marketer distinguishes among a variety of market segments, chooses one or more of the segments and then develops products and marketing mixes customized to each segment.

3.4. Benefits of Market Segmentation

The size and differential needs of the purchasing public, hundreds of millions of people in the United States alone, make it difficult for any one company to serve everyone. Market segmentation aims to define a specific subset of the purchasing public that aligns well with the services or products a business offers. Businesses often analyze demographics to perform market segmentation, although psychographic factors, geographic differences and even behavioral variances can indicate viable market segments.

Cost Reduction

The old standby of mass marketing in an attempt to capture with widest possible cross-section of consumers produces mixed results and runs up enormous costs. Market segmentation, by contrast, limits the field of customers and allows a business to direct financial resources into specific communication channels that reach out directly to consumers in that market segment. A company that makes precision machining tools would waste money marketing placing ads in general interest magazines, as the average consumer has no use for precision machining equipment. Magazines aimed at machinists and machine shops represent a far smaller investment compared with mass marketing and speak directly to the company's desired customer base.

Product Development

Focusing in on a specific market segment allows a business to tailor existing products and services to meet the particular needs of those customers. Segmentation also allows the business to design future products and services to address the exact needs of the target market. A spa that caters to professionals, for example, might institute expanded evening hours to accommodate the demanding schedules working professionals often face. Consumers in the market segment also can provide input for proposed products, through focus groups or surveys, to help a business determine if the product provides value to them.

New Markets

Market segmentation can help a business identify underserved markets, which provide a golden opportunity for a business to establish itself as first in the market. As the book "The 22 Immutable Laws of Marketing" points out, businesses that first offer a product or service to a market tend to control a commanding market share even when competitors move in. For example, a pizza place that offers delivery service to an area that could not get delivery before stands a good chance of remaining the go-to pizza delivery place for residents in that area.

Business Focus

Market segmentation also encourages the business to focus, as trying to serve too many markets or provide too many products dilutes the business brand. If a restaurant tries to offer food ranging from burgers and takeout Chinese to high-end Italian cuisine, it fails to capture any single market and loses its ability to differentiate itself. Catering to a narrowly defined market means the business must narrowly define its offerings to suit those customers. The restaurant that serves only high-end Italian food to dine-in customers attracts a market segment that seeks a specific product and experience while allowing the business to improve its core competencies.

3.5. Basis of Market Segmentation

The segmentation of consumer markets requires the creation of sub-groups from a larger population to more specifically target them. There are virtually dozens of ways that a market might be segmented and the segments chosen will depend on the business and the products or services it offers. Basically, segmentation is all about identifying specific groups of people based on common characteristics.

Demographic	Behavioural	Psychographic	Geographic
Age	Purchase	Lifestyle	Needs
Education	Consumption	Personality Traits	Preferences
Income	Lifestyle	Values	Interests
Family Size	Usage	Opinions	Based on Location
Race		Interests	
Gender			
Occupation			
Nationality			

Demographics

One common way of segmenting a market is through the use of demographics. Demographics are quantitative characteristics of a group of people. These characteristics might include sex, age, income or geography (where they live). Businesses that segment their market based on demographics are attempting to target specific market segments that are more likely to be interested in what they have to offer. The cosmetics industry, for example, primarily targets women. The hunting industry might be more likely to target men. Luxury car makers target their markets based on income. Marketers are likely to consider multiple demographic characteristics when segmenting their consumer markets.

Psychographics

Psychographics are qualitative attributes of a market and refer to the way people think and what they like to do. Psychographics is sometimes categorized with the acronym IAO which stands for Interests, Activities and Opinions. It can be difficult for marketers to segment their markets into these types of categories on their own. Nielsen is one organization that offers access to consumer lists based on their specific classifications. They have divided U.S. households into 66 distinct types or segments to help marketers focus on market segments based on psychographic characteristics. Psychographics are personal attributes related to personality, values, attitudes, interests, or lifestyles.

Purchase Behaviors

An important way for businesses to segment their consumer markets is through purchase behavior. Keeping good records of customers and their purchases, allows marketers to identify those who have purchased certain types of products or spent at certain levels and to then target them with similar offers. Marketers are also able to target customers of other businesses through by renting lists, which can be used in direct marketing efforts through traditional mail or, increasingly, online.

Pulling it together

The more segments that marketers are able to identify and combine to specifically target groups of individuals most likely to be interested in what they have to offer, the more effective and cost effective their marketing efforts can be. Toward this end, businesses attempt to learn as much as they can about their customers where they live, their age, their income levels, what they purchase, what their hobbies are and what their likes and dislikes are. This information can then be used to "clone" these customers by reaching out to non-customers who share similar traits and characteristics.

3.6. Market Segmentation for Organizational Markets

Just like for consumer markets, business or organizational markets should be segmented in order for the firm to effectively develop a successful marketing program. The segmentation bases/variables for business markets vary a little in terminology, but are quite similar in concept and application to the process of segmenting consumer markets. The main segmentation bases/variables used in business markets include: geographic location, business description (sometimes referred to as demographics), behavioral/operating practices, culture/personality, and organizational goals.

Broad category of business market Segmentation base	Which factors are being considered?
Geographic location	Where does the organization operate? (*Could be multiple locations)*
Business description	What sort of business is it, where does it fit into its industry?
Behavioral/operating practice	How does the organization undertake its purchasing decisions?
Culture/personality	What is the management style of the organization?

Main Category	Segmentation Base	Question to help define segment groups
Geographic location/s	Country/continent	In which countries do they operate?
	Region/area of the country	In which regions do they operate?
	Number of outlets	Does the film have one office only or potentially 1,000s of outlets?
	Geographic spread	Does the firm operate in one geographic area, or spread over a wide area?
Business description	Industry	What industry do they operate in?
	Size (by staff or outlets)	How many staff do they have, or how many outlets do they have?
	Size (revenues/profits)	What is their financial position?
	Products sold	What is their product mix?
	Equipment/technology	What is the main forms of manufacturing and/or IT equipment do they use?
	Company ownership	Are they a public or private company? Are they a subsidiary?

Behavioral/ operating practice	Do they have a centralize purchase decision-making process?
	Are they generally loyal to suppliers or do they frequently switch?
	Are they fast or slow decision makers?
	Do they use franchising?
Culture/ personality	Are they a lead user (an early adopter) or more of a market follower?
	Do they make highly analytical decisions or are they more initiative?
	How socially and environmentally conscious are they?
Organizational goals	Do they have aggressive growth goals?
	Do they want to be seen as a market innovation?
	How important is brand equity to them

3.7. Target Marketing

In business it is a matter of being able to communicate your message in a persuasive way. Companies therefore need to be able to adapt to their target audiences' needs, wants and values. In order for companies to do so, they may ask themselves questions like; how the customers are? What do they buy? And where can they be found? It is not possible for the companies to reach out to all customers in large, broad, or diverse markets and therefore by dividing the customers into groups or segment(s), the company can choose which group they wish to target. Kotler and Armstrong define market segmentation as "dividing a market into distinct groups of buyers who have distinct needs, characteristics, or behavior and who might require separate products or marketing mixes". The overall aim of this chapter is to study the concepts of the market segmentation followed by the next steps of the market segmentation process.

4

CONSUMER BEHAVIOUR

4.1. Consumer Behavior – Meaning and Definition

Consumer Behavior may be defined as "the interplay of forces that takes place during a consumption process, within a consumers' self and his environment. - this interaction takes place between three elements viz. knowledge, affect and behavior; - it continues through pre-purchase activity to the post purchase experience; - it includes the stages of evaluating, acquiring, using and disposing of goods and services". The "consumer" includes both personal consumers and business/industrial/organizational consumers. Consumer behavior explains the reasons and logic that underlie purchasing decisions and consumption patterns; it explains the processes through which buyers make decisions. The study includes within its purview, the interplay between cognition, affect and behavior that goes on within a consumer during the consumption process: selecting, using and disposing off goods and services.

i) The subject deals with issues related to cognition, affect and behavior in consumption behaviors, against the backdrop of individual and environmental determinants. The individual determinants pertain to an individual's internal self and include psychological components like personal motivation and involvement, perception, learning and memory, attitudes, self-concept and personality, and, decision making. The environmental determinants pertain to external influences surrounding an individual and include sociological, anthropological and economic components like the family, social groups, reference groups, social class, culture, sub-culture, cross-culture, and national and regional influences.

ii) The subject can be studied at micro or macro levels depending upon whether it is analyzed at the individual level or at the group level.

iii) Consumer behavior is dynamic and interacting in nature. The three components of cognition, affect and behavior of individuals alone or in groups keeps on changing; so does the environment. There is a continuous interplay or interaction between the three components themselves and with the environment. This impacts consumption pattern and behavior and it keeps on evolving and it is highly dynamic.

iv). Consumer behavior involves the process of exchange between the buyer and the seller, mutually beneficial for both.

v). As a field of study it is descriptive and also analytical/ interpretive. It is descriptive as it explains consumer decision making and behavior in the context of individual determinants and environmental influences. It is analytical/ interpretive, as against a backdrop of theories borrowed from psychology, sociology, social psychology, anthropology and economics; the study analyzes consumption behavior of individuals alone and in groups. It makes use of qualitative and quantitative tools and techniques for research and analysis, with the objective is to understand and predict consumption behavior.

vi). It is a science as well as an art. It uses both, theories borrowed from social sciences to understand consumption behavior, and quantitative and qualitative tools and techniques to predict consumer behavior.

4.2. Consumer Behaviour versus Buyer Behaviour

Your consumer and business customers approach purchasing in two very different ways. To successfully market your business to both types of clients, you need to understand the differences between the consumer and business buying processes. The business processes you use and the kinds of products you offer enter into the way that businesses and consumers purchase your products and view your business.

Planning

Most purchases made by a business are planned in advance, where the same purchases might be impulse buys for a consumer. For example, a business will plan an employee lunch, choose the menu in advance and have the order in place to be catered on a particular day. A consumer's decision on where to go for lunch is often made just minutes before the lunch break. To be able to accommodate both business and consumer purchases, you need to have a structure in place that allows businesses to plan their purchases while still offering impulse options to consumers.

Decision-making

In many cases, the consumer decision-maker is the person that ultimately buys the product. For example, the mother of a family may decide to buy a new sandbox for the children, so she is either the one that goes out to make the purchase or is on hand with the father to make the final choice. A business purchasing process starts with an idea and then goes through a formal approval process. The person that makes the final purchase is often a purchasing agent or departmental representative.

Support

Many businesses require support contracts when purchasing certain types of items. For example, if a business purchases a copier then the copier may need to have at least a three-year warranty on the product before the company can finalize the purchase. A consumer is not restricted by support needs when it comes to buying products, but that does not mean that support is unimportant to a consumer. Adequate support for a product can be sufficient to an end consumer as part of the final purchase contract. For a business, the support issues may need to be spelled out in a more comprehensive manner.

4.3. Buyer and User

Buyer personas are focused on prospects looking to solve a problem or meet an objective that your products, solutions or services help them to achieve. Buyer personas encompass all of the differing roles or stakeholders involved in the purchase decision and are usually represented by decision maker, influencer, champion, and gatekeeper roles. Distinctions can also be made as to economic buyer and functional buyer. User personas are designed to address the perspectives of those who work with your products, solutions or services on a daily basis. The goal is to help these "end users" achieve more complete use of the product, gain more value than they initially anticipated, as well as to help them become champions for continued use,(new additions, extensions or feature upgrades. They got what they needed to solve the original problem from your product, now how do they gain more value, or use more features? This persona is often the influencer in an account-based-marketing retention sale.

4.4. Consumer Behavior versus Consumption Behavior

The difference between Consumer Buyer Behavior and Organizational Buyer Behavior In this essay we will be talking about the difference between consumer buyer behavior and organizational buyer behavior and how marketers can harvest this knowledge to create the right marketing strategies for each category of market. The main difference between consumer buyer behavior and organizational buyer behavior is that consumer buying consists of activates involved in buying and using of products for personal and household use, where organizational buyers purchase primarily for organizational purpose. Consumer behavior is complex and a company has to fit their product more closely and satisfy their customer needs more fully than the competitors. Marketers will also need to know whether their controllable variables, e.g. marketing mix variables, will affect buying behaviour. Culture is the broadest environmental factor witch influences buyer behaviour, consumption choices cannot be understood without considering the culture. It is the prisms with witch customers perceive the product. The culture of consumers determines the priorities he attaches to different products. The link between consumer behaviour and culture is a two-way street. In one direction the products that are produced to fit a consumer's culture are better accepted, in the other direction products and innovation that are created in a specific culture on a given time show us a clear domination in the cultures ideals. (Michael Solomon, Culture, 2006) Social class refers to the grouping together of individuals or families who have certain common social or economic characteristics. Societies can be divided in haves and have-nots. Social Class is determined by income, family background and occupation. The social class is not only determining how much money is spent by the individual but also how it is spent.

4.5. Significance of Consumer Behaviour

Consumer behavior covers a broad variety of consumers based on diversity in age, sex, culture, taste, preference, educational level, income level, etc. Consumer behavior can be defined as "the decision process and physical activity engaged in evaluating, acquiring, using or disposing of goods and services." With all of the diversity to the surplus of goods and services offered to us, and the freedom of choices, one may speculate how individual marketers actually reach us with their highly definite marketing messages. Understanding consumer behavior helps in identifying whom to target, how to target, when to reach them, and what message is to be given to them to reach the target audience to buy the product.

The following illustration shows the determinants of consumer behavior.

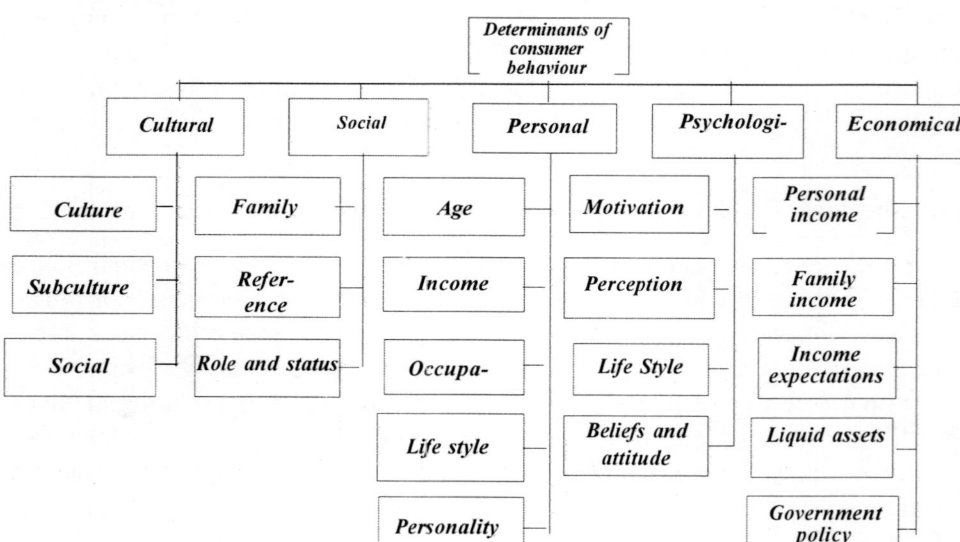

Figure: Determinants of Consumer Behaviour

The study of Consumer Behavior helps in understanding how individuals make decisions to spend their available resources like time, money, and effort while purchasing goods and services. It is a subject that explains the basic questions that a normal consumer faces " what to buy, why to buy, when to buy, where to buy from, how often to buy, and how they use it.

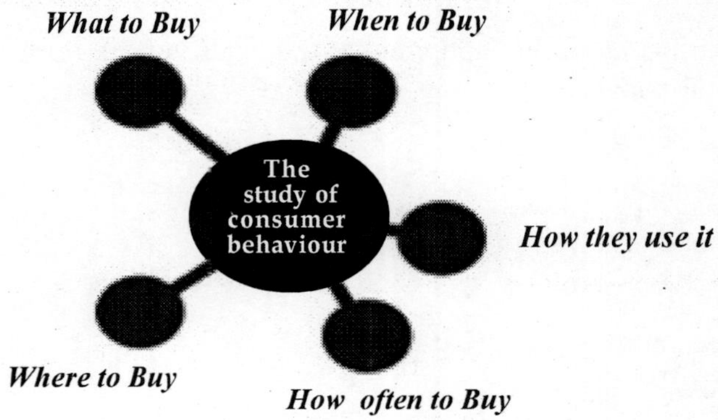

Figure: Study of Consumer Behaviour

Consumer behavior is a complex and multidimensional process that reflects the totality of consumer decisions with respect to acquisition, consumption, and disposal of goods and services.

Dimensions of Consumer Behavior

Consumer behavior is multidimensional in nature and it is influenced by the following subjects "

- Psychology is a discipline that deals with the study of mind and behavior. It helps in understanding individuals and groups by establishing general principles and researching specific cases. Psychology plays a vital role in understanding how consumers behave while making a purchase.
- Sociology is the study of groups. When individuals form groups, their actions are sometimes relatively different from the actions of those individuals when they are operating individually.
- Social Psychology is a combination of sociology and psychology. It explains how an individual operates in a group. Group dynamics play an important role in purchasing decisions. Opinions of peers, reference groups, their families and opinion leaders influence individuals in their behavior.
- Cultural Anthropology is the study of human beings in society. It explores the development of central beliefs, values and customs that individuals inherit from their parents, which influence their purchasing patterns.

4.6. Factors Influencing Consumer Behavior

The consumer behavior or buyer behavior is influenced by several factors or forces. They are: 1. Internal or Psychological factors 2. Social factors 3. Cultural factors 4. Economic factors 5. Personal factors

There are five questions that support any understanding of consumer behavior.

i) Who is the market and what is the extent of their power with regard to the organization?

ii) What do they buy?

iii) Why do they buy?

iv) Who is involved in the buying?

v) How do they buy?

vi) When do they buy?

vii) Where do they buy?

The answers of these questions provide the understanding of the ways in which buyers are most likely to respond to marketing stimuli. The stimulus-response model of buyer behavior is shown below.

Marketing Stimull	Other Stimull
Product	Political
Price	Economic
Place	Social
Promotion	Technological

Buyer's Black Box

Buyer's Characteristics	*Buyer's Decision process*
Psychological	Problem recognition
Social	Information search
Cultural	Evaluation of alternatives
Economic	Purchase decision
Personal	Post-purchase behaviour

Buyer's Decisions
Product and Brand choice
Dealer choice
Purchase timing
Purchase among

Figure : Buyer Behaviour

According to this model, stimuli in the form of both the external environment and the elements of the marketing mix enter the buyer's 'black box' and interact with the buyer's characteristics and decision processes to produce a series of outputs in the form of purchase decisions. The task faced by the marketing planner involves understanding how the black box operates, for which two principal components of the box must be considered; firstly the factors that the individual brings to the buying situation and secondly the decision processes that are used. The consumer behaviour or buyer behaviour is influenced by several factors or forces. They are: I. Internal or Psychological factors II. Social factors III. Cultural factors IV. Economic factors V. Personal factors:

I. Internal or psychological factors

The buying behaviour of consumers is influenced by a number of internal or psychological factors. The most important ones Motivation and Perception.

a) Motivation

A need becomes a motive when it is aroused to a sufficient level of intensity. A motive is a need that is sufficiently pressing to drive the person to act. There can be of types of needs:

i. Biogenic needs

They arise from physiological states of tension such as thirst, hunger

ii. Psychogenic needs

They arise from psychological states of tension such as needs for recognition, esteem in the words of William J Stanton, "A motive can be defined as a drive or an urge for which an individual seeks satisfaction. It becomes a buying motive when the individual seeks satisfaction through the purchase of something". A motive is an inner urge (or need) that moves a person to take purchase action to satisfy two kinds of wants viz. core wants and secondary wants. Let us take two examples:

Examples of core and secondary want are as follows.

Products	Core want	Secondary want
Glasses	Protection to eyes	It should look goo
Shoes	Protection to feet	Elegance in style

So, motivation is the force that activates goal-oriented behavior. Motivation acts as a driving force that impels an individual to take action to satisfy his needs. So it becomes one of the internal factors influencing consumer behavior.

b) Perception

Human beings have considerably more than five senses. Apart from the basic five (touch, taste, smell, sight, hearing) there are senses of direction, the sense of balance, a clear knowledge of which way is down, and so forth. Each sense is feeding information to the brain constantly, and the amount of information being collected would seriously overload the system if one took it all in. The brain therefore selects from the environment around the individual and cuts out the extraneous noise. In effect, the brain makes automatic decisions as to what is relevant and what is not. Even though there may be many things happening around you, you are unaware of most of them; in fact, experiments have shown that some information is filtered out by the optic nerve even before it gets to the brain. People quickly learn to ignore extraneous noises: for example, as a visitor to someone else's home you may be sharply aware of a loudly ticking clock, whereas your host may be entirely used to it, and unaware of it except when making a conscious effort to check that the clock is still running. Therefore the information entering the brain does not provide a complete view of the world around you. When the individual constructs a world-view, she then assembles the remaining information to map what is happening in the outside world. Any gaps (and there will, of course, be plenty of these) will be filled in with imagination and experience. The cognitive map is therefore not a 'photograph'; it is a construct of the imagination. This mapping will be affected by the following factors:

a. Subjectivity

This is the existing world-view within the individual, and is unique to that individual.

b. Categorization

This is the 'pigeonholing' of information, and the pre-judging of events and products. This can happen through a process known as chunking, whereby the individual organizes information into chunks of related items. For example, a picture seen while a particular piece of music is playing might be chunked as one item in the memory, so that sight of the picture evokes the music and vice versa.

c. Selectivity

This is the degree to which the brain is selecting from the environment. It is a function of how much is going on around the individual, and also of how selective (concentrated) the individual is on the current task. Selectivity is also subjective: some people are a great deal more selective than others.

d. Expectation

These lead individuals to interpret later information in a specific way.

e. Past experience

This leads us to interpret later experience in the light of what we already know. Psychologists call this the law of primacy, Sometimes sights, smells or sounds from our past will trigger off inappropriate responses: the smell of bread baking may recall a village bakery from twenty years ago, but in fact the smell could have been artificially generated by an aerosol spray near the supermarket bread counter. An example of cognitive mapping as applied to perception of product quality might run as follows. The consumer uses the input selector to select clues and assign values to them. For quality, the cues are typically price, brand name and retailer name. There are strong positive relationships between price and quality in most consumers' perceptions, and brand name and quality; although the retailer name is less significant, it still carries some weight. For example, many consumers would feel confident that Big Bazaar would sell higher-quality items than the local corner shop, but might be less able to distinguish between Food Bazaar and Giant hyper store. The information is subjective in that the consumer will base decisions on the selected information. Each of us selects differently from the environment and each of us has differing views. Information about quality will be pigeonholed, or categorized: the individual may put Scoda Octavia in the same category as Mercedes Benz or perhaps put Sony in the same slot as Aiwa.

II. Social factors

Man is a social animal. Hence, our behaviour patterns, likes and dislikes are influenced by the people around us to a great extent. We always seek confirmation from the people around us and seldom do things that are not socially acceptable. The social factors influencing consumer behavior are a) Family, b) Reference Groups, c) Roles and status.

a) Family

There are two types of families in the buyer's life viz. nuclear family and Joint family. Nuclear family is that where the family size is small and individuals have higher liberty to take decisions whereas in joint families, the family size is large and group decision-making gets more preference than individual. Family members can strongly influence the buyer behavior, particularly in the Indian contest. The tastes, likes, dislike, life styles etc. of the members are rooted in the family buying behavior. The family influence on the buying behavior of a member may be found in two ways

i) The family influence on the individual personality, characteristics, attitudes and evaluation criteria and

ii) The influence on the decision-making process involved in the purchase of goods and services. In India, the head of the family may alone or jointly with his wife decides the purchase. So marketers should study the role and the relative influence of the husband, wife and children in the purchase of goods and services.

An individual normally lives through two families:

Family of orientation

This is the family in which a person takes birth. The influences of parents and individual's upbringing have a strong effect on the buying habits. For instance, an individual coming form an orthodox Tamil or Gujarati vegetarian family may not consume meat or egg even though she may appreciate its nutritional values.

Family of procreation

This is the family formed by an individual with his or her spouse and children. Normally, after marriage, an individual's purchasing habits and priorities change under the influence of spouse. As the marriage gets older, the people usually settle in certain roles. For instance, a father normally takes decisions on investment whereas the mother takes decision on health of children. From a marketing viewpoint, the level of demand for many products is dictated more by the number of households than by the number of families. The relevance of families to marketing is therefore much more about consumer behavior than about consumer demand levels .In terms of its function as a reference group, the family is distinguished by the following characteristics:

i. Face-to-face contact

Family members see each other every day and interact as advisers, information providers and sometimes deciders. Other reference groups rarely have this level of contact.

ii. Shared consumption

Durables such as refrigerators, washing machines, televisions and furniture are shared, and food is collectively purchased and cooked. Purchase of these items is often collective; children even participate in decision making on such major purchases as cars and houses.

iii. Subordination of individual need

Because consumption is shared, some family members will find that the solution chosen is not one that fully meets their needs.

iv. Purchasing agent

Because of the shared consumption, most families will have one member who does most, or all of the shopping. Traditionally, this has been the mother of the family, but increasingly the purchasing agents are the older children of the family and even pre-teens are sometimes taking over this role.

The reason for this is the increase in the number of working mothers who have less time for shopping. This has major implications for marketers, since pre-teens and young teens generally watch more TV than adults and are therefore more open to marketing communications. Role specialization is critical in family decision making because of the sheer number of different products that must be bought each year in order to keep the family supplied. What this means in practice is that, for example, the family member responsible for doing the cooking is also likely to take the main responsibility for shopping for food. The family member who does the most driving is likely to make the main decision about the car and its accessories, servicing, fuelling and so forth; the family gardener buys the gardening products, and so on. Culture has a marked effect on family decision-making styles. Religion and nationality will often affect the way decisions are made. Indian cultures tend to be male dominated in decision-making, whereas European and North American cultures show a more egalitarian pattern of decision-making. There are two issues here for the marketer: first, what is the effect on the marketing mix of the multiethnic society like in India; and secondly, what is the effect when dealing internationally? This is a somewhat sensitive area and the marketers are still getting to grips with. Social class creates patterns of decision-making. Among very wealthy families, there appears to be a greater tendency for the husbands to make the decisions, but at the same time the norms of purchase tend to be well established and therefore discussion is unnecessary. Lower-class families, with low incomes, tend to be more matriarchal, with the wives often handling the financial decisions about rent, insurance, grocery and food bills without reference to the husbands. Middle-class families tend to show greater democratic involvement in decision-making. These social class distinctions are gradually breaking down, however, as a result of increasing wealth and mass education. The family may well adopt different roles according to the decision-making stage. At the problem recognition stage of, for example, the need for new shoes for the children, the children themselves may be the main contributors. The mother may then decide what type of shoes should be bought, and the father may be the one who takes the children to buy the shoes. It is reasonable to suppose that the main user of the product might be important in the initial stages, with perhaps joint decision making at the final purchase.

Other determinants might include such factors as whether both parents are earning. The double income families generally take decisions jointly because each has a financial stake in the outcome. Gender role orientation is clearly crucial to decision making. Husbands (and wives) with conservative views about gender roles will tend towards the assumption that most decisions about expenditure will be made by the husband. Even within this type of decision-making system, however, husbands will usually adjust their own views to take account of their wife's attitudes and needs. The family is a flexible concept, and families go through life cycles. There have been various versions of the family life cycle, but most are based on the original work of Wells and Gubar. Following table shows the stages of the family life cycle.

4.7. Types of Consumer Behavior

a. Complex Buying Behavior

Consumers go through complex buying behaviour when they are highly involved in a purchase and aware of significant differences among brands. Consumers are highly involved when the product is expensive, bought infrequently, risky and highly self-expressive. Typically the consumer does not know much about the product category and has much to learn. F01 example, a person buying a personal computer may not know what attribute to look for. Many of the product features like "16K.memory" "disc storage", "screen resolution" carry no meaning to him or her. This buyer will pass through a learning process characterized by first developing beliefs about the product, then attitudes, and then making a thoughtful purchase choice. The marketer of a high-involvement product must understand the information-gathering and evaluation behaviour of high-involvement consumers. The marketer needs to develop strategies that assist the buyer in learning about the attributes of the product class, their relative importance, and the high standing of the company's brand on the more important attributes. The marketer needs to differentiate the brand's features, use mainly print media and long copy to describe the brand's benefits, and motivate store sales personnel and the buyer's acquaintances to influence the final brand choice.

b. Dissonance-Reducing Buying Behavior

Sometimes the consumer is highly, involved in a purchase but sees little difference in the brands. The high involvement is again based on the fact that the purchase is expensive, infrequent, and risky. In this case, the buyer will shop around to learn what is, available but will buy fairly quickly because brand differences are not pronounced. The buyer may respond primarily to a good price or to purchase convenience. After the purchase, the consumer might experience dissonance that stems from noticing certain disquieting features of the product or hearing favorable things about other brands. The consumer will be alert to information that might justify his or her decision. The consumer will first act, then acquire new beliefs and end up with a set of attitudes. Here marketing communications should aim to supply beliefs and evaluations that help the consumer feel good about his or her brand choice.

c. Habitual Buying Behavior

Many products are bought under conditions of low consumer involvement and the absence of significant brand differences. Consider the purchase of salt. Consumers have little involvement in this product category. They go to the store and reach for the brand. If they keep reaching for the same brand, it is out of habit, not strong brand loyalty. There is good evidence that consumers have low involvement with most low-cost, frequently purchased products. Consumer behavior in these cases does not pass through the normal belief/attitude/behavior sequence. Consumers do not search extensively for information about the brands, evaluate their characteristics, and make a weighty decision on which brand to buy. Instead, they are passive recipients of information as they watch television or see print ads. Ad repetition creates brand familiarity rather than brand conviction. Consumers do not form a strong attitude towards a brand but select it because it is familiar. After purchase, they may not even evaluate the choice because they are not highly involved with the product. So the buying process is brand beliefs formed by passive learning, followed by purchase behavior, which may be followed by evaluation. Marketers of low-involvement products with few brand differences find it effective to use price and sales promotions to stimulate product trial, since buyers are not highly committed to any brand. In advertising a low-involvement product, a number of things should be observed. The ad copy should stress only a few key points Visual symbols and Imagery are important because they can easily be remembered and associated with the brand. The ad campaigns should go for high repetition with short- duration messages. Television is more effective than print media because it is a low-involvement medium that is suitable for passive learning. Advertising planning should be based on classical conditioning theory where the buyer learns to identify a certain product by a symbol that is repeatedly attached to it.

d. Variety-Seeking Buying Behavior

Some buying situations are characterized by low consumer involvement but significant brand differences. Here consumers are often observed to do a lot of brand' switching. An example occurs in purchasing cookies. The consumer has some beliefs, chooses a brand of cookies without much evaluation, and evaluates it during consumption. But next time, the consumer may reach for another brand out of boredom or a wish for a different taste. Brand switching occurs for the sake of variety rather than dissatisfaction. The marketing strategy is different for the market leader and the minor brands in this product category. The market leader will try to encourage habitual buying behavior by dominating the shelf space, avoiding out-of-stock conditions, and sponsoring frequent reminder advertising. Challenger firms will encourage variety seeking by offering lower prices, deals, coupons, free samples and advertising that presents reasons for trying something new.

4.8. Theories of Buying Behavior

There are a multitude of theories on the buying behavior of individuals and businesses are constantly analyzing them to figure out how to persuade the consumer to buy their products and services. Often a customer will feel a need to purchase a product and go through a series of steps before making the purchase.

However, different consumers will come to different buying decisions based on a number of factors like cultural influences, environmental elements and even their own personality.

Generic Theory of Buying Behavior

For many purchases, the consumer will follow a generic model of decision-making by going through a process to make a decision. Typically, the buyer will recognize a need to make a purchase that initiates research on products and pricing. As an example, the decision to buy a washing machine might come after the old one breaks and needs a costly repair. The consumer will investigate the new washing machines on the market, evaluate features, benefits and pricing and ultimately make a decision to purchase. How the consumer feels about the product after the purchase is also an issue. If he is satisfied with its performance, he will be more likely to purchase that brand in the future.

Cultural Theory of Buying Behavior

Cultural influences can affect the buying behavior of the individual. A person's culture is his set of values and beliefs learned in the context of a community. These values and beliefs lead to certain buying behaviors. Your social class based on your occupation, income and education can influence buying behavior as can your membership in a group such as family and friends at work or at school. Often, there is an opinion leader in the group who has influence over the buying behavior of others because of specialized knowledge of sheer force of personality.

Environmental Theory of Buying Behavior

The same buyer can exhibit different buying behavior based upon the situation. For example, you may love to eat peanuts as a snack, but you would not consider buying them when you are trying to impress a new friend. Normally, you might compare prices in the supermarket when purchasing juice or water, but after a long day at the office you might just grab the first bottle you see at a convenience store at a higher price.

Internal Theory of Buying Behavior

Some people love to shop and will go the last mile to examine every product out there and compare pricing before making a decision. Others have a personality that encourages them to select a product for purchase when they find one that is good enough although it may not be the best in terms of price or features. The lifestyle of the buyer also influences buying decisions. Consumers living in a family neighborhood where many people own SUVs may be predisposed to buy one, too.

4.9. Buying Motives

A buying motive is the reason why the customer purchases the goods. So, motive refers to thought, urge, feeling, emotion and drive which make the buyer to react in the form of a decision. Motivation explains the behavior of why they are going to buy the goods. They buy the goods due to several motives such as economic, social, psychological, etc. For example: In winter seasons we are motivated to purchase the woolen clothes to protect from the cold. Likewise, we are motivated to purchase the fans in summer season to get relief from the hot. Knowledge of buying motives of the customers is important for the producers and suppliers. The needs and desires of customers and their buying behavior should be properly discussed. This will help to take proper step for drawing the attention and sale of goods. So, buying motive is concerned with the reasons that impulse the buyer to take the decision for the action. It motivates or induces the customers that may be affected due to several reasons such as pride, fashion, fear, safety, love, affection, comfort, convenience and economy. After analyzing and evaluating it, the producers as well as suppliers can effort to develop the product and advertisement creativity.

4.10. Types of Buying Motives

There are the following different roles that persons can play in a buying decision:

a. **Initiator:** The initiator is a person who first suggests or thinks of the idea of buying the particular product. For example, publisher of a book initiates the professor to ask the students of his class to purchase the book. Here publisher is the initiator, the first person to initiate the buying process.

b. **Influencer:** Influencer is a person who explicitly or implicitly has some influence on the final buying decision of others. Students are influenced by the advice of the professor while taking a decision to purchase a book. Here professor is the influencer.

c. **Decider:** The decider is a person who ultimately determines any part or whole of the buying decision, i.e., whether to buy, what to buy, how to buy, when to buy or where to buy. Children are the deciders for buying the toys, house lady for kitchen provisions, and head of the family for durable or luxury items.

d. **Buyer:** The buyer is the person who actually purchase. Buyer may be the decider or he may be some other person. Children (deciders) are the deciders for purchasing the toys, but purchases are made by the parents.

e. **User:** User is the person who actually uses or consumes the services or products.

Buying motive is the urge or motive to satisfy a desire or need that makes people buy goods or services. Behind every purchase there is a buying motive.It refers to the thoughts, feelings, emotions and instincts, which arouse in the buyers a desire to buy an article. A buyer does not buy because s/he has been persuaded by the salesman, but s/he buys for the aroused desire in him or her. Motives should be distinguished from instincts. A motive is simply a reason for carrying out a particular behavior and not an automatic response to a stimulus, whereas instincts are pre-programmed responses, which are inborn in the individual and involuntary. Thus hunger is an instinct whereas desire to purchase pizza is a buying motive. According to Prof. D. J. Duncan, "Buying Motives are those influences or considerations which provide the impulse to buy, induce action and determine choice in the purchase of goods and services." Buying motives are can be divided by the following way:

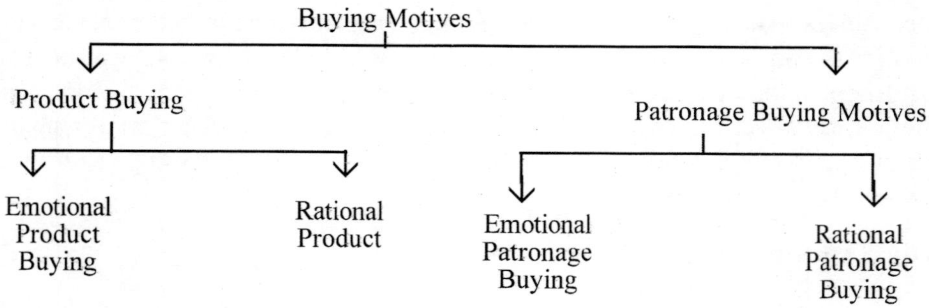

Figure: Classification of Buying Motives

Product Buying Motives

Product buying motives refer to those influences and reasons, which prompt (i.e. induce) a buyer to choose a particular product in preference to other products. They include the physical attraction of the product (i.e. the design, shape, dimension, size, colour, package, performance, price etc. of the product) or the psychological attraction of the product (i.e. the enhancement of the social prestige or status of the purchaser through its possession), desire to remove or reduce the danger or damage to life or body of the possessor, etc. In short, they refer to all those characteristics of a product, which induce a buyer to buy it in preference to other products. Product buying motives may be sub-divided into two groups, viz., (1) emotional product buying motives and (2) rational product buying motives.

A. Promotional Product Buying Motives: When a buyer decides to purchase a product without thinking over the matter logically and carefully (i.e., without much reasoning), she is said to have been influenced by emotional product buying motives.

B. Rational Product Buying Motives: When a buyer decides to buy a certain thing after careful consideration (i.e. after thinking over the matter consciously and logically), s/he is said to have been influenced by rational product buying motives.

Patronage Buying Motives

Patronage buying motives refer to those considerations or reasons, which prompt a buyer to buy the product wanted by him from a particular shop in preference to other shops. In other words, they are those considerations or reasons, which make a buyer, patronize a particular shop in preference to other shops while buying a product. Patronage buying motives also may be sub-divided into two groups' viz. a) Emotional patronage buying motives and b) Rational patronage buying motives.

A. **Emotional Patronage Buying Motives:** When a buyer patronizes a shop (i.e. purchases the things required by him from a particular shop) without applying his mind or without reasoning, he is said to have been influenced by emotional patronage buying motives.

B. **Rational Patronage Buying Motives:** When a buyer patronizes a shop after careful consideration (i.e. after much logical reasoning and careful thinking) he is said to have been influenced by rational patronage buying motives.

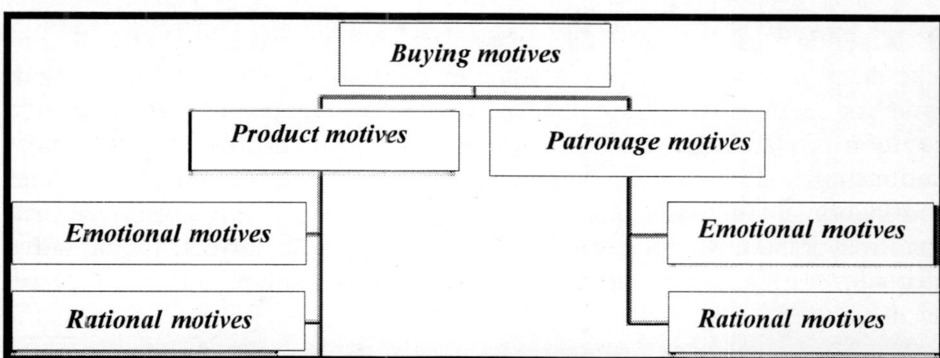

Figure: Product and Patronage Buying Motive

5

MARKETING ORGANIZATION AND PLANNING

5.1. Marketing Organization – Meaning and Definition

Marketing organization is a group of marketing persons brought together to make decisions on marketing areas like product, price, place, and promotion. Marketing organization is the foundation of effective sales planning for systematic execution of plans and policies. Marketing organization provides a system of relationships among various marketing functions to be performed by proper coordination among marketing persons. Marketing organization can be defined as a formal or informal group of individuals working together to reach quantitative and qualitative marketing objectives by making decisions on product, price, place, and promotion.

5.2. Need for Marketing Organization

Streamlines Product Development

A marketing strategy helps you create products and services with the best chances for making a profit. This is because marketing strategy starts with marketplace research, taking into consideration your optimal target customer, what your competition is doing and what trends might be on the horizon. Using this information, you determine the benefit customers and clients want, what they're willing to pay and how you can differentiate your product or service from the competition.

Helps Determine Optimal Prices

Part of a marketing strategy is setting the right price for your product or service based on what you learned in your market research. If you learned that customers want a high-end product in your category, your pricing strategy might require you to sell at prices that create a high-end perceived value. If your target customer is bargain conscious and is willing to accept fewer bells and whistles on your product in exchange for paying less, your pricing strategy will require you to sell at or below the competition's price.

Establishes Effective Distribution

Once you know what product features you'll offer, who your target customer is and what your price points will be, you can select where you want to sell to maximize your marketing effectiveness. Younger customers will be more likely to shop using a smartphone or on a website, paying with PayPal or a credit card. Older customers might prefer to shop at retail outlets. If your market research shows you need to be in retail stores but you don't have a sales force, you can use a wholesaler or distributor.

Assists with Marketing Communications

Your market research will help you create your brand, or image you want to establish about your business. Without marketplace research and a strategic marketing plan, you might respond to solicitations from advertising salespeople on an individual, reactionary basis, sending messages that don't fit in with the brand identity you've created based on your product development efforts. A marketing strategy lets you determine if a particular magazine, radio station or website fits into your selling plans.

Organizational Impact

When you have a marketing strategy, your departments can better work with each other, because they are all working from the same plan. For example, your advertising people will talk with your product development people to determine what message you should send about your benefit. Your sales people will talk with the people responsible for managing your image to determine if they can offer discounts, coupons or rebates without damaging your brand.

5.3. Factors Influencing Size of Marketing Organization

Factors influencing marketing org can be categorized into internal and external factors.

Internal

a. Top Management Philosophy: Organizational planning and its working is greatly influenced by philosophy which can be good or bad eg: Centralization Vs Decentralization

b. Product policy: the width of product line of an org determines its size as the product offerings becomes increasingly diverse. Eg: There could be a need to move away from straight functional approach to product group approach.

c. People: The size of the organization is not an important factor in terms of number of people but it is important with respect to human values which are critical and correct decisions regarding people cannot be made unless taking into consideration the following.

- Number
- Qualifications
- Capabilities
- Personality
- Attitude
- Fear
- Suspicion
- Ambition

Are some of the above intangible factors which affect the marketing organization?

External Factors

a. Business Environment: With regards to business environment three points are important.

1. The type of environment in which the firm is operating in terms of operations and size.

2. The Nature of particular requirement for success in a given business which again determines the size.

3. The rate of change in industries being served which again decides on its size and working.

b. Markets: This is the factor which again affects the marketing organization i.e. one should note about its

a. Size

b. Scope

c. Nature

d. Location

Based on the above aspects we need to design the size of the organization.

c. Consumer requirements and expectations: Consumers have their own set of requirements and expectations from the organization. The more varied and vivid services they expect that the usual requirements. as a marketer we need to increase the workload depending upon the consumer requirements and expectations

d. Channels of distribution: It is the type of channel of distribution which a marketing firm selects based on its size. Egg : Incase the company opts for indirect channel or channels it depends on outside sales force and hence the organization gets thinner .When the organization selects direct channel its size is increased as it has its own sales force.

5.4. Marketing Organization Structure

Organization is the vehicle for accomplishing the goals and objectives of the business. Organization is essential, when human beings have to collaborate and work for a common purpose. In fact, an organization is often defined as "a group of persons working together towards the attainment of certain common objectives." When the enterprise expands, some pattern of organization should be adopted. Generally, the following are the types of organization.

5.5. Functional Organization

The limitations of line organization have been removed under this system. All types of work of the organization are grouped and managed by the top executive. There are separate functional departments for major functions of the enterprise; example personnel department, purchase department etc. Each department does its function for the entire organization. Sales department does the function for the whole enterprise. The functional Organization works through the line organization. Functional organization is based on expert knowledge and makes the greatest use of division of labour resulting in high efficiency and specialization.

Merits

a) Greatest use of division of labour is possible.

b) The system is based on expert knowledge.

c) Functional efficiency of the worker can be maintained.

d) Mass production is made by standardization and specialization.

e) Separation of mental and manual functions is possible.

f) Methods and operations can be standardized.

Demerits

a) Too many experts and bosses (high officials) create confusion in the mind of the worker.

b) It is difficult to fix responsibility on workers.

c) Discipline and morale of the workers are seriously affected, because of contradictory orders from different experts.

d) There is heavy overhead expense.

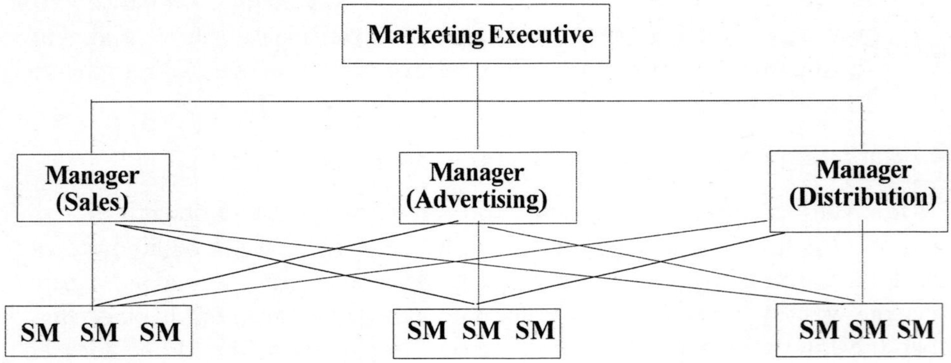

Figure: Functional Type Organization

5.6. Product Based Organization

Certain companies produce different varieties of products and it is advantageous to boost the sales on the basis of product or product groups. A separate product manager is appointed for each product. He attends to the production and marketing of his products when the market is competitive, the product type organization with the product manager can concentrate its attention on the performance of a particular product or brand. Sales promotion, advertising, marketing research etc., remain as the centralized activity for the product group.

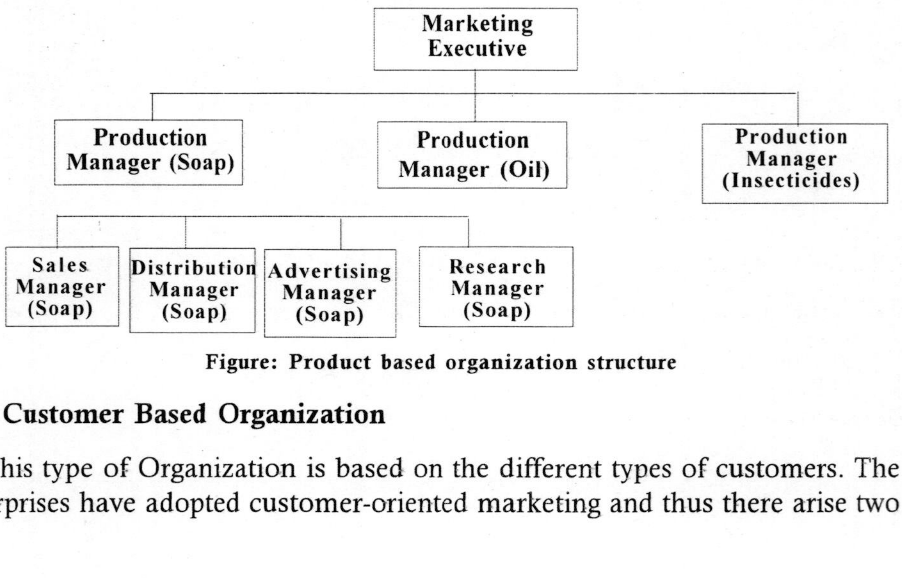

Figure: Product based organization structure

5.7. Customer Based Organization

This type of Organization is based on the different types of customers. The enterprises have adopted customer-oriented marketing and thus there arise two sets of Organizations through which the needs of customers or market are met; i.e., sub-division of markets on the basis of government and non-government customers, industrial individual customers, rich and poor customers and on the basis of sex, income, taste, age etc. A firm may have different groups of customers, who have different needs and problems. Thus, each section can look into the needs of each group of consumers and facilitate their buying-wholesale section, retail section etc.

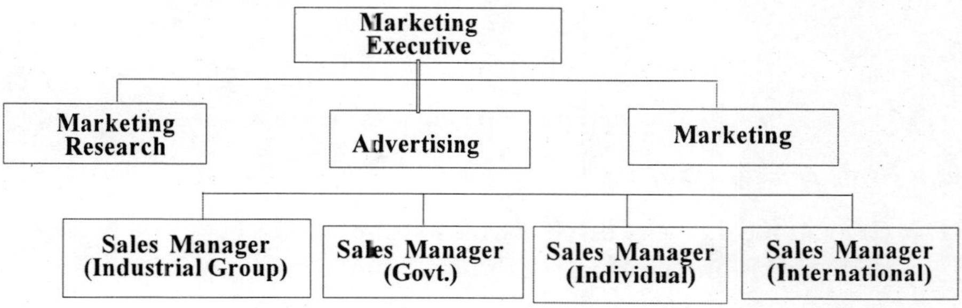

Figure: Customer Based Organization

Merits (Consumer type)

a) This type of Organization can encourage consumers with clearly defined services.

b) The specialists can understand the needs of a particular segment of customers.

c) This type of Organization is useful to serve different type of customers.

Demerits (Consumer type)

a) Coordination between sales and other functions of marketing is difficult.

b) More man-power is required thus expenditure is high.

5.8. Geographic Organization

The structure is based on territorial or regional basis. When business activities are expanded, the various parts of the market area are divided into territories. The whole world into continents, continent into regions, region into zones, zone into districts etc. This type of Organization gives importance to the consumer's needs and desire, especially in pharmaceutical companies. In this way, the market is fragmented into different sales territories like national market into regions, region into districts, district into areas as shown in the chart next. Salesmen are controlled by the respective district sales managers (DSM), DSM are controlled by their regional sales manager (RSM), RSM are controlled by the marketing executive. This type of Organization enjoys the knowledge of likes and dislikes of people in the particular areas. A firm can modify or alter the products, on the basis of the needs of the buyers who are represented by sales manager. The competitors can be counteracted soon.

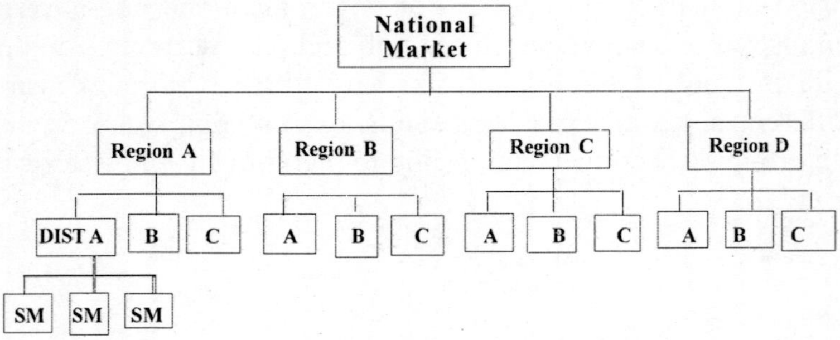

Source: Geographic Organization

Merits (Geographical Type)

a) Geographical type of divisions allows a manager to pay special attention to the needs and problems of the local markets.

b) Geographic type of organization provides opportunities for local talent to be utilized.

c) Geographic division helps managers gain extensive knowledge of diverse activities.

d) This type of Organization improves an organization's relationship with customers.

Demerits (Geographical Type)

a) This type of Organization requires more people to work.

b) There arise communication problems.

c) Cost of operations is high.

d) Top managers at HO find it difficult to control and supervise the activities in different locations.

5.9. Essentials of a Good Marketing Organization Structure

Communication

The flow of information is essential to an organization's success. The organization structure should be designed to ensure that individuals and departments that need to coordinate their efforts have lines of communication that are built into the structure. The financial planning and analysis department might report to the Chief Financial Officer and the Senior Vice President of Marketing, because both of these members of the top management team depend on information and reports provided by financial planning.

Reporting Relationships

Reporting relationships must be clear so all members of the organization understand what their responsibilities are and know to whom they are accountable. These clear relationships make it easier for managers to supervise those in lower organization levels. Each employee benefits by knowing whom they can turn to for direction or help. In addition managers are aware of who is outside the scope of their authority, so they do not overstep their bounds and interfere with another manager's responsibilities.

Growth and Expansion

Companies that grow rapidly are those that make the best use of their resources, including management talent. A sound organization structure ensures that the company has the right people in the right positions. The structure may suggest weak spots or deficiencies in the company's current management team. As the company grows, the organization structure must evolve with it. Many times more layers of management are created, when one department head has too many individuals reporting to him at one time to give each employee the attention and direction needed for the employee to succeed.

Task Completion

A well-designed organization structure facilitates the completion of projects. Project managers can better identify the human resources available to them if the scopes of each department's responsibility and each team member's capabilities are clear. A project to develop a new product would require market research. The project manager needs to know who in the organization can provide this research, and whose permission must be obtained for the research to be done.

Fits Company's Needs

Companies in different industries require different mixes of talent and a relatively greater emphasis on certain management functions. A software company often has a large development staff. Structuring the reporting relationships within the development team so creativity and productivity are maximized, and deadlines are met, is vital to that type of company's success. Companies often have to go through a reorganization phase in which individual positions or even whole departments are repositioned on the organization chart in an effort to better utilize the company's human resources and make the operation run more smoothly.

5.10. Marketing Planning

A marketing plan is a comprehensive document or blueprint that outlines a company's advertising and marketing efforts for the coming year. It describes business activities involved in accomplishing specific marketing objectives within a set time frame. "Marketing Planning is the process of developing marketing plan incorporating overall marketing objectives, strategies, and programs of actions designed to achieve these objectives." Marketing Planning involves setting objectives and targets, and communicating these targets to people responsible to achieve them. It also involves careful examination of all strategic issues, including the business environment, the market itself, the corporate mission statement, competitors, and Organizational capabilities.

5.11. What is Marketing Planning?

A marketing plan is a business document written for the purpose of describing the current market position of a business and its marketing strategy for the period covered by the marketing plan. Marketing plans usually cover a period of one to five years.

5.12. Types of Marketing Planning

Direct Marketing

Direct marketing is used by a company that wants to promote its products and services directly to the consumer. Methods for delivering this type of marketing include email, mobile messaging, and interactive websites, promotional materials addressed personally to customers, fliers and public advertisements. Direct marketing can be accomplished over the telephone, with printed materials or through TV and radio advertisements.

Indirect Marketing

Indirect marketing is a passive/aggressive marketing strategy that puts less focus on a product or service and more focus on your company. Companies participate in indirect marketing strategies by donating to charities and sponsoring events. Indirect marketing keeps the name of the company or brand in front of the public without asking consumers for a purchase. A contest that gives away prizes with no purchase necessary is another indirect marketing plan.

Cause Marketing

Cause marketing is a form of indirect marketing that links a company to social issues or causes. A company that advertises its products as being friendly on the environment is using this marketing plan to attract those customers who have the same environmental concerns. The goal of a cause marketing campaign is to rely on the public conscience as a means for attracting customers.

Relationship Marketing

Relationship marketing is a strategy where a company places emphasis on customer satisfaction and the company's appreciation of the customer. This type of marketing strategy often involves offering discounts to current customers, sending birthday wishes to current customers and offering current customers low-cost upgrades to products they have already purchased. This is a marketing plan used by software companies and car dealerships.

Niche Marketing

The purpose of a niche marketing plan is to reach a target audience that has been forgotten or to offer products or services with a limited audience.

5.13. Process of Marketing Planning

Marketing planning process is a series of stages that are usually followed in a sequence. Organizations can adapt their marketing plan to suit the circumstances and their requirements. Marketing planning process involves both the development of objectives and specifications for how to achieve the objectives. Following are the steps involved in a marketing plan.

a) ***Mission***

Mission is the reason for which an Organization exists. Mission statement is a straightforward statement that shows why an Organization is in business, provides basic guidelines for further planning, and establishes broad parameters for the future. Many of the useful mission statements motivate staff and customers.

b) ***Corporate Objectives***

Objectives are the set of goals to be achieved within a specified period of time. Corporate objectives are most important goals the Organization as a whole wishes to achieve within a specified period of time, say one or five years. All the departments of an Organization including marketing department works in harmony to achieve the corporate objectives of the Organization. Marketing department must appreciate the corporate objectives and ensure its actions and decisions support the overall objectives of the Organization. Mission statement and corporate objectives are determined by the top level management (including Board of Directors) of the Organization. The rest of the steps of marketing planning process are performed by marketing department. All the actions and decisions of the marketing department must be directed to achieve Organization mission and its corporate objectives.

c) ***Marketing Audit***

Marketing audit helps in analyzing and evaluating the marketing strategies, activities, problems, goals, and results. Marketing audit is done to check all the aspects of business directly related to marketing department. It is done not only at the beginning of the marketing planning process but, also at a series of points during the implementation of plan. The marketing audit clarifies opportunities and threats, so that required alterations can be done to the plan if necessary.

d) *SWOT Analysis*

The information gathered through the marketing audit process is used in development of SWOT Analysis. It is a look at Organization's marketing efforts, and its strengths, weaknesses, opportunities, and threats related to marketing functions.

- Strengths and Weaknesses are factors inside the Organization that can be controlled by the Organization. USP of a product can be the example of strength, whereas lack of innovation can be the example of weakness.
- Opportunities and Threats are factors outside the Organization which are beyond the direct control of an Organization. Festive season can be an example of opportunity to make maximum sales, whereas increasing FDI in a nation can be the example of threat to domestic players of that nation.

e) *Marketing Assumptions*

A good marketing plan is based on deep customer understanding and knowledge, but it is not possible to know everything about the customer, so lot of different things are assumed about customer.

For example:

- Target Buyer Assumptions - assumptions about who the target buyers are.
- Messaging/Offering Assumptions - assumptions about what customers think are the most important features of product to be offered.

f) *Marketing Objectives and Strategies*

After identification of opportunities and challenges, the next step is to develop marketing objectives that indicate the end state to achieve. Marketing objective reflects what an Organization can accomplish through marketing in the coming years.

Objective identifies the end point to achieve. Marketing strategies are formed to achieve the marketing objectives. Marketing strategies are formed to determine how to achieve those end points. Strategies are broad statements of activities to be performed to achieve those end points.

g) *Forecast the Expected Results*

Marketing managers have to forecast the expected results. They have to project the future numbers, characteristics, and trends in the target market. Without proper forecasting, the marketing plan could have unrealistic goals or fall short on what is promised to deliver.

- Forecasting Customer Response - Marketing managers have to forecast the response that the average customers will have to marketing efforts. Without some idea how the marketing will be received, managers can't accurately plan the promotions.
- Forecasting Marketing cost - To make the marketing plan stronger, accurate forecast of marketing cost is required to be done.
- Forecasting the Market - To accurately forecast the market, marketing managers have to gain an intimate understanding of customers, their buying behaviour, and tendencies.
- Forecasting the Competition - Forecast of competition like - what they market, how they market, what incentives they use in their marketing can help to counter what they are doing.

h) Create Alternative Plan

A alternate marketing plan is created and kept ready to be implement at the place of primary marketing plan if the whole or some part of the primary marketing plan is dropped.

i) Marketing Budget

The marketing budget is the process of documenting the expected costs of the proposed marketing plan. One common method to allocate marketing budgeting is based on a percentage of revenue. Other methods are - comparative, all you can afford, and task method.

j) Implementation and Evaluation

At this stage the marketing team is ready to actually start putting their plans into action. This may involve spending money on advertising, launching new products, interacting with potential new customers, opening new retail outlets etc.

5.14. Factors Affecting Marketing Planning

A. **Demographics**—How will the composition of your market change and what opportunities or hurdles will this create? How will population and housing demand evolve?

B. **Current and projected economic conditions**—How will inflation, employment, taxes, and other economic factors effect supply, demand, and pricing?

C. **Size, growth potential, and prosperity of the market**—Will the size of your market continue to support current business and/or allow the opportunity for business growth? What are the growth options for housing availability in your market? Is there vacant land available? Are there geographic limitations on growth (a mountain range)? Are there zoning, use fees, and other restrictions that might fuel or limit growth?

D. **Market potential**—Strengths and weakness of major competitors. How can you capitalize on a competitor's weakness?

E. **Market share**—What percentage of current transactions in your market are handled by your company and what factors could change that percentage either positively or negatively?

F. **Present customer composition**— How do factors such education, buying frequency, age, income level, occupations and hobbies affect the level of future demand among existing customers?

5.15. Importance of Marketing Planning

Marketing planning is a systematic and disciplined exercise to formulate marketing strategies. Marketing planning can be related to the Organization as a whole or to strategic business units (SBU). Marketing planning is a forward looking exercise, which determines the future strategies of an Organization with special reference to its product development, market development, channel design, sales promotion and profitability.

- It helps in avoiding future uncertainties.
- It helps in management by objectives.
- It helps in achieving objectives.
- It helps in coordination and communication among the departments.
- It helps in control.
- It helps the customers in getting full satisfaction.

5.16. Difficulties in Marketing Planning

a. Can be time-consuming

b. Constant change in the market makes assumptions difficult.

c. Danger of either being too simplistic or too complicated.

d. The plan can be ignored as circumstances take over.

e. Identifies weaknesses in your business skills

f. Leads to faulty marketing decisions based on improperly analyzed data.

g. Creates unrealistic financial projections if information is interpreted incorrectly.

h. Identifies weaknesses in your overall business plan.

6

MARKETING INFORMATION SYSTEM

6.1. Marketing Information System (MIS) – Meaning and Definition

The results of marketing research that are used to plan for future marketing or product development activities. The information may come from a single source or through a system of collection. Marketing information is an ongoing and repetitive process of collection and processing and presenting of pertinent information. But marketing research is an intermittent or irregular activity on a project to project basis and it is concerned with solving specific and typical marketing problems.

6.2. Need for Marketing Information System

Marketing information includes all the date, in terms of facts, opinions, views, guidelines and policies, which are necessary to make vital marketing decisions. The data is collected from customers, competitors, company sales force and other staff, government sources, specialized agencies and sources. MIS provides relevant, reliable and required information in respect of business environment-both internal and external environments. Such information is vital for successful decision making. The following are the benefits or advantages of MIS.

a) **Helps to recognize trends:** MIS helps managers to recognize marketing trends. The changing trends may be in respect of prices, product design, packaging, promotion schemes, etc. managers can take effective decisions in respect of prices, product designs, etc., in response to changing trends in the environment.

b) **Facilitates Marketing Planning and Control:** Effective market planning is required in terms of product planning, pricing, promotion and distribution. Such planning will be possible only f the company is possessing adequate and relevant information.

c) **Quick supply of information:** A firm has to take quick decision for this purpose; it requires fast flow of information which is facilitated by a properly designed MIS. Due to timely supply of marketing information, the marketing managers can make quick and effective decisions.

d) **Quality of decision making:** In every aspect of marketing, there is need to make constant and correct decisions. A properly designed marketing information system promptly supplies reliable and relevant information. With the help of computers and other data processing equipments, the marketing managers can make the right decisions at the right time.

e) **Tapping of business Opportunities:** There are number of business opportunities which have remained untapped for various reasons are due to unavailability of sufficient information. MIS makes it possible to tap business opportunities as it can supply required and reliable data.

f) **Provides Marketing Intelligence:** Marketing intelligence refers to information of the events that are happening in the external environment, i.e., changes in customer tastes, expectations, competitors' strategies, government policies, international environment, etc. with the help of MIS specialists, it is possible to collect marketing intelligence which is vital to make effective marketing decisions.

g) **Help managers to Recognize Change:** A business firm may be handling or marketing a wrong line of products. As such the company will not be able to make profits. And if it is does, profits may not be adequate. A firm which is well equipped with MIS will be able to realize the need to change the line of business.

h) **Integration of Information:** Firms, which are largely decentralized can gather information which is scattered at many centers or departments and integrate it for effective decision making. Such integration is possible if there is a centralized MIS.

6.3. Significance of Marketing Information

The existence of an adequate information system which would secure data acquisition and analyses, as well as the transformation of above mentioned data into useful information is an essential condition for a company to function effectively. Successful companies should be flexible enough to adapt to the changes brought by intensive alternations in business environment. The design of marketing information system has been initiated for this particular purpose. The main task of this application is to improve the efficiency of a company's operations through the implementation of the research process. Marketing information system is the fundamental precondition for the successful realization of the research project, i.e. the means used by producers in order to collect information about the, needs of the consumers. Marketing information system represents efforts of the companies to provide pertinent decision-making information to marketing managers on regular basis.

6.4. Characteristics of Good Marketing Information

The characteristics of a good Marketing Information System are stated in the following.

a) It handles both internal and external data.

b) It is concerned with preventing as well as solving problems.

c) It operates continuously as a system.

d) It tends to be future oriented.

e) It includes other subsystems besides marketing research.

6.5. Components of Marketing Information System

A marketing information system (MIS) is intended to bring together disparate items of data into a coherent body of information. An MIS is, as will shortly be seen, more than raw data or information suitable for the purposes of decision making. An MIS also provides methods for interpreting the information the MIS provides. Moreover, as Kotler's definition says, an MIS is more than a system of data collection or a set of information technologies:

"A marketing information system is a continuing and interacting structure of people, equipment and procedures to gather, sort, analyze, evaluate, and distribute pertinent, timely and accurate information for use by marketing decision makers to improve their marketing planning, implementation, and control". The following figure illustrates the major components of an MIS, the environmental factors monitored by the system and the types of marketing decision which the MIS seeks to underpin.

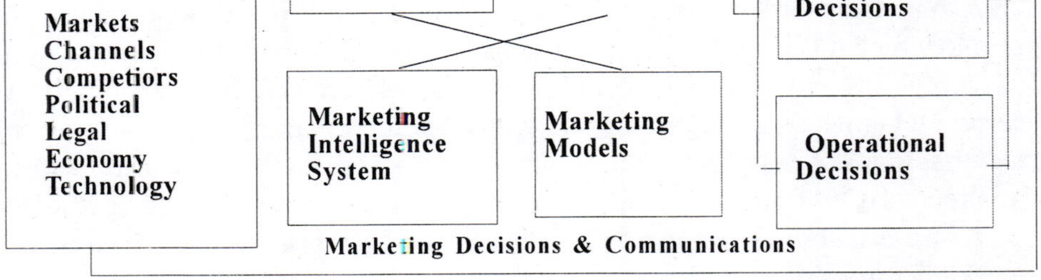

Figure: The marketing information systems and its subsystems

The explanation of this model of an MIS begins with a description of each of its four main constituent parts: the internal reporting systems, marketing research system, marketing intelligence system and marketing models. It is suggested that whilst the MIS varies in its degree of sophistication - with many in the industrialized countries being computerized and few in the developing countries being so - a fully fledged MIS should have these components, the methods (and technologies) of collection, storing, retrieving and processing data notwithstanding.

Internal reporting systems: All enterprises which have been in operation for any period of time nave a wealth of information. However, this information often remains under-utilized because it is compartmentalized, either in the form of an individual entrepreneur or in the functional departments of larger businesses. That is, information is usually categorized according to its nature so that there are, for example, financial, production, manpower, marketing, stockholding and logistical data. Often the entrepreneur, or various personnel working in the functional departments holding these pieces of data, does not see how it could help decision makers in other functional areas. Similarly, decision makers can fail to appreciate how information from other functional areas might help them and therefore do not request it. The internal records that are of immediate value to marketing decisions are: orders received, stockholdings and sales invoices. These are but a few of the internal records that can be used by marketing managers, but even this small set of records is capable of generating a great deal of information. Below, is a list of some of the information that can be derived from sales invoices.

- Product type, size and pack type by territory
- Product type, size and pack type by type of account
- Product type, size and pack type by industry
- Product type, size and pack type by customer
- Average value and/or volume of sale by territory
- Average value and/or volume of sale by type of account
- Average value and/or volume of sale by industry
- Average value and/or volume of sale by sales person

By comparing orders received with invoices an enterprise can establish the extent to which it is providing an acceptable level of customer service. In the same way, comparing stockholding records with orders received helps an enterprise ascertain whether its stocks are in line with current demand patterns. Marketing research systems: The general topic of marketing research has been the prime subject of the textbook and only a little more needs to be added here. Marketing research is a proactive search for information. That is, the enterprise which commissions these studies does so to solve a perceived marketing problem. In many cases, data is collected in a purposeful way to address a well-defined problem (or a problem which can be defined and solved within the course of the study). The other form of marketing research centres not around a specific marketing problem but is an attempt to continuously monitor the marketing environment. These monitoring or tracking exercises are continuous marketing research studies, often involving panels of farmers, consumers or distributors from which the same data is collected at regular intervals. Whilst the ad hoc study and continuous marketing research differs in the orientation, yet they are both proactive.

Marketing intelligence systems: Whereas marketing research is focused, market intelligence is not. A marketing intelligence system is a set of procedures and data sources used by marketing managers to sift information from the environment that they can use in their decision making. This scanning of the economic and business environment can be undertaken in a variety of ways, including the following.

Unfocused scanning

The manager, by virtue of what he/she reads, hears and watches exposes him/herself to information that may prove useful. Whilst the behaviour is unfocused and the manager has no specific purpose in mind, it is not unintentional

Semi-focused scanning

Again, the manager is not in search of particular pieces of information that he/she is actively searching but does narrow the range of media that is scanned. For instance, the manager may focus more on economic and business publications, broadcasts etc. and pay less attention to political, scientific or technological media.

Informal search

This describes the situation where a fairly limited and unstructured attempt is made to obtain information for a specific purpose. For example, the marketing manager of a firm considering entering the business of importing frozen fish from a neighboring country may make informal inquiries as to prices and demand levels of frozen and fresh fish. There would be little structure to this search with the manager making inquiries with traders he/she happens to encounter as well as with other ad hoc contacts in ministries, international aid agencies, with trade associations, importers/exporters etc.

Formal search

This is a purposeful search after information in some systematic way. The information will be required to address a specific issue. Whilst this sort of activity may seem to share the characteristics of marketing research it is carried out by the manager him/herself rather than a professional researcher. Moreover, the scope of the search is likely to be narrow in scope and far less intensive than marketing research

Marketing intelligence is the province of entrepreneurs and senior managers within an agribusiness. It involves them in scanning newspaper trade magazines, business journals and reports, economic forecasts and other media. In addition it involves management in talking to producers, suppliers and customers, as well as to competitors. Nonetheless, it is a largely informal process of observing and conversing. Some enterprises will approach marketing intelligence gathering in a more deliberate fashion and will train its sales force, after-sales personnel and district/area managers to take cognizance of competitors' actions, customer complaints and requests and distributor problems. Enterprises with vision will also encourage intermediaries, such as collectors, retailers, traders and other middlemen to be proactive in conveying market intelligence back to them.

Marketing models: Within the MIS there has to be the means of interpreting information in order to give direction to decision. These models may be computerized or may not. Typical tools are:

- Time series sales modes
- Brand switching models
- Linear programming
- Elasticity models (price, incomes, demand, supply, etc.)
- Regression and correlation models
- Analysis of Variance (ANOVA) models
- Sensitivity analysis
- Discounted cash flow
- Spreadsheet 'what if models

These and similar mathematical, statistical, econometric and financial models are the analytical subsystem of the MIS. A relatively modest investment in a desktop computer is enough to allow an enterprise to automate the analysis of its data. Some of the models used are stochastic, i.e. those containing a probabilistic element whereas others are deterministic models where chance plays no part. Brand switching models are stochastic since these express brand choices in probabilities whereas linear programming is deterministic in that the relationships between variables are expressed in exact mathematical terms.

7

MARKETING RESEARCH

7.1. Marketing Research – Meaning and Definition

It is very important to understand at the outset that the, modern concept of marketing revolves around the customer. Satisfaction of customer is the main aim of marketing. For achieving this goal, marketing research is undertaken. In fact, marketing management is nothing but marketing research. With the expansion of business, marketing management becomes complex. It has to rely heavily on marketing research for solving problems in the field of marketing.

7.2. Features of Marketing Research

The relevant features of Marketing Research are stated in the following.

a) Continuous process

Marketing research is not only continuous but also a scientific and system-atic process. It is scientific and systematic because it has well-defined procedures. It is a process of generating and evaluating data, and then refining it. It is professionally organized. It is a continu-ous process because every firm is faced with problems and opportunities.

b) Wide scope

Marketing is a specialized activity. It encompasses several functions. Thus, market-ing research has a wide scope. It includes product research, market research, consumer research, promotion research, international market research, price research and distribution research.

c) Aid to decision-making

It helps the managers take practical decisions. Decisions based on experience and research is better than decisions based on intuition. Functions such as description, evaluation, explanation and prediction by the marketing researcher help in practical decision-making. Thus, it an essential tool not only for marketing managers but also for other functional managers.

d) Uncertainty of conclusions

Consumer is the focal point of marketing research. However, con-sumer behaviour is difficult to judge precisely. It is not a physical science, but social science. Due to this inherent nature, it suffers from certain levels of inaccuracy.

e) Applied research

Marketing research is not a fundamental research because it does not reveal conceptual aspects. It is an applied research, as it begins with defining or identifying a problem or opportunity, and ends with a follow-up of recommendations made from research. Moreover, it is related to the commercial aspects.

f) Commercial intelligence

Marketing research is equivalent of military intelligence. It provides vital insights and information of product, price, place and promotional aspects. It is the soul of modem marketing management.

g) Statistical tools

Various mathematical and statistical tools are used for data analysis and inter-pretation. Percentages, ratios, averages, z-test, t-test, chi-square tests, etc. are used for presenta-tion and interpretation of findings. The use of computer software has made it more convenient for in-depth analysis, cross-sectional studies, detection of errors in sampling and questionnaires.

h) Research approaches

A researcher has several options of research methodology. Methods include the field survey method, the observation method and the experimental research. The choice depends on factors such as time availability, funds, number of respondents to be covered, location of respondents and literacy levels.

i) Links a company to the consumers and public

Marketing research is a function that links a company to the consumers, customers and public, through information. It evaluates marketing actions, marketing performances and marketing processes. This evaluation results in collection of information that brings company closer to its customer and society.

7.3. Objectives of Marketing Research

Marketing research is undertaken for attaining the following objectives

(a) To Provide Basis for Proper Planning

Marketing and sales forecast research provides sound basis for the formulation of all marketing plans, policies, programmes and procedures.

(b) To Reduce Marketing Costs

Marketing research provides ways and means to reduce marketing costs like selling, advertisement and distribution etc.

(c) To Find Out New Markets for the Product

Marketing research aims at exploring new markets for the product and maintaining the existing ones.

(d) To Determine Proper Price Policy

Marketing research is considered helpful in the formulation of proper price policy with regard to the products.

(e) To Study in Detail Likes and Dislikes of the Consumers

Marketing research tries to find out what the consumers, (the men and women who constitute the market) think and want. It keeps us in touch with the consumers, minds and to study their likes and dislikes.

(f) To Know the Market Competition

Marketing research also aims at knowing the quantum of competition prevalent in the market about the product in question. The company may need reliable information about competitor's moves and strategies which are of immense significance for further planning.

(g) To Study the External Forces and Their Impact

Marketing research provides valuable information by studying the impact of external forces on the organization. External forces may include conditions developing in foreign markets, govt, policies and regulations, consumer incomes and spending habits, new products entering in the market and their impact on the company's products. Prof. Gilies has rightly pointed out that, "The basic objective of marketing research is to supply management with information which will lead to a fuller understanding of the distribution habits and attitudes of present and potential buyers and users, and their reactions to products, packing, selling and advertising methods".

7.4. Scope of Marketing Research

Scope of marketing research means the possible applications of marketing research in corporate environment. Bulk of research is done to measure consumer needs and wants. Besides, marketing research is carried out to assess the impact of past marketing actions. Some research is done to understand the competitive, technological, social, economic, cultural, political or legal environments of the market. Another way of looking at the scope of marketing research is the look at the particular decision area, where research results are used.

They may be outlined as follows:

Sales Analysis

Much research is done in these areas which are broadly referred to as sales analysis measurement of market potential/demand projection, determination of market characteristics, market share estimation, studies of business trends, etc.

Sales Methods and Policies

Marketing research studies are also conducted with a view to evaluating the effectiveness of present distribution system. Such studies are used in establishing or revising sales territories. They are also helpful in establishment of sales quotas, design of territory boundary, compensation to sales force, physical distribution, cost analysis, etc. It is also done to assess the effectiveness of different promotional activities, such as premiums, deals, coupons, samples, etc.

Product Management

Market research is also conducted in order to better manage the existing and new products to assess consumer feedback, to assess consumer reaction before launching a new product, etc. Sometimes pricing studies, packaging research, and design or physical characteristics studies have also been conducted.

Advertising Research

These include media research, and advertising copy research.

Corporate Research

Corporate research studies about the social value research, political studies {e.g., research to ascertain the public opinion about the election results), and consumer service studies (e.g., many banks and large industrial houses have conducted market research to know the consumer's changing needs, for service and possible grievances about existing operations).

Syndicated Research

Several research agencies collect and tabulate marketing information on a continuing basis. Reports are sent periodically (i.e., weekly, monthly or quarterly) to clients who pay subscription for them.

7.5. Significance of Marketing Research

The most important task of a marketer is to get the right product at the right place with the right price to the right person. Besides, it was also necessary to go back and find whether consumer is getting optimum satisfaction, so that consumer remains loyal. These aspects made it imperative for the marketers to conduct marketing research. The following points explain the significance of marketing research:

a. ***Identifying problem and opportunities in the market***

It helps in identifying new market opportunities for existing and new products. It provides information on market share, nature of competition, customer satisfaction levels, sales performances and channel of distribution. This helps the firms is solving problems.

b. ***Formulating market strategies***

Today, markets are no more local. They have become global. Manufactures find it difficult to contact customers and control distribution channels. Competition is equally severe. The consumer needs are difficult to predict. Market segmentation is a complicated task in such wide markets. The marketing intelligence provided through marketing research not only helps in framing but also in implementing the market strategies.

c. ***Determining consumer needs and wants***

Marketing has become customer-centric. However, large-scale production needs intermediaries for mass distribution. Due to prevalence of multi channels of distribution, there is an information gap. Marketing research helps in collecting information on consumers from structured distribution research and helps in making marketing customer oriented.

d. ***For effective communication mix***

In an era of micro- rather than mass-marketing, communica-tion plays a vital role. Marketing research uses promotional research to study media mix, advertising effectiveness and integrated communication tools. Research on such aspects will help in promoting effectively a company's product in the market.

e. ***Improving selling activities***

Marketing research is used to analyze and evaluate performances of a company within a market. It also studies effectiveness of a sales force. It helps in identifying sales territories. Such information helps the companies in identifying areas of shortcoming in sales. It also examines alternative methods for distribution of goods.

f. ***Sales forecasting***

The most challenging task for any production manager is to keep optimum levels of inventory. However, production is undertaken in anticipation of demand.

Therefore, scientific forecast of sales is required. Marketing research helps in sales forecasting by using market share method, sales force estimate method and jury method. This can also help in fixing sales quotas and marketing plans.

g. *To revitalize brands*

Marketing research is used to study and find out the existing brand position. It finds out the recall value of brands. It explores the possibilities of brand extension or prospects of changing existing brand names. The main purpose of marketing is to create brand loyalty. Marketing research helps in developing techniques to popularize and retain brand loyalty.

h. *To facilitate smooth introduction of new products*

Marketing research helps in testing the new products in one or two markets on a small scale. This helps in finding out consumer response to new product and develops a suitable marketing mix. It reveals the problems of the customers regarding new products. Thus, it controls the risk involved in introducing a new product.

i. *Determine export potentials*

The development in transport and communication has helped in globalization and digitalization of world trade. This has helped in boosting the growth of international markets. Marketing research helps in conducting market survey for export. It. collects information on marketing environment prevailing in a country. By collecting data on consumers from different countries, it indicates export potentials.

j. *Managerial decision-making*

Marketing research plays a vital role in the decision-making processes by supplying relevant, up-to-date and accurate data to the decision-makers. Managers need up-to-date information to access customer needs and wants, market situation, technological change and extent of competition.

7.6. Limitations of Marketing Research

Following are the main limitations of Marketing Research.

- Marketing Research (MR) is not an exact science though it uses the techniques of science. Thus, the results and conclusions drawn upon by using MR are not very accurate.
- The results of MR are very vague as MR is carried out on consumers, suppliers, intermediaries, etc. who are humans. Humans have a tendency to behave artificially when they know that they are being observed. Thus, the consumers and respondents upon whom the research is carried behave

artificially when they are aware that their attitudes, beliefs, views, etc are being observed.

- MR is not a complete solution to any marketing issue as there are many dominant variables between research conclusions and market response.
- MR is not free from bias. The research conclusions cannot be verified. The reproduction of the same project on the same class of respondents give different research results.
- Inappropriate training to researchers can lead to misapprehension of questions to be asked for data collection.
- Many business executives and researchers have ambiguity about the research problem and its objectives. They have limited experience of the notion of the decision-making process. This leads to carelessness in research and researchers are not able to do anything real.
- There is less interaction between the MR department and the main research executives. The research department is in segregation. This all makes research ineffective.
- MR faces time constraint. The firms are required to maintain a balance between the requirement for having a broader perspective of customer needs and the need for quick decision making so as to have competitive advantage.
- Huge cost is involved in MR as collection and processing of data can be costly. Many firms do not have the proficiency to carry wide surveys for collecting primary data, and might not also able to hire specialized market experts and research agencies to collect primary data. Thus, in that case, they go for obtaining secondary data that is cheaper to obtain.
- MR is conducted in open marketplace where numerous variables act on research settings.

7.7. Marketing Research Process / Steps Involved in Marketing Research

Marketing Research (MR) is generally conducted with the help of some process or stages to obtain the desired objective of the marketing research. Some of the major steps involved in marketing research process are as follows.

a) Identification and Defining the Problem

b) Statement of Research Objectives

c) Planning the Research Design or Designing the Research Study

d) Planning the Sample

e) Data Collection

f) Data Processing and Analysis

g) Formulating Conclusion, Preparing and Presenting the Report

Marketing research exercise may take many forms but systematic enquiry is a feature common to all such forms. Being a systematic enquiry, it requires a careful planning of the orderly investigation process. Though it is not necessary that all research processes would invariably follow a given sequence, yet marketing research often follows a generalized pattern which can be broken down and studied as sequential stages. The various stages or steps in the marketing research process are discussed below.

a. *Identification and Defining the Problem*

The market research process begins with the identification "of a problem faced by the company. The clear-cut statement of problem may not be possible at the very outset of research process because often only the symptoms of the problems are apparent at that stage. Then, after some explanatory research, clear definition of the problem is of crucial importance in marketing research because such research is a costly process involving time, energy and money. Clear definition of the problem helps the researcher in all subsequent research efforts including setting of proper research objectives, the determination of the techniques to be used, and the extent of information to be collected. It may be noted that the methods of explanatory research popularly in use are survey of secondary data, experience survey, or pilot studies, i.e., studies of a small initial sample. All this is also known as 'preliminary investigation'.

b. *Statement of Research Objectives*

After identifying and defining the problem with or without explanatory research, the researcher must take a formal statement of research objectives. Such objectives may be stated in qualitative or quantitative terms and expressed as research questions, statement or hypothesis. For example, the research objective, "To find out the extent to which sales promotion schemes affected the sales volume" is a research objective expressed as a statement. On the other hand, a hypothesis is a statement that can be refuted or supported by empirical finding. The same research objective could be stated as, "To test the proposition that sales are positively affected by the sales promotion schemes undertaken this winter."

Example of another hypothesis may be: "The new packaging pattern has resulted in increase in sales and profits." Once the objectives or the hypotheses are developed, the researcher is ready to choose the research design.

c. *Planning the Research Design or Designing the Research Study*

After defining the research problem and deciding the objectives, the research design must be developed. A research design is a master plan specifying the procedure for collecting and analysing the needed information. It represents a framework for the research plan of action.

The objectives of the study are included in the research design to ensure that data collected are relevant to the objectives. At this stage, the researcher should also determine the type of sources of information needed, the data collection method (e.g., survey or interview), the sampling, methodology, and the timing and possible costs of research.

d. *Planning the Sample*

Sampling involves procedures that use a small number of items or parts of the 'population' (total items) to make conclusion regarding the 'population'. Important questions in this regard arewho is to be sampled as a rightly representative lot? Which is the target 'population'? What should be the sample size how large or how small? How to select the various units to make up the sample?

e. *Data Collection*

The collection of data relates to the gathering of facts to be used in solving the problem. Hence, methods of market research are essentially methods of data collection. Data can be secondary, i.e., collected from concerned reports, magazines and other periodicals, especially written articles, government publications, company publications, books, etc. Data can be primary, i.e., collected from the original base through empirical research by means of various tools. There can be broadly two types of sources:

(i) Internal sources: existing within the firm itself, such as accounting data, salesmen's reports, etc.

(ii) External sources: outside the firm.

f. *Data Processing and Analysis*

Once data have been collected, these have to be converted into a format that will suggest answers to the initially identified and defined problem. Data processing begins with the editing of data and its coding. Editing involves inspecting the data-collection forms for omission, legibility, and consistency in classification. Before tabulation, responses need to be classified into meaningful categories. The rules for categorizing, recording and transferring the data to 'data storage media' are called codes. This coding process facilitates the manual or computer tabulation. If computer analysis is being used, the data can be key punched and verified. Analysis of data represents the application of logic to the understanding of data collected about the subject. In its simplest form analysis may involve determination of consistent patterns and summarizing of appropriate details. The appropriate analytical techniques chosen would depend upon informational requirements of the problem, characteristics of the research designs and the nature of the data gathered. The statistical analysis may range from simple immediate analysis to very complex multivariate analysis.

g. *Formulating Conclusion, Preparing and Presenting the Report*

The final stage in the marketing research process is that of interpreting the information and drawing conclusion for use in managerial decision. The research report should clearly and effectively communicate the research findings and need not include complicated statement about the technical aspect of the study and research methods. Often the management is not interested in details of research design and statistical analysis, but instead, in the concrete findings of the research. If need be, the researcher may bring out his appropriate recommendations or suggestions in the matter. Researchers must make the presentation technically accurate, understandable and useful.

7.8. Characteristics of Good Marketing Research

First, marketing research is systematic. Thus systematic planning is required at all the stages of the marketing research process. The procedures followed at each stage are methodologically sound, well documented, and, as much as possible, planned in advance. Marketing research uses the scientific method in that data are collected and analyzed to test prior notions or hypotheses. Experts in marketing research have shown that studies featuring multiple and often competing hypotheses yield more meaningful results than those featuring only one dominant hypothesis. Marketing research is objective. It attempts to provide accurate information that reflects a true state of affairs. It should be conducted impartially. While research is always influenced by the researcher's research philosophy, it should be free from the personal or political biases of the researcher or the management. Research which is motivated by personal or political gain involves a breach of professional standards. Such research is deliberately biased so as to result in predetermined findings. The objective nature of marketing research underscores the importance of ethical considerations. Also, researchers should always be objective with regard to the selection of information to be featured in reference texts because such literature should offer a comprehensive view on marketing. Research has shown, however, that many marketing textbooks do not feature important principles in marketing research

7.9. Methods of Conducting Marketing Research

Marketing research is primarily used to enable managers to take decisions. However, some limitations such as the inability to define the problem accurately, unavailability of past researches, etc., may force researchers to gather more background information about the problem in hand. In such cases, exploratory research is used first. Thereafter, conclusive research is done either through surveys or experiments, enabling managers to take decisions. Decision making is not possible through exploratory research.

Types of Research Methods

Exploratory research	Descriptive research	Experimental research
• Gather preliminary information • Define problem with more clarity • Use when paucity of data exists • Use of secondary data and qualitative research	• Qualitative research • Describe consumer attitudes, beliefs, recall, brand image, etc. • Use of large and representative sample • Instruments such as questionnaires	• Esmtimate causal relationships • Control groups and experimental groups

Figure: Types of Research Methods

Exploratory Research

The agency conducts exploratory research, which is a preliminary exploration of the research area prior to quantitative data collection stage. It is normally done after the client accepts the agency's research proposal, but it can also take place before the client-agency briefing meeting and submission of the proposal. It can also be used in the problem definition process.

Hypothesis generated at this stage can be tested further by undertaking quantitative research. The idea is not to collect data and form conclusions but to get better understanding of the client's target market, its customers and its competitors. So when the agency starts collecting data, it knows who its respondents are, what it has to know about them and what it has to ask from them. During the exploratory research, the agency tries to identify and understand the respondents who would be interviewed in the data collection stage. It also tries to get a comprehensive understanding of the industry in which the client operates its target markets and its competitors. Exploratory research helps in getting rid of the prejudices that the agency might possess about the research area. Such prejudices involuntarily misguide the research proceedings and are a major deterrence in understanding the realities of the research area.

Exploratory research is also often useful under such circumstances when enough information does not exist about the area being researched. Therefore, the agency conducts its exploratory research diligently. Exploratory research is used when the available data is insufficient for proceeding further. It enables the MR firm to gain better insights about the problem in hand.

i. *Secondary research*

Secondary data is compiled by other people, for other purposes and is not meant specifically for the research in question. Secondary data is generally used to understand the problem, to define the problem better, to develop an appropriate approach to the problem, to formulate a suitable research design or to answer certain questions. It can also be used to interpret primary data more insightfully. Internal records of the company are important sources of secondary data and so are reports of previous researches carried out by the company. Therefore, it is important that a company maintains data like revenue, profit and expenses of its products and major customers. Government, trade associations, newspapers, magazines and internet are important external sources of secondary data. It is easy and rather inexpensive to obtain secondary data, therefore an agency should spend some time carrying out secondary research. It may also happen that an agency might get most of the data of a research project from secondary sources and may be saved from conducting primary research. But, if it does not conduct secondary research diligently, it may carry out primary research to obtain data that is already available through secondary sources.

ii. *Qualitative research*

In a focus group: unstructured or semi-structured discussions are conducted between a representative group of consumers and a trained moderator, who is often a psychologist. The idea is to let consumers discuss their preferences, behavior, motivations, attitudes and beliefs in an uninhibited manner, in an unthreatening environment. And it is possible that a company learns about its customers' nuanced needs and behavior, which they might not have been able to reveal in a survey. The moderator leads the discussion and ensures that the group stays on course and discusses the issues that are on the agenda of the focus group. But the moderator understands that the group cannot be allowed to become inhibited, and therefore, allows the members to discuss issues which are important to them, but which are not on the agenda of the focus group. Focus groups are valuable due to the unexpected findings that emanate from free-flowing discussions among customers. Such discussions are likely to reveal complex and subtle relationships between consumers and products. The discussions are not based on percentages, averages or other numbers that are impersonal in nature. And as marketers are directly in contact with their customers, focus groups often stimulate new ideas for them.

The resultant data from focus group discussions is interpreted by experts. The data obtained from discussions is helpful when designing the questionnaire for conducting quantitative research, which will focus on what is important to the respondent. The instrument is thus worded in the language that the respondent uses and understands. However, focus groups are not representative of the population, and hence cannot be the sole basis for decision making. For instance, the size of the target audience holding a particular type of view cannot be gauged by conducting focus group discussions. In a depth interview, a consumer is interviewed at length about an issue. As in a focus group, the idea is to understand customers' nuanced needs, behavior and motivations, but an agency resorts to the more expensive depth interview, when the issue is such that presence of other members inhibits honest answers and viewpoints. Also, when an agency has to understand an individual's response to a stimulus such as an advertisement, or has to understand his decision making process as when an executive buys an expensive equipment, it sanctions a depth interview. Depth interviews are also used when an agency is not able to get a group together for instance, when it is dealing with busy CEOs, it mandates a depth interview. The questionnaire is usually in the form of an outline, allowing respondents to freely express their views about the topics being questioned. Thus, there is a lot of flexibility for the researcher in this method, and responses that are obtained may yield new ideas which otherwise could not have been obtained by means of structured questionnaires. Depth interviews are difficult to standardize as no two interviewers are likely to proceed in an absolutely similar manner, and their biases are also likely to reflect in the results if the interviewers are not adequately trained. The result of the qualitative research has to be studied carefully as it is based on small sample sizes. Much depends on the ability to interpret subjective data and may vary from one analyst to the other. More interesting or surprising viewpoints may be disproportionately reported. The quality of the data obtained also depends on the skills of the interviewer. Qualitative methods of data collection take longer amount of time and are more expensive. The agency consults experts, who may not belong to the company's target market, but who are knowledgeable about the issues being researched, because they have expended considerable time and resources studying it. They are very insightful and possess insider knowledge about the markets in which they possess expertise. Consumers want to look good when they talk about themselves, therefore their opinions about themselves and their behavior can be biased. Since experts are not consumers themselves, their opinions about the target market are unbiased. Fertile grounds for experts are universities, institutions and media. Lead users of a product are also consulted as they develop a sophisticated understanding of the product and the uses it can be put to. They are also able to predict the trajectory that consumer needs would take, and the type of technologies that would be needed to serve those needs. They are way ahead into the future of the markets and technologies that they are experts of, and companies would do well to tap their insights. Observation is an uninstructive method of studying consumer behavior and is extremely useful when the agency is unfamiliar with the research area. Observation studies are usually conducted in retail stores to track consumer purchases. Various data such as the amount of time spent by the customer, number of choices considered, amount of the product purchased, shopping influences, amount of money spent, reasons for selection or rejection, etc., can be observed. Much depends on the skills of the researcher in gathering and interpreting data.

Descriptive Research

Descriptive research describes something. Such research may be, for instance, meant to describe customers' beliefs, attitudes, recall of advertisements and knowledge about its content. However such researches are not merely fact finding exercises, but are meant to gather data for specific objectives.

Descriptive research differs from exploratory research in terms of the formality and structure with which the research is planned. Data obtained from such researches are usually used in taking marketing decisions. Relationships among various variables are examined in such researches, though cause-effect relationship cannot be established. Descriptive research is quantitative in nature, involving surveys using questionnaires and statistical analysis. Large and representative sample sizes permit generalization of results, aiding in the decision making process, and the collection as well as interpretation of data is objective.

Experimental Research

Experimental research establishes cause and effect. It involves setting up of control procedures to isolate the impact of a factor, like price discount on a dependent variable like sales. The idea is to eliminate other explanations of change in the dependent variable. For example, a product is sold on discount in a few stores, and it is sold on undiscounted price in a few similar stores. It is important that customers visiting the two set of stores are similar in as many ways as possible. Statistical significance testing is done to test whether the difference in sales is caused by the discount, or it is a simple random variation.

The Main Data Collection Stage

The main issue in the data collection stage is the technique to collect data from the chosen sample representative.

Sampling process

The sampling process aims at deciding who and how many people should be interviewed. First, the universe, i.e., the group which forms the subject of study has to be clearly defined. The universe depends on the objectives of the study. The sampling frame must be chosen next. This comprises the list or other records of the chosen universe from which a sample can be selected.

Sample size

Next, it is important to determine the sample size. This involves arriving at the number of respondents who must be surveyed to yield a representative sample of all demographic subgroups of respondents who are being studied. Though it is expensive to interview a large sample size, the larger the sample size, the more is the sample representativeness of the population, and more strongly can the results of the survey be extrapolated to the population. Best results are obtained by interviewing everyone in the population.

The agency has to be mindful of sampling error, which is the error caused by not interviewing everyone in the population. The number of people interviewed is based on a balance between sampling error and cost the more the number of people interviewed, the less the sampling error, but more is the cost of conducting the survey and vice versa.

Sample selection

After selecting the sample size, it must be determined as to how the sample will be selected for response. The sample can be selected by using either the probability methods or by using the non-probability methods. The probability method is used when every sampling unit has an equal probability of being selected. The selection of every item in the sample is independent of the person who conducts the survey. There are three probability sampling methods:

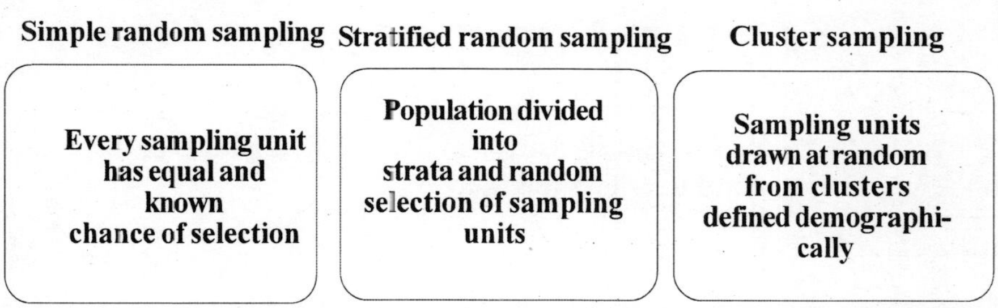

Figure: Types of Sampling

i. *Simple random sampling*

The agency assigns a number to each individual in the sampling frame, and the numbers are drawn at random to complete the sample. Therefore, everyone on the list has an equal probability of being part of the sample.

ii. *Stratified random sampling*

The agency divides the population into groups, such as those on the basis of age, gender or income and respondents are chosen randomly from each group. The number of respondents from each group corresponds to the size of the group, i.e., if the population has twice the number of youths than old people, the sample would also have twice the number of youths than old people. The method ensures that each group gets representation in the sample corresponding to its size in the population.

iii. *Cluster sampling*

The population is divided into mutually exclusive groups, such as residential blocks, and the researcher randomly selects residential blocks to be interviewed.

In the nonprobability sampling methods, every sampling unit does not have an equal probability of being selected. Thus, there is some researcher bias in selecting the sample item. There are three nonprobability sampling methods:

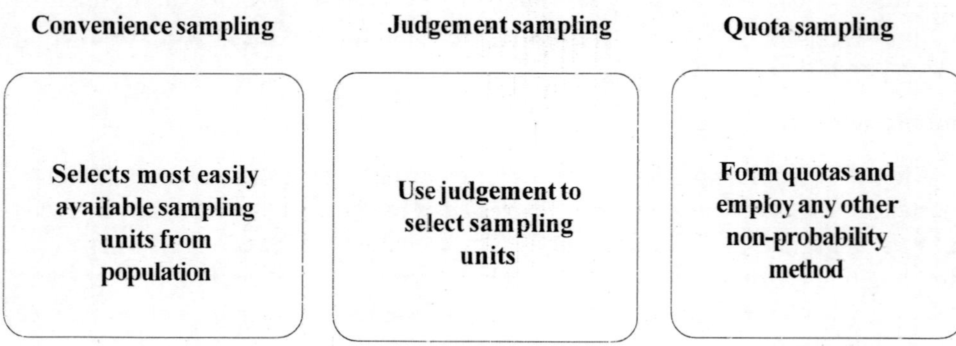

Figure: Types of nonprobability sampling methods

i. *Convenience sample*

The researcher selects the most easily available sampling units or respondents from the population and interviews them.

ii. *Judgment sample*

The researcher uses his judgment to select population members from whom appropriate information can be obtained.

iii. *Quota sampling*

There is no sampling frame, but the agency knows the percentage of population that lies in various groups in terms of age, gender or income. The sample is made by selecting individuals on the basis of this percentage. For instance, a sample will contain roughly 50:50 females to males, because that is roughly the ratio of males and females in the population.

This is a non-random method, because all members of the population do not have an equal chance of selection the interviewer selects members according to his convenience and availability of members, but ensures that the ratios among groups are maintained. This method is adopted when the population is widely dispersed. The difference between quota sampling and stratified sampling method is in the method of selection of the sampling units. In the former, the sampling units are selected by non-random methods such as by convenience or judgment, while in the latter, they are selected on a random basis.

Survey Methods

Survey method involves determining how to interview the respondents who have been selected.

Face to face interviews

Response rates are higher as the personal element in a face to face interview makes refusal to respond less likely. Such interviews can be self-administered, i.e., completed by the respondent himself, or administered by the researcher. In sample surveys, personal interviews are used frequently. Probing of the respondent is easier with face to face interviews. Clarifying probes help interviewers to understand what the interviewee is saying. Exploratory probes stimulate interviewees to give full answers. Probing is possible but restricted due to time pressures and a less personalized situation in telephonic interviews. Visual aids can also be used in face to face interviews. However, interviewer bias may creep in during selection of respondents and administration of the questionnaire. Preparing a structured questionnaire can eliminate some element of the interviewer bias. Experimental design, i.e., testing effectiveness of a stimulus would normally be conducted by this method, rather than by a mail survey, where there is high non-response rate and lack of control over who completes the questionnaire, which could invalidate the results. Use of many open-ended questions in a mail survey would lower response rates, and time restrictions for telephone interviews limit their use for conducting interviews. But personal interviews are expensive. The presence of an interviewer can cause bias, i.e., the respondent may give socially desirable answers and that may lead to misreporting of sensitive information.

Telephone interviews

Telephonic interviews have response rates and cost that lie in between those of face to face interviews and mail surveys. Telephonic interviews allow some degree of flexibility when interviewing, as there is a two way flow of information between the interviewer and the respondent, which is absent in mail surveys, but this flexibility is lesser than in personal interviews. Use of visual aids is not possible. There are limits to the number of questions asked before the respondent either terminates the interview or gives quick and sometimes invalid answers to speed up the process. The use of computer aided interviewing is growing. The presence of accurate databases helps telephonic interviews immensely. Certain type of surveys, for instance, feedback studies, and studies that explore prospective customers, can be done by using telephones.

Mail surveys

These are least expensive and can cover widely dispersed population. Response rate is very low and there is danger of unrepresentative sample. The questionnaire is fully structured and probing is not possible. Control over who fills the questionnaire is low. Visual aids can be supplied and because of self-completion, the interviewer bias is less. Response rate can be increased by prior notification by telephone, monetary and non-monetary incentives, by providing stamped return envelopes, granting anonymity to respondents, close-ended questions in the questionnaire and follow up telephone calls.

Questionnaire Design

Three conditions are necessary to get a true response to question-respondents must understand the question; they must be able to provide information and must be willing to provide it. Questions need to be framed in the language that the respondent understands. Researcher must not ask about issues that respondents cannot remember, or are outside their sphere of experience. Researchers need to consider the best way to elicit sensitive or personal information.

Design stage

The questionnaire may be self-administered, i.e., the respondent fills up the questionnaire himself, or it may be in the form of an interview whereby the researcher asks questions of the respondent. Whatever be the mode of administration, the sequence of questions, wording, number of questions and the length of the questionnaire, type of questions (open or close-ended questions or statements), as well as the techniques used to measure the responses affect the quality of the information obtained.

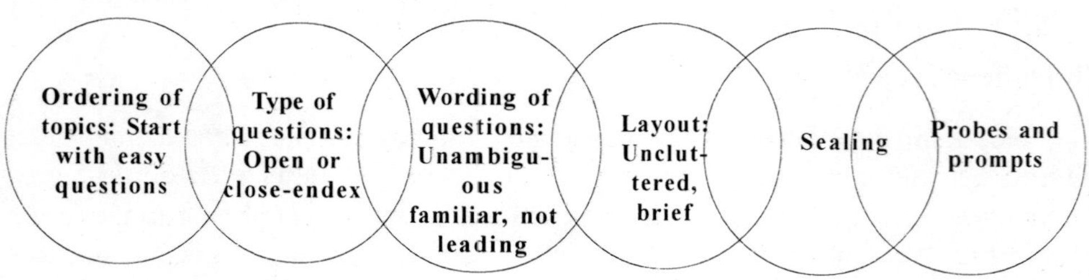

Figure: Qualities of a good questionnaire

i. *Ordering of topics*

The questionnaire starts with questions which the respondents might find easy to answer. Respondents do not want to sound ignorant, and if they are confronted with a question that they have a difficulty in answering right in the beginning of the interview, they may just decline to go further. The interviewer asks awkward questions before attitude measurement. He asks questions related to unaided awareness before aided ones. Classified information such as age, occupation should always be asked at the end.

ii. ***Type of questions***

Close-ended questions limit the range of answers that respondents can give. They have to choose their answers from the options given in the questionnaire, which may not be their true answer. Open-ended questions allow respondents to answer questions in their own way. They can elaborate and explain.

iii. ***Take care in wording of questions***

Guard against ambiguity, leading questions, asking two questions in one and using unfamiliar words. Instructions should be printed in capital letters or underlined so that they are easily distinguished from questions.

iv. ***Layout***

The questionnaire should not appear cluttered. In a mail questionnaire, it is a mistake to squeeze in too many questions in one page to reduce the number of pages. Response is likely to be lower if the questionnaire is heavy, than if the number of pages is extended.

v. ***Scaling***

Attitudes and beliefs can be measured by means of scales, for instance, a scale ranging from 'Strongly agree' to 'strongly disagree'.

vi. ***Probes and prompts***

They seek to explore or clarify what a respondent has said. Respondents may use vague words or phrases. 'Probe' is used to get clarifications, and 'prompts' are used to elicit responses to a question.

vii. ***Pilot Stage***

Once the preliminary questionnaire has been designed, it should be tested with a representative subsample to identify faults. Piloting tests questionnaire design and helps to estimate costs. If the pilot proves satisfactory, the final questionnaire is administered to a chosen sample. Usually, the reliability and validity of the instrument is checked during the pilot stage. Other problems such as response and non-response errors, the ability of respondents to understand the instrument, length and time taken to complete the instrument are assessed in this stage.

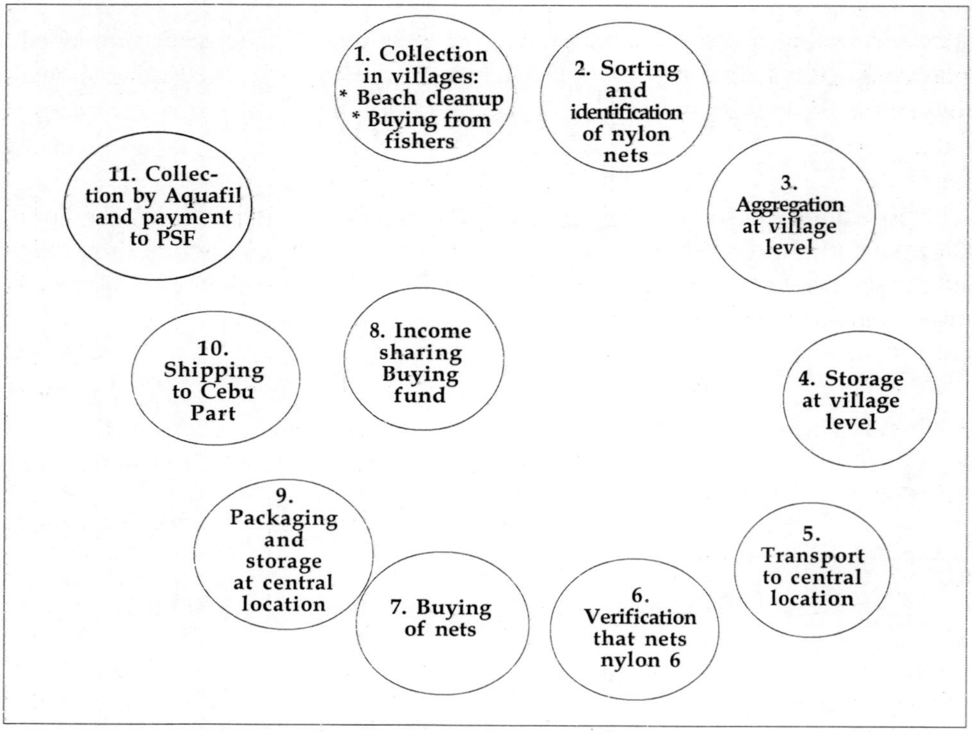

Figure: Networks model pilot stage

If the first pilot study identifies some drawbacks in the instrument, i.e., the questionnaire, a second pilot may have to be conducted to rectify the errors and retest the new questionnaire that has been formulated.

Data Analysis and Interpretation

Before analysis and interpretation, the data has to be prepared. The raw data that has been collected must be edited. Preliminary checks must be conducted to improve the quality of the data collected. It must also be verified that the sampling instructions have been adhered to. Such checks must be done during the data collection process as well as at the end. Thereafter, the data has to be codified and tabulated. These procedures must be done by those who are familiar with the entire research, from the objectives to the research design. Basic marketing research analysis can be carried out using software analysis packages. Sophisticated analysis is conducted using packages such as SPSS. Analysis may be carried out to find mean, standard deviation, and frequency tables, cross tabs and to conduct other advanced statistical analysis. Several sophisticated statistical analysis may be used to formulate decisions such as segmentation of the relevant target audience, identifying key factors in new product launches, tracking brand image, etc. An agency needs to exercise caution when it is interpreting the results of its marketing research endeavor. Agencies commonly infer cause and effect, when only association has been established by the data. For example, data may show that sales rise when number of salespeople is increased, but it does not mean that increasing the size of the sales force will necessarily lead to increase in sales. The company's increased sales might have been the result of increased advertising spend, higher margin for retailers, or even lackluster performance of a competing brand. An agency also needs to exercise caution when it is interpreting means and percentages. Since in most marketing research projects, a sample is surveyed and not the whole population, a mean or percentage is just an estimate, subject to sampling error, i.e., the error due to taking a sample rather than interviewing the entire population. Statistical hypothesis testing allows sampling differences to be evaluated in the light of sampling errors to establish whether they are likely to be real differences, i.e., statistically significant differences, or they are likely to be a result of taking a sample rather than interviewing the entire population.

Report Writing and Presentation

The results of the research have to be presented in the form of a report or a presentation.

The key elements in a research project are:

- Title page, containing the topic of the research study, time of the study, to whom is the report being submitted to and by whom has the research been done.
- List of contents, containing a detailed list of the contents of the report along with page numbers, list of tables and list of figures in die report.
- Preface, comprising outline of clients' brief, statement of objectives, scope and methods of research.
- Executive summary, comprising a summary of conclusions and recommendations. The purpose of the executive summary is to summarize the key issues and findings of the report for executives who do not have the time to read the complete report.
- Previous related research, detailing how previous research has had an influence on this research. This section should list out the methodology, context, results and conclusions of related researches done earlier to provide a relevant perspective for the present study.
- Research methods, which explains the methodology used for the purpose of the present research. This includes details about the type of study, sampling issues, data sources, data collection methods, use of instruments, preparation of the instruments and method of administration.
- Research findings, which should detail the results of the study according to the objectives with which the study was initiated.

- Conclusions of the study, along with suitable recommendations.

Appendices, including reports, articles, tables and figures that are not directly related to the study, or can interrupt the flow of the report, though they are useful as background information.

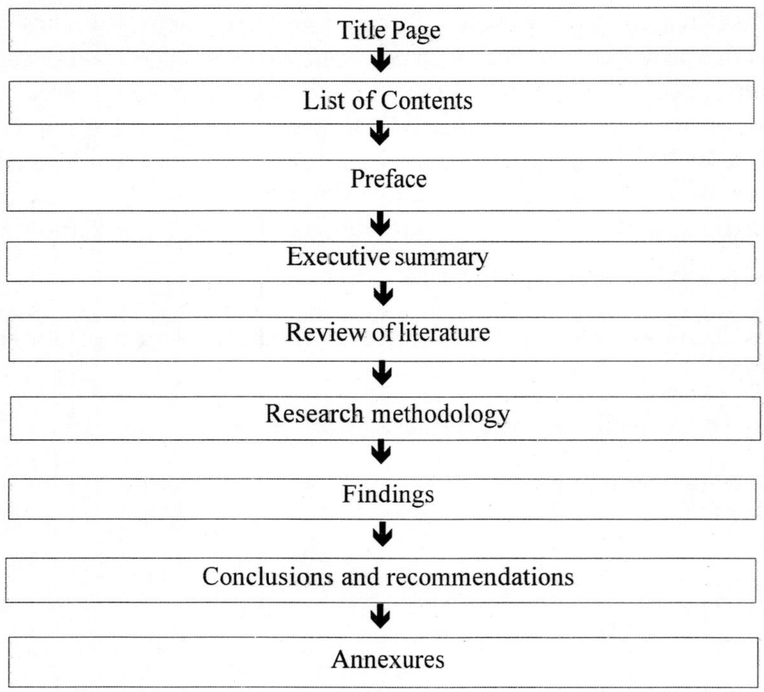

Figure: Key elements of a research report

The report should be written in the language which the reader will understand. Jargon should be avoided. The most important parts of the report are the findings and conclusions based on the survey. These should be presented in a clear and lucid manner. As far as possible, the results should clearly point to some outcomes or suggestions that can help the management in taking decisions or solving the problems that were outlined in the objectives of the study. Sometimes results may point towards additional research being required.

7.10. Marketing Research V/S Market Research

Marketing research is a broader term including market research. Marketing research is concerned with all the major functions of marketing. Market research is primarily concerned with knowing the capacity of the market to absorb a particular product. Marketing research is not only concerned with the jurisdiction of the market but also covers nature of the market, product analysis, sales analysis, time, place and media of advertising, personal selling and marketing intermediaries and their relationships etc. Marketing research serves the purpose of 'intelligence wing of the marketing management. Its scope is very broad as compared to market-research. It is concerned with collection of market information systematically and impartially, analysis and evaluation of relevant data and use such data for the benefit of the organization. It is a careful and objective study of various areas of marketing activities. What, when, where and how to sell the end product and the services are four questions to which the marketing research wing provides an answer. Thus, market research and marketing research are different from each other. Market research is a narrow concept whereas marketing research is a broad one and its scope is much wider. It includes nature of the market, product analysis, sales analysis, time, place and media of advertising, personal selling, pricing, sales organization, packaging, brand names, etc.

7.11. Need and Importance of Marketing Research

The following advantages offered by marketing research show its importance.

a) Facilitates planned production

By forecasts of probable sales in the coming years.

b) Discovery of causes of consumer's resistance

It helps in identifying the reasons for consumer resistance to existing or new products.

c) Correction of defects

It reveals defects and therefore makes corrective action possible.

d) Reveals the nature of demand

It brings out whether the product is in constant demand throughout the year or has a seasonal demand.

e) Effectiveness of existing channels of distribution

For example, in the case of TVs it may be discovered that after sale service is not satisfactory. Then, arrangements may be made to remove such grievances of the customers.

f) Product utility

It indicates why exactly the product is being purchased by the people and what exact service do they get out of it. For example, a market research conducted by Hindustan Lever Ltd., revealed that their 'Sunlight Soap' which was originally intended to serve as a washing soap, was being used as toilet soap by many people.

g) New uses of the product

Marketing research may reveal certain new uses for the existing products.

h) Market information

It provides complete information about the market and the changes that are likely to occur in demand for a certain product.

i) Discovery of potential market

It provides information about the possibility of potential (future) market.

j) Discovery of new lines of production

It helps in the discovery of supplementary lines of products.

7.12. Advantages of Marketing Research

- Marketing research helps the management of a firm in planning by providing accurate and up- to-date information about the demands, their changing tastes, attitudes, preferences, buying.
- It helps the manufacturer to adjust his production according to the conditions of demand.
- It helps to establish correlative relationship between the product brand and consumers' needs and preferences.
- It helps the manufacturer to secure economies in the distribution in its products.
- It makes the marketing of goods efficient and economical by eliminating all type of wastage.
- It helps the manufacturer and dealers to find out the best way of approaching the potential.
- It helps the manufacturer to find out the defects in the existing product and take the required corrective steps to improve the product.
- It helps the manufacturer in finding out the effectiveness of the existing channels of distribution and in finding out the best way of distributing the goods to the ultimate consumers.
- It guides the manufacturer in planning his advertising and sales promotion efforts.
- It is helpful in assessing the effectiveness of advertising programmes.
- It is helpful in evaluating the relative efficiency of the different advertising media.
- It is helpful in evaluating selling methods.

- It reveals the causes of consumer resistance.
- It minimizes the risks of uncertainties and helps in taking sound decisions.
- It reveals the nature of demand for the firm's product. That is, it indicates whether the demand for the product is constant or seasonal.
- It is helpful in ascertaining the reputation of the firm and its products.
- It helps the firm in determining the range within which its products are to be offered to the consumers. That is, it is helpful in determining the sizes, colours, designs, prices, etc., of the products of the firm.
- It would help the management to know how patents, licensing agreements and other legal restrictions affect the manufacture and sale of the firm's products.
- It is helpful to the management in determining the actual prices and the price ranges.
- It is helpful to the management in determining the discount rates.
- It is helpful to the management in ascertaining the price elasticity for its products.
- It helps the firm in knowing the marketing and pricing strategy of competitors.
- It is helpful in knowing the general conditions prevailing in the mark.
- It is helpful to the management in finding out the size of the market for its products.
- It helps the firm in knowing its market share over various time periods.
- It is quite helpful to a firm in launching a new product.
- It helps the firm in knowing the transportation, storage and supply requirements of its products.
- It helps the firm in exploring new uses for its existing products and thereby, increasing the demand for its products.
- It is helpful to a firm in making sales forecasts for its products and thereby, establishing harmonious adjustment between demand and supply of its products.
- It helps the firm in exploring new markets for its products.

7.13. Essential Stages of Marketing Research Process

Some of the most essential stages of marketing research process are as follows. The process of marketing research starts with the identification of a problem. Simultaneously the company also identifies whether the required information can be collected by the internal staff, or an external MR agency needs to be commissioned.

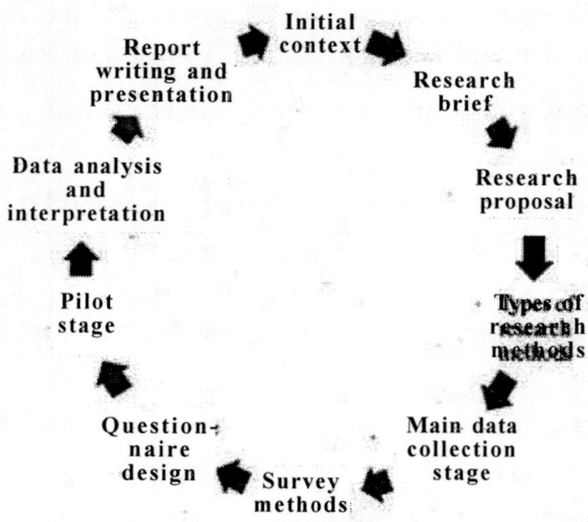

Figure: Stages in Marketing Research Process

I. Initial Contact

There is a realization that a marketing problem requires information to help find its solution. The marketing department asks the marketing research team to carry out a research, or seeks the services of a marketing research agency. If it is agreed that the services of a marketing research agency is required, the marketing department briefs the agency about the problem it wants the agency to investigate. It discusses the nature of the problem in detail, and delineates its research needs. It is imperative that the agency learns as much about the client's business as it can before it agrees to meet the client. The agency talks to existing clients who are in the same industry as the prospective client, and carries out exploratory research, like a search in the business press and on the internet to know more about the client.

II. Research Brief

The marketing department and the research agency meet to discuss why the research is needed, what it will be used for, when it is needed and how much is to be paid for it. The marketing department explains its problem and its research objectives minutely and meticulously. It is important that the marketing department keeps in mind that while it understands the nuances of its problem, the agency will understand only as much as it is told. For example, if the company's problem is to attract customers to a new product, it should brief the agency about the target market for which the product has been designed, the benefits and features of the product, its advertising and sales strategy for the product and a complete profile of its competitors. The corresponding research objectives would be to identify customers who can use the product and to identify the features of the product that appeal to them most. The marketing department also explains as to how detailed the research should be, and how long the agency can take to complete the research. The marketing department ensures that the agency understands its requirements by encouraging it to ask questions, and at the end of the meeting they collaborate to write down their expectations from each other. It is important that the marketing department hands over its requirement in writing to the agency, so that the latter always keeps in mind what it has to achieve for its client, and not let the research project go astray and esoteric. The written document can also be used to settles disputes between them, if there are any, at any time during the research project.

Prerequisites for commissioning a good research

The research brief should be clear about the marketing problem for which research needs to be done. Additionally, the company must also take into consideration diverse perspectives of at least two or three MR agencies to ascertain the accuracy of their research designs.

i. Terms like market, market share and competitors should be clearly defined for the purpose of the research.

ii. Some researchers in the MR agency may be specialists in a particular data gathering method like group discussion, and they may bend research problems to use their favourite methods. This may be expensive in addition to being inappropriate for the research objectives under consideration. The company must familiarize itself with the MR agency and people handling its research project.

iii. Allow the researcher to ask even naive questions. Clearing doubts about the problem to be examined or related background information can avoid costlier problems in the future.

iv. Brief two or three agencies to get diverse viewpoints on the research problem.

III. Research Proposal

The agency formulates a research proposal, in which it delineates as to what it will achieve for its client and how it will go about doing so. For example, it may agree to identify demographic variables of the customers of the client's new product by a certain date and at a certain price. This is almost always written so that both parties understand each other's commitments. A client is likely to be impressed by the research proposal if it demonstrates that the agency has understood the client's problems and its research objectives clearly. A good research proposal unambiguously describes how the research will be conducted-What will be the sample size? Which survey methods would be used? How would data be analyzed? How long will the research take? In what form would the report be presented? And how much will the company have to pay? The client judges the intent and competence of the agency by what is contained in the research proposal. Therefore the agency should be forthright and avoid camouflaging of any type it should simply state what it is going to achieve for the client, how, and by when. The agency should ensure that the client understands the nuances of the proposal, and the client should ensure that the proposal contains everything that it wants the agency to do. The client should be aware of the fact that the agency will do what it has promised in the research proposal, but no more, so it should be exhaustive in listing its requirements, and ensure that the agency has promised to meets all its requirements in the research proposal. If there is any doubt about an issue, the client should ask the agency for clarification. The research proposal should first define the problem. For doing this, the researcher must consider the purpose for which the study is being conducted, the available information, additional information required and how such information would aid the client in the decision making process. The problem can be formulated without much consultation, though frequently it may involve discussions with decision makers in the company, experts outside the client's company, use of secondary data or even some exploratory research, for instance, a few focus groups. This should be followed by developing an approach to the problem. This involves developing a framework for analyzing the problem. Relevant questions, for which answers are needed by conducting the research, must be clearly propounded in this step. The research design should explain the methods of collecting data, sampling plan and a plan for data analysis. The client should be clearly told about the sources from where the relevant data can be obtained, the time frame within which the entire study will be completed and the modus operandi of conducting the study.

8

PRODUCT DECISIONS

8.1. Product – Meaning and Definition

A product can be defined as a collection of physical, service and symbolic attributes which yield satisfaction or benefits to a user or buyer. A product is a combination of physical attributes say, size and shape; and subjective attributes say image or "quality". A customer purchases on both dimensions. As cited earlier, an avocado pear is similar the world over in terms of physical characteristics, but once the label CARMEL, for example, is put on it, the product's physical properties are enhanced by the image CARMEL creates. In "postmodernisation" it is increasingly important that the product fulfils the image which the producer is wishing to project. This may involve organisations producing symbolic offerings represented by meaning laden products that chase stimulation-loving consumers who seek experience - producing situations. So, for example, selling mineral water may not be enough. It may have to be "Antarctic" in source, and flavoured. This opens up a wealth of new marketing opportunities for producers. A product's physical properties are characterised the same the world over. They can be convenience or shopping goods or durables and nondurables; however, one can classify products according to their degree of potential for global marketing:

a) Local products - seen as only suitable in one single market.

b) International products - seen as having extension potential into other markets.

c) Multinational products - products adapted to the perceived unique characteristics of national markets.

d) Global products - products designed to meet global segments.

Quality, method of operation or use and maintenance (if necessary) are catchwords in international marketing. A failure to maintain these will lead to consumer dissatisfaction. This is typified by agricultural machinery where the lack of spares and/or foreign exchange can lead to lengthy downtimes. It is becoming increasingly important to maintain quality products based on the ISO 9000 standard, as a prerequisite to export marketing. Consumer beliefs or perceptions also affect the "world brand" concept. World brands are based on the same strategic principles, same positioning and same marketing mix but there may be changes in message or other image. World brands in agriculture are legion. In fertilizers, brands like Norsk Hydro are universal; in tractors, Massey Ferguson; in soups, Heinz; in tobacco, BAT; in chemicals, Bayer. These world brand names have been built up over the years with great investments in marketing and production. Few world brands, however, have originated from developing countries. This is hardly surprising given the lack of resources. In some markets product saturation has been reached, yet surprisingly the same product may not have reached saturation in other similar markets. Whilst France has long been saturated by avocadoes, the UK market is not yet, hence raising the opportunity to enter deeper into this market.

8.2. Elements of Product

The elements of a product must have the following credentials.

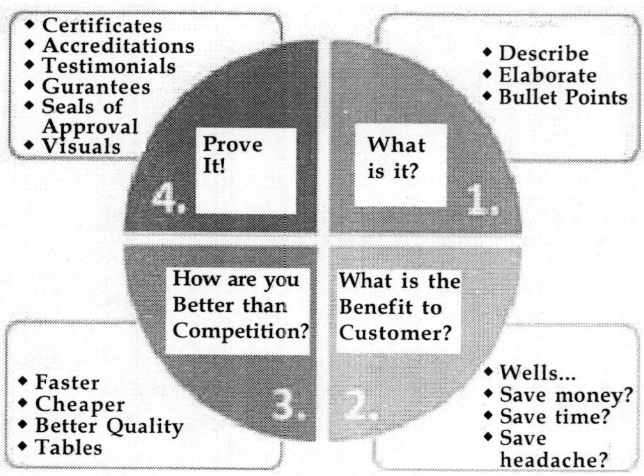

Figure: Elements of product

Customers, whether looking for a product or a service, are looking for 4 primary pieces of information on any given page. The four elements below work for either products or services:

a) Description – Service: What do you do? / Product: What do you sell?

b) Benefit – What is the benefit of this product/service to the customer?

c) Comparison – Why is this product/service better than your competitors?

d) Proof – Prove it!

Every product or service: (P/S) must describe what you do or sell. This is what most websites achieve, though many don't go much farther. In and of itself, describing your P/S is key. After all, if you don't describe the scope of your product or service, customers can't understand the direct benefit to them.

Describe: You must describe your product in detail. This helps in two fundamental ways: one, it helps robots spider your web pages in more detail; two, it helps customers know what you're selling.

Elaborate: Don't be afraid to put in as much detail as necessary. Use this logic: if it will help sell the product, leave it in. If it doesn't, pull it out.

Bullet Points: Bullet points help a person's eyes break down information. Therefore, when you can use bullet points, do so.

Element	**Products**	**Services**
What is your P/S?	Price, size, color, variety, how it fits into other products, short description, long description, great title, catchphrase that sums up the product, image, multiple images if you have them, in stock?, add to cart button, what it's used for, how it combines with other products, "customers that bought this product also bought…," audio description, video	Type of service, who would use such a service, how it fits into other services, the nature of the service in action, video, audio, breakdown of service into sub-elements, milestones of service, how the service 'rolls out' for the customer, where you would use this service.

8.3. Significance of Product

The concept of product life-cycle highlights that sooner or later all products die and that if management wishes to sustain its revenues, it must replace the declining products with the new ones. The product life-cycle concept indicates as to what can be expected in the market for a new product at various stages. i.e., introduction, growth, maturity and decline. Thus, the concept of product life-cycle can be used as a forecasting tool. It can alert management that its product will inevitably face saturation and decline, and the host of problems these stages pose. The product life-cycle is also a useful framework for describing the typical evolution of marketing strategy over the stages of product life-cycle. This will help in taking sound marketing decisions at different stages of the product life-cycle.

After a product has been developed, it is launched in the market with the help of various promotional devices such as advertising, sales promotion, publicity and personal selling. In other words, product development must be followed by the successful introduction of the product in the market. For this, planning for introduction of the product starts during the process of product development itself. Every firm makes sale projections during introduction, growth and maturity stage of the product life-cycle. To achieve the projected sales target, it formulates promotional, pricing and distribution policies. Thus, the concept of product life-cycle facilitates integrated marketing policies relating to product, price, place and promotion/distribution.

The advantages of PLC to a firm are as follows:

When the product life-cycle is predictable, the management must be cautious in taking advance steps before the decline stage, by adopting product modification, pricing strategies, style, quality, change, etc. The firm can prepare an effective product plan by knowing the product life-cycle of a product. The management can find new uses of the product for the expansion of market during growth stage and for extending the maturity stage. The management can adopt latest technological changes to improve the product quality, features and design.

8.4. Product Classification

In every part of the world there are different systems of **product classification**. The concept of "product classification" consists of dividing products according to specific characteristics so that they form a structured portfolio. In general, manufacturers use an informal product classification system but there are also many standardized methods of product classification devised by various industry organizations. Some examples of such standardized methods of classification of products are the GS1 Global Product Classification, the International (Nice) Classification of Goods and Services, North American Product Classification System, etc. A very well known system for classification of products is the Harmonized Commodity Description and Coding System (HS) created by the World Customs Organizations.

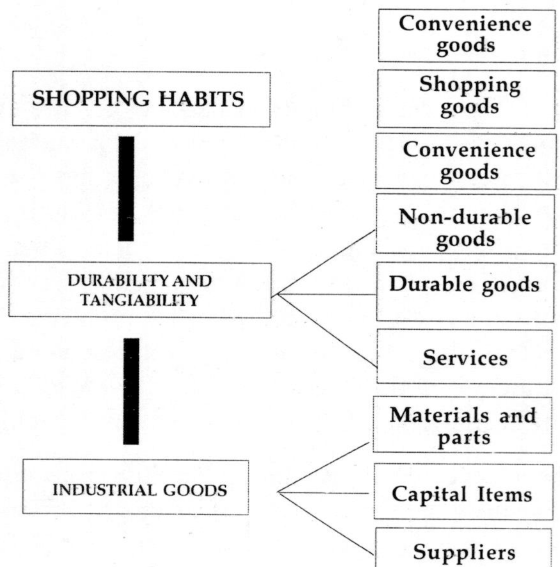

Figure: Product Classification Framework

The main reason for using such kind of system can vary from registering trademarks to numerous different purpose. A basic product classification can be made based on consumer and business products. The consumer products are afterwards divided based on preference for shopping habits or durability and tangibility. The business products are the industrial goods. The informal classification of products based on variables such as shopping habits, durability and tangibility as well as industrial goods is presented in the following.

Classification of products on the basis of shopping habits

Based on the first variable, the shopping habits, the products can be classified into convenience goods, shopping goods and unsought goods. At the end of the week when you go to the supermarket to complete the necessary shopping for the next week, you probably buy condiments, soap, etc. These kinds of product, which has become a habit and for which you don't think too much before buying are part of the convenience goods category. Another example would be when you enter into a shop, and when going to the cash machine you see some umbrellas and take one just because outside was raining and you went out unprepared. This is also an excellent example of impulse buying. Generally for convenience goods, once customers makes a choice for their preferred brand, then stay loyal to that brand because it is convenient to keep repeating the choice over time. Other examples of such convenience purchases include bread, cold drinks, chewing gum, etc. The shopping goods are another category of products. Compared with the convenience goods, the shopping goods are not so frequent. A relevant example can be clothing, electronics, etc.. This category relies heavily on advertising and trained sales people who can influence customer's choices. For the unsought goods consumers don't put much thought into purchasing them and generally don't have compelling impulse to buy them. An example in this category would be life insurances.

Classification of products on the basis of durability and tangibility

Based on the second variable of durability and tangibility there are non-durable and durable goods as well as services. The non-durable category consists of tangible goods that are low priced and purchased frequently such as shampoos, deodorants, etc. Compared with these ones, the durable goods are also tangible goods but are targeted for many uses. For this category, more personal selling is required as well as guarantee to be provided, resulting in higher margin. Relevant example can be the couches or chairs. About the third category, i.e. services, we are going to speak in another article.

Classification of products based on industrial consumption

The last category of products mentioned as the industrial goods classification involves the materials (raw materials such as wood, cooper, aluminium) and parts (tiers, computer chips), capital items such as installations and equipment (cranes, bulldozers), accessory equipment (hand tools, computers, calculators), process materials (food preservatives), operating supplies (papers, pencils, oil).

8.5. Product item, Product line and Product mix

Concept of Product Item

Product items are various varieties offered within product line, which are similar in one or other ways. Such varieties are based on quality, size, colour, capacity, price, model, performance, and so on.

Table: Product Mix, Product Line, and Product items

No.	Name of product Lines	Product Items	Total Items in Each Line
1.	A	A1,A2,A3,A4,A5,A6,A7	7
2.	B	B1, B2, B3, B4	4
3.	C	C1,C2,C3,C4,C5,C6,C7,C8	8
4.	D	D1,D2,D3,D4,D5,D6	6
5.	E	E1,E2,E3,E4,E5	5
		TOTAL	30

Number of product line	:	**5**
Number of product items	:	**30**
Product mix length	:	**30**
Product mix width	:	**5**
Product mix dpth	:	**30/5-6**
Product mix consistency	:	**?**

Figure: Product Mix, Product Line, and Product Items

Product Line

Product line is a group of product items that can satisfy the same needs and wants, they have more or less similar features. For example, Bajaj Auto Ltd., in its two wheeler product line, makes Discover, Boxer, Boss, Pulsar, Cub scooter, Bajaj Sunny, etc. According to Philip Kotler "Product line is a group of products that are closely related because they function in a similar way, are sold to same customer groups, are marketed through the same type of outlets, or fall within given price range." Thus, product line is the group of similar products. The similarity may be seen in one or more ways. Product line consists of product items belonging to same class.

The definition suggests following five ways the items are closely related:

a) They function in similar manner.

b) They offer similar benefits, or meet similar expectations.

c) They are sold to similar customer groups.

d) They are marketed by similar outlets.

e) They fall within same price range.

Characteristics of Product Line

Main characteristics of product line can be listed as:

a) Product line consists of closely related product items. Difference is only found in terms of colour, size, shape, model, performance, weight, and capacity.

b) It is a compose of various similar items.

c) Product items are complementary to one another. For example, tube, tyre, and related materials.

d) There is difference in price. For example, Hero Honda charges different price for different models.

e) The purpose of offering similar items in each of the product line may be to attract customers by offering more varieties, and to create a good image or reputation.

f) Different items of a product line can be manufactured using same technology and/or inputs.

g) Product items in each of the product lines are distributed in same distribution channel. That is, similar outlets market them.

h) Product items in each product line function in same manner. They need same technical skills to use them.

i) They are sold to similar customer groups. They satisfy needs of the same groups.

j) They have more or less same use or utility. They are used for the same purpose.

Product Mix

Product mix of a company is made of all product lines and items. It includes the total number of varieties or models offered by the company.

Let us define the term:

Philip Kotler:

"A product mix is the set of all product lines and items that a particular seller offers for the sale to buyers."

William Stanton:

"The product mix is the full list of all products offered for the sale by the company." Thus, product mix means total number of products items offered by the company. For example, HMT Company produces watches, machines, tractors, plants, tools, and equipment's, and many other products. In each product group, a number of varieties are offered. The set of all these products (main range) and product varieties in each range can be said as product mix.

Product Mix Dimensions

Product mix of a particular company includes major product lines.

Product mix has various dimensions, such as:

i. Product Mix Length

It refers to the total number of items (in all the product lines) in product mix. For example product mix of Bajaj Company has more than 100 items in various product lines, such as fans, bulbs and tubes, heaters, motorbikes, shooters, rich-show, processing machines, and many other ranges.

ii. Product Mix Width or Breadth

It indicates the total number of product lines a company carries. For example, two wheelers (including various models) constitute one of the product lines of Bajaj Company.

iii. Product Mix Depth

It refers to a number of varieties in forms of sizes, colors, and models offered within each product line. It can be said as the average number of product items offered by the firm in each product line.

iv. Product Mix Consistency

It refers to degree to which different product lines are related in one or other ways. It indicates how closely various product lines are related. The consistency can be judged on the basis of production requirements, uses of products, distribution channels, or some other ways. For example, product lines of Philips India Ltd., include radios, bulbs and tubes, different television sets, VCR, CD-DVD player, tape recorders, etc., can have higher consistency. While Hindustan Machines and

Tools produce wrist watches as well as tractors, it is called inconsistent product mix.

8.6. Product Line Policies and Strategies

Product line Policy pricing refers to the practice of reviewing and setting prices for multiple products that a company offers in coordination with one another. Rather than looking at each product separately and setting its price, product-line pricing strategies aim to maximize the sales of different products by creating more complementary, rather than competitive, products. If you offer more than one product or service, consider the impact that one product's or service's price will have on the others.

Perceived Value

Some consumers want the best product available and are willing to pay more for it, while other shoppers just want a basic product and buy primarily based on affordability. Creating a product line that offers low-end, mid-range and high-end pricing can lead consumers to believe that different products have different values. The business will have to offer more features on its top-end product to justify a higher price if all of the products are sold under the same name and in the same place. Alternately, the business might sell different versions of a similar product under two different names; one might be sold with colorful packaging and the other without it.

Captive Pricing

Some businesses sell products in their line at a low price to get consumers to use the base product and then they encourage them to buy add-ons or complementary products. For example, a salon owner might offer affordable haircuts to get customers into her shop to spend money on perms, colorings, nail treatments and hair care products. While they are in the store, these customers might make impulse purchases at the counter while checking out.

Loss Leaders

Selling a product at or below cost to lure customers in and drive other sales is an example of product-line pricing. A restaurant, for example, might offer a low-priced entrée with the purchase of a drink and dessert that have higher profit margins. A landscaper might offer a fall aerating and reseeding package at a price well below the competition to land a summer lawn-cutting contract.

Domino Effect

Part of the rationale of product-line pricing is that changing the price of one product can affect the rest of the products in the line. For example, if you set your base product price too high, you might lose enough sales of that product to lose your total gross profits, because your add-ons and related products are where you make your best margins. If you set your add-on prices too high, you might lose sales of your base product. A pet sitter, for example, might raise her standard fee for daytime pet sitting and consequently lose customers who might have hired her for overnight stays, grooming or training services.

8.7. Factors Influencing Product Decision

Some of the major factors influencing pricing decisions of a company are as follows:

A company's price level sends signals about the quality of its products to the customer. A customer always compares the company's prices with those of its competitors. The competitors also keep an eye on the price levels of a company. Very low prices may invite price wars, while high prices without sufficient additional features or quality invite bad publicity. Distribution channel members also exert pressure on prices by demanding higher margins.

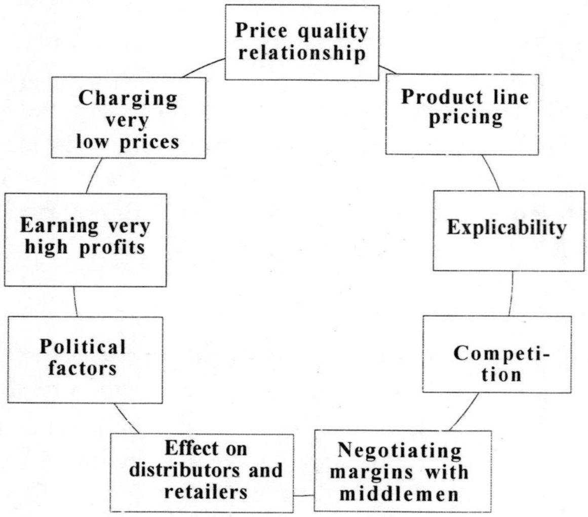

Figure: Factors influencing pricing decisions

a) ***Price-quality relationship***

Customers use price as an indicator of quality, particularly for products where objective measurement of quality is not possible, such as drinks and perfumes. Price strongly influences quality perceptions of such products. If a product is priced higher, the instinctive judgment of the customer is that the quality of the product must be higher, unless he can objectively justify otherwise.

b) ***Product line pricing***

A company extends its product line rather than reduce price of its existing brand, when a competitor launches a low price brand that threatens to eat into its market share. It launches a low price fighter brand to compete with low price competitor brands. The company is able to protect the image of its premium brand, which continues to be sold at a higher price. At a later stage, it produces a range of brands at different price points, which serve segments of varying price sensitivities. And when a customer shows the inclination to trade up, it persuades him to buy one of its own premium brands. Similarly, if a customer of one of its premium brands wants to trade down, it encourages him to buy one of its value brands. But, it is not easy to maintain a portfolio of brands in the same product category. The company needs to endow each of its brands with an independent personality, and identify it with a segment. A company's brands should not be floating around, willing to grab any customer that they can, but they should be specifically targeted at segments customers of the target segment should like the brand, but customers of other segments should not like it enough to buy it.

c) *Explicability*

The company should be able to justify the price it is charging, especially if it is on the higher side. Consumer product companies have to send cues to the customers about the high quality and the superiority of the product. A superior finish, fine aesthetics or superior packaging can give positive cues to the customers when they cannot objectively measure the quality of the offering. A company should be aware of the features of the product that the customers can objectively evaluate and should ensure superior performance of those features. In industrial markets, the capability of salespeople to explain a high price to customers may allow them to charge higher prices. Where customers demand economic justifications of prices, the inability to produce cost arguments may mean that high price cannot be charged. A customer may reject a price that does not seem to reflect the cost of producing the product. Sometimes it may have to be explained that premium price was needed to cover R&D expenditure, the benefits of which the customer is going to enjoy.

d) *Competition*

A company should be able to anticipate reactions of competitors to its pricing policies and moves. Competitors can negate the advantages that a company might be hoping to make with its pricing policies. A company reduces its price to gain market share.

One or more competitors can decide to match the cut, thwarting the ambitions of the company to gamer market share. But all competitors are not same and their approaches and reactions to pricing moves of the company are different. The company has to take care while defining competition. The first level of competitors offers technically similar products. There is direct competition between brands which define their businesses and customers in similar way. Reactions of such competitors are very swift and the company will have to study each of its major competitors and find out their business objectives and cash positions. Competitors who have similar ambitions to increase their market share and have deep pockets will swiftly reduce price if any one of them reduces prices. A telephone company offering landline services has all telephone companies offering landline services as its first level of competitors. The second level of competition is dissimilar products serving the same need in a similar way. Such competitors' initial belief is that they are not being affected by the pricing moves of the company. But once it sinks in that they are being affected adversely by the pricing moves of a company that seemingly belongs to another industry, they will take swift retaliatory actions. The telephone company has the mobile phone operators as its second level of competitors. The third level of competition would come from products serving the problem in a dissimilar way. Again such competitors do not believe that they will be affected. But once convinced that they are being affected adversely, swift retaliation should be expected. The retaliation of third level is difficult to comprehend as their business premises and cost structures are very different from the company in question. Companies offering e-mail service are competitors at the third level of the telephone company. A company must take into account all three levels of competition.

e) ***Negotiating Margins***

A customer may expect its supplier to reduce price, and in such situations the price that the customer pays is different from the list price. Such discounts are pervasive in business markets, and take the form of order-size discounts, competitive discounts, fast payment discounts, annual volume bonus and promotions allowance. Negotiating margins should be built, which allow price to fall from list price levels but still permit profitable transactions. It is important that the company anticipates the discounts that it will have to grant to gain and retain business and adjust its list price accordingly. If the company does not build potential discounts into its list price, the discounts will have to come from the company's profits.

f) ***Effect on distributors and retailers***

When products are sold through intermediaries like retailers, the list price to customers must reflect the margins required by them sometimes list prices will be high because middlemen want higher margins. But some retailers can afford to sell below the list price to customers. They run low-cost operations and can manage with lower margins. They pass on some part of their own margins to customers.

g) ***Political factors***

Where price is out of line with manufacturing costs, political pressure may act to force down prices. Exploitation of a monopoly position may bring short term profits but incurs backlash of a public enquiry into pricing policies. It may also invite customer wrath and cause switching upon the introduction of suitable alternatives.

h) ***Earning very high profits***

It is never wise to earn extraordinarily profits, even if current circumstances allow the company to charge high prices. The pioneer companies are able to charge high prices, due to lack of alternatives available to the customers. The company's high profits lure competitors who are enticed by the possibility of making profits. The entry of competitors in hordes puts tremendous pressure on price and the pioneer company is forced to reduce its price. But if the pioneer had been satisfied with lesser profits, the competitors would have kept away for a longer time, and it would have got sufficient time to consolidate its position.

i) ***Charging very low prices***

It may not help a company's because if it charges low prices when its major competitors are charging much higher prices. Customers come to believe that adequate quality can be provided only at the prices being charged by the major companies. If a company introduces very low prices, customers suspect its quality and do not buy the product in spite of the low price. If the cost structure of the company allows, it should stay in business at the low price. Slowly, as some customers buy the product, they spread the news of its adequate quality.

The customers' belief about the quality-price equation starts changing. They start believing that adequate quality can be provided at lower prices. The companies which have been charging higher prices come under fire from customers. They either have to reduce their prices or quit.

8.8. Product Life Cycle (PLC)

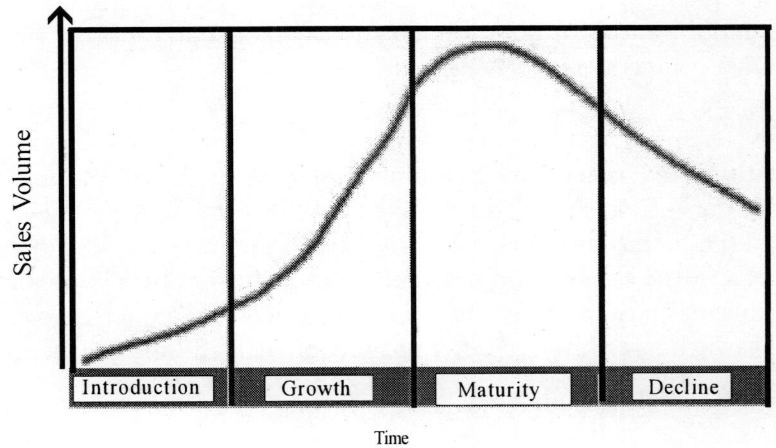

Figure: Product Life Cycle

As consumers, we buy millions of products every year. And just like us, these products have a life cycle. Older, long-established products eventually become less popular, while in contrast, the demand for new, more modern goods usually increases quite rapidly after they are launched. Because most companies understand the different product life cycle stages, and that the products they sell all have a limited lifespan, the majority of them will invest heavily in new product development in order to make sure that their businesses continue to grow. The product life cycle has 4 very clearly defined stages, each with its own characteristics that mean different things for business that are trying to manage the life cycle of their particular products.

Introduction Stage

This stage of the cycle could be the most expensive for a company launching a new product. The size of the market for the product is small, which means sales are low, although they will be increasing. On the other hand, the cost of things like research and development, consumer testing, and the marketing needed to launch the product can be very high, especially if it's a competitive sector.

Growth Stage

The growth stage is typically characterized by a strong growth in sales and profits, and because the company can start to benefit from economies of scale in production, the profit margins, as well as the overall amount of profit, will increase. This makes it possible for businesses to invest more money in the promotional activity to maximize the potential of this growth stage.

Maturity Stage

During the maturity stage, the product is established and the aim for the manufacturer is now to maintain the market share they have built up. This is probably the most competitive time for most products and businesses need to invest wisely in any marketing they undertake. They also need to consider any product modifications or improvements to the production process which might give them a competitive advantage.

Decline Stage

Eventually, the market for a product will start to shrink, and this is what's known as the decline stage. This shrinkage could be due to the market becoming saturated (i.e. all the customers who will buy the product have already purchased it), or because the consumers are switching to a different type of product. While this decline may be inevitable, it may still be possible for companies to make some profit by switching to less-expensive production methods and cheaper markets.

Product Life Cycle Examples:

It's possible to provide examples of various products to illustrate the different stages of the product life cycle more clearly. Here is the example of watching recorded television and the various stages of each method:

- Introduction – 3D TVs
- Growth – Blue ray discs/DVR
- Maturity – DVD
- Decline – Video cassette

The idea of the product life cycle has been around for some time, and it is an important principle manufacturers need to understand in order to make a profit and stay in business. However, the key to successful manufacturing is not just understanding this life cycle, but also proactively managing products throughout their lifetime, applying the appropriate resources and sales and marketing strategies, depending on what stage products are at in the cycle.

8.9. Marketing Strategies adopted during PLC

Product passes through four stages of its life cycle. Every stage poses different opportunities and challenges to the marketer. Each of stages demands the unique or distinguished set of marketing strategies. A marketer should watch on its sales and market situations to identify the stage in which the product is passing through, and accordingly, he should design appropriate marketing strategies. Here, strategy basically involves four elements – product, price, promotion, and distribution. By appropriate combination of these four elements, the strategy can be formulated for each stage of the PLC. Every stage gives varying importance to these elements of marketing mix. Let us analyze basic strategies used in each of the stages of the PLC, as described by Philip Kotler.

Marketing Strategies for Introduction Stage

Introduction stage is marked with slow growth in sales and a very little or no profit. Note that product has been newly introduced, and a sales volume is limited; product and distribution are not given more emphasis. Basic constituents of marketing strategies for the stage include price and promotion. Price, promotion or both may be kept high or low depending upon market situation and management approach. Following are the possible strategies during the first stage.

		Promotion: High	Promotion: Low
Price	High	Rapid Siddming Strategy	Slow Siddming Strategy
	Low	Rapid Penetration Strategy	Slow Penetration Strategy

Figure: Marketing Stragies for Introduction Stage

I. *Rapid Skimming Strategy*

This strategy consists of introducing a new product at high price and high promotional expenses. The purpose of high price is to recover profit per unit as much as possible. The high promotional expenses are aimed at convincing the market the product merits even at a high price. High promotion accelerates the rate of market penetration, in all; the strategy is preferred to skim the cream (high profits) from market.

This strategy makes a sense in following assumptions:

(a) Major part of market is not aware of the product.

(b) Customers are ready to pay the asking price.

(c) There possibility of competition and the firm wants to build up the brand preference.

(d) Market is limited in size.

II. *Slow Skimming Strategy*

This strategy involves launching a product at a high price and low promotion. The purpose of high price is to recover as much as gross profit as possible. And, low promotion keeps marketing expenses low. This combination enables to skim the maximum profit from the market.

This strategy can be used under following assumptions:

(a) Market is limited in size.

(b) Most of consumers are aware of product.

(c) Consumers are ready to pay high price.

(d) There is less possibility of competition.

III. *Rapid Penetration*

The strategy consists of launching the product at a low price and high promotion. The purpose is the faster market penetration to get larger market share. Marketer tries to expand market by increasing the number of buyers.

It is based on following assumptions:

(a) Market is large.

(b) Most buyers are price-sensitive. They prefer the low-priced products.

(c) There is strong potential for competition.

(d) Market is not much aware of the product. They need to be informed and convinced.

(e) Per unit cost can be reduced due to more production, and possibly more profits at low price.

IV. ***Slow Penetration***

The strategy consists of introducing a product with low price and low-level promotion. Low price will encourage product acceptance, and low promotion can help realization of more profits, even at a low price.

Assumptions of this strategy

(a) Market is large.

(b) Market is aware of product.

(c) Possibility of competition is low.

(d) Buyers are price-sensitive or price-elastic, and not promotion-elastic.

Marketing Strategies for Growth Stage

This is the stage of rapid market acceptance. The strategies are aimed at sustaining market growth as long as possible. Here, the aim is not to increases awareness, but to get trial of the product. Company tries to enter the new segments. Competitors have entered the market. The company tries to strengthen competitive position in the market. It may forgo maximum current profits to earn still greater profits in the future.

Several possible strategies for the stage are as under:

a) Product qualities and features improvement

b) Adding new models and improving styling

c) Entering new market segments

d) Designing, improving and widening distribution network

e) Shifting advertising and other promotional efforts from increasing product awareness to product conviction

f) Reducing price at the right time to attract price-sensitive consumers

g) Preventing competitors to enter the market by low price and high promotional efforts

Marketing Strategies for Maturity Stage

In this stage, competitors have entered the market. There is severe fight among them for more market share. The company adopts offensive/aggressive marketing strategies to defeat the competitors.

Following possible strategies are followed:

a) To Do Nothing

To do nothing can be an effective marketing strategy in the maturity stage. New strategies are not formulated. Company believes it is advisable to do nothing. Earlier or later, the decline in the sales is certain. Marketer tries to conserve money, which can be later on invested in new profitable products. It continues only routine efforts, and starts planning for new products.

b) Market Modification

This strategy is aimed at increasing sales by raising the number of brand users and the usage rate per user. Sales volume is the product (or outcome) of number of users and usage rate per users. So, sales can be increased either by increasing the number of users or by increasing the usage rate per user or by both. Number of users can be increased by variety of ways.

There are three ways to expand the number of users:

i. Convert non-users into users by convincing them regarding uses of products

ii. Entering new market segments

iii. Winning competitors' consumers

Sales volume can also be increased by increasing the usage rate per user.

This is possible by following ways:

i. More frequent use of product

ii. More usage per occasion

iii. New and more varied uses of product

c) Product Modification

Product modification involves improving product qualities and modifying product characteristics to attract new users and/or more usage rate per user.

Product modification can take several forms:

i. Strategy for Quality Improvement

Quality improvement includes improving safety, efficiency, reliability, durability, speed, taste, and other qualities. Quality improvement can offer more satisfaction.

ii. Strategy for Feature Improvement

This includes improving features, such as size, colour, weight, accessories, form, get-up, materials, and so forth. Feature improvement leads to convenience, versatility, and attractiveness. Many firms opt for product improvement to sustain maturity stage.

Product improvement is beneficial in several ways like:

a) It builds company's image as progressiveness, dynamic, and leadership.

b) Product modification can be made at very little expense.

c) It can win loyalty of certain segments of the market.

d) It is also a source of free publicity and

e) It encourages sales force and distributors.

V. *Marketing Mix Modification*

This is the last optional strategy for the maturity stage. Modification of marketing mix involves changing the elements of marketing mix. This may stimulate sales. Company should reasonably modify one or more elements of marketing mix (4P's) to attract buyers and to fight with competitors. Marketing mix modification should be made carefully as it is easily imitated.

Marketing Strategies for Decline Stage

Company formulates various strategies to manage the decline stage. The first important task is to detect the poor products. After detecting the poor products, a company should decide whether poor products should be dropped. Some companies formulate a special committee for the task known as Product Review Committee. The committee collects data from internal and external sources and evaluates products. On the basis the report submitted by the committee, suitable decisions are taken.

Company may follow any of the following strategies:

a) Continue with the Original Products

This strategy is followed with the expectations that competitors will leave the market. Selling and promotional costs are reduced. Many times, a company continues its products only in effective segments and from remaining segments they are dropped. Such products are continued as long as they are profitable.

b) Continue Products with Improvements

Qualities and features are improved to accelerate sales. Products undergo minor changes to attract buyers.

c) Drop the Product

When it is not possible to continue the products either in original form or with improvement, the company finally decides to drop the products.

Product may be dropped in following ways:

i. Sell the production and sales to other companies.

ii. Stop production gradually to divert resources to other products

iii. Drop product immediately.

8.10. Product Planning and Development

The following discussion light upon the seven main steps in product planning and development. The steps are:

a) Generation of New Product Ideas

b) Screening of Ideas

c) Product Concept Development

d) Commercial Feasibility

e) Product Development

f) Test Marketing

g) Commercialisation

a) Generation of New Product Ideas

The first step in product planning and development is generation of ideas for the development of new/innovative products.

Ideas may come from internal sources like company's own Research and Development (R&D) department, managers, sales-force personnel etc.; or from external sources like, customers, dealers, competitors, consultants, scientists etc. At this stage, the intention of management is to generate more and more new and better product ideas; so that the most practical and profitable ideas may be screened subsequently.

b) Screening of Ideas

Screening of ideas means a close and detailed examination of ideas, to determine which of the ideas have potential and are capable of making significant contribution to marketing objectives. In fact, generation of ideas is not that significant as the system for screening the generated ideas. The ideas should be screened properly; as any idea passing this stage would cost the firm in terms of time, money and efforts, at subsequent stages in product planning and development.

c) Product Concept Development

Those product ideas which clear the screening stage must be developed into a product concept identifying physical features, benefits, price etc. of the product.

At this stage product idea is transformed into a product concept i.e. a product which target market will accept.

d) Commercial Feasibility

At this stage, the purpose is to determine whether the proposed product idea is commercially feasible, in terms of demand potential and the costs of production and marketing. Management must also ensure that product concept is compatible with the resources of the organization technological, human and financial.

e) Product Development

Product development encompasses the technical activities of engineering and design. At this stage, the engineering department converts the product concept into a concert form of product in view of the required size, shape, design, weight, colour etc. of the product concept. A model or prototype of the product is manufactured on a limited scale. Decisions are also made with regard to packaging, brand name, label etc. of the product.

f) Test Marketing

A sample of the product is tested in a well-chosen and authentic sales environment; to find out consumers' reaction. In view of consumers' reactions, the product may be improved further.

g) Commercialisation

After the management is satisfied with the results of test marketing, steps are taken to launch a full-fledged programme for the production, promotion and marketing of the product. It is the stage where the new product is born; and it enters it life cycle process.

1. **Generation of new product ideas**
2. **Screening of ideas**
3. **Product concept development**
4. **Commercial Feasibility**
5. **Product development**
6. **Test marketing**
7. **Commercialisation**

Figure: Steps in product planning and development- at a glance

8.11. New Product Development (NPD) and Planning

Every entrepreneur knows that *productivity* is one of the key ingredients for successful product development. One of the two key processes in Robert's Rules of Innovation is the NEW PRODUCT DEVELOPMENT PROCESS. A formalized, NPD process – also referred to and best practice is a must, from simple to sophisticated. The New Product Development process is often referred to as The Stage-Gate innovation process, developed by Dr. Robert G. Cooper as a result of comprehensive research on reasons why products succeed and why they fail. When teams collaborate in developing new innovations, having the following eight ingredients mixed into your team's new product developmental repertoire will ensure that it's overall marketability will happen relatively quick, and accurately making everyone productive across the board.

Step I: ***Generating***

Utilizing basic internal and external SWOT analyses, as well as current marketing trends, one can distance themselves from the competition by generating ideologies which take affordability, ROI, and widespread distribution costs into account.

Lean, mean and scalable are the key points to keep in mind. During the NPD process, keep the system nimble and use flexible discretion over which activities are executed. You may want to develop multiple versions of your road map scaled to suit different types and risk levels of projects.

Step II: ***Screening the Idea***

Wichita, possessing more aviation industry than most other states, is seeing many new innovations stop with Step 2: screening. Do you go/no go? Set specific criteria for ideas that should be continued or dropped. Stick to the agreed upon criteria so poor projects can be sent back to the idea-hopper early on. Because product development costs are being cut in areas like Wichita, "prescreening product ideas,"means taking your Top 3 competitors' new innovations into account, how much market share they're chomping up, what benefits end consumers could expect etc. An interesting industry fact: Aviation industrialists will often compare growth with metals markets; therefore, when Boeing is idle, never assume that all airplanes are grounded, per se.

Step III: ***Testing the Concept***

As Gaurav Akrani has said, "Concept testing is done after idea screening." And it is important to note, it is different from test marketing. Aside from patent research, design due diligence, and other legalities involved with new product development; knowing where the marketing messages will work best is often the biggest part of testing the concept. Does the consumer understand, need, or want the product or service?

Step IV: ***Business Analytics***

During the New Product Development process, build a system of metrics to monitor progress. Include input metrics, such as average time in each stage, as well as output metrics that measure the value of launched products, percentage of new product sales and other figures that provide valuable feedback. It is important for an organization to be in agreement for these criteria and metrics. Even if an idea doesn't turn into product, keep it in the hopper because it can prove to be a valuable asset for future products and a basis for learning and growth.

Step V: *Beta / Marketability Tests*

Arranging private tests groups, launching beta versions, and then forming test panels after the product or products have been tested will provide you with valuable information allowing last minute improvements and tweaks. Not to mention helping to generate a small amount of buzz. WordPress is becoming synonymous with beta testing, and it's effective; Thousands of programmers contribute code, millions test it, and finally even more download the completed end-product.

Step VI: *Technicalities + Product Development*

Provided the technical aspects can be perfected without alterations to post-beta products, heading towards a smooth step 7 is imminent. According to Akrani, in this step, "The production department will make plans to produce the product. The marketing department will make plans to distribute the product. The finance department will provide the finance for introducing the new product". As an example; In manufacturing, the process before sending technical specs to machinery involves printing MSDS sheets, a requirement for retaining an ISO 9001 certification (the organizational structure, procedures, processes and resources needed to implement quality management). In internet jargon, honing the technicalities after beta testing involves final database preparations, estimation of server resources, and planning automated logistics. Be sure to have your technicalities in line when moving forward.

Step VII: *Commercialize*

At this stage, your new product developments have gone mainstream, consumers are purchasing your good or service, and technical support is consistently monitoring progress. Keeping your distribution pipelines loaded with products is an integral part of this process too, as one prefers not to give physical (or perpetual) shelf space to competition. Refreshing advertisements during this stage will keep your product's name firmly supplanted into the minds of those in the contemplation stages of purchase.

Step VIII: *Post Commercialization*

Review the NPD process efficiency and look for continues improvements. Most new products are introduced with introductory pricing, in which final prices are nailed down after consumers have 'gotten in'. In this final stage, you'll gauge overall value relevant to COGS (cost of goods sold), making sure internal costs aren't overshadowing new product profits. You continuously differentiate consumer needs as your products age, forecast profits and improve delivery process whether physical, or digital, products are being perpetuated. This is further to note that the entire new product development (NPD) process is an ever evolving testing platform where errors will be made, designs will get trashed, and loss could be recorded. Having your entire team working in tight synchronicity will ensure the successful launch of goods or services, even if reinventing your own wheel. Productivity during product development can be achieved if, and only if, goals are clearly defined along the way and each process has contingencies clearly outlined on paper.

8.12. New Product Failure

Even though the commonly quoted product failure rates of 80 to 95% (the latter figure attributed to Professor Clayton Christensen, a statement he now denies making) may be nothing more than urban myths, the actual mortality rate of new products remains high. According to Crawford C. Merle, 35% products fail to deliver a significant return. In the article entitled "Identifying industrial new product success," R. G. Cooper estimates the product failure rate at 48%. And in his book "Winning at New Products" he writes: "about half of all resources allocated to product development and commercialization in the U.S. goes to products that a firm cancels or produces an inadequate financial return." However, StatGate International claims that 28 to 34% of middle to bottom performers fails commercially. And 20 to 21% get killed prior to launch. But why do so many products fail to produce any meaningful financial. The 7 key reasons major brands' products fail on the market are discussed in the following.

Reason I: ***Failure to Understand Consumer Needs and Wants***

After spending years researching and trialling the product, in 1970 AT&T finally launched the Picture phone.

The company's executives believed that a million units would be in use within 10 years of launch. They pulled it off market 3 years later due to a lack of consumer interest.

Why did Picture phone failed?

As it turns out, users found the equipment too bulky, its controls unfriendly, and picture too small to actually enjoy viewing. Blinded by their own vision the company ignored negative user feedback right from trials, and developed a product that failed to meet customers' needs and wants. It seems that AT&T didn't learn anything from this mistake. The company re-launched Picturephone in 1992. Unfortunately, to similar results).

Reason II: ***Fixing a Non-Existent Problem***

In 1990 Maxwell House launched Ready to Drink Coffee. The premise behind the product was simple: To create a new, convenient way for customers to enjoy coffee instantly, without having to actually make themselves a cuppa at home. Sounds genius, right? A customer could buy the product at their local supermarket, bring it home, microwave it, and ... voila, their coffee was ready. So why did it flop? You see, turns out that you can't microwave coffee in its original packaging. Instead customers had to pour the product from the packaging into a mug before putting it into the microwave. An activity no different than pouring yourself a cup of fresh coffee from the coffeemaker. Which are exactly what customers kept doing, forcing the company to abandon the product?

Reason III: ***Targeting the Wrong Market***

I'm sure you remember how Microsoft decided to take on the iPod in 2006. The company launched Zune which promised to do everything that Apple's device could do too. And yet, in spite of great promises, Zune failed on the market.

Why did Zune fail?: Microsoft admits that they were just chasing Apple and created a product that offered no reasons for customers to switch. What's the lesson from this mistake? It's hard to know how the market will react to a product and marketing messaging. Hence why it's crucial to test these things beforehand. Ask potential users for feedback and test their response to the marketing message. And then, listen to that feedback.

Reason IV: ***Incorrect Pricing***

The Apple Newton PDA flopped because it was priced too high. Although some observers cite poor handwriting recognition as another reason for the product's failure, the steep $700 price tag contributed significantly.

Customers could afford the Newton. But what's worse, is its pricing affected its market positioning too. You see, a high price might suggest too sophisticated product to customer needs. And so, it could force potential buyers to look for alternatives they'd perceive more relevant to them.

Reason V: ***Weak Team and Internal Capabilities***

In 2007, Joost promised to be the peer to peer TV network of the future, and seemed off to a flying start. Unfortunately, Joost had various problems with its architecture, player, content library… you name it. As a result, it never took off. 2 years after its launch, whatever was left of it was sold to Adconian. A lesson? Lack of skills can limit any potential solutions your team can create. Similarly, lack of resources and internal support can hinder your efforts to produce a product that satisfies customer needs.

Reason VI: ***Prolonged Development or Delayed Market Entry***

Taking too long to launch may also cause a product to fail. By the time it hits the market, customer needs could change, the economy could have taken a downturn, or the market segments may have evolved. That's the fate of Google Lively, the search giant's answer to Second Life. After prolonged development, Lively finally launched in 2008, just as the recession started to take its toil. As a result, the company pulled the product after just 5 months to "focus on core search, ads and apps business."

Reason VII: ***Poor Execution***

Bad design, poor user experience, sloppy implementation, feature creep, and lack of quality control all contribute to product failure.

8.13. Organization for New Product Development (NPD)

A traditional organization achieves efficiency and control of work by division of labour. Employees or departments carry out work in one business area, such as design, marketing or production. New product development relies on bringing together different disciplines to make sure the new product has the required functionality and appeals to a target market. As a result, companies have to implement specific organizational structures that promote effective new product development and strategies. Example: revenue forecasting strategies for travel & tourism businesses

a) ***Develop New Products in Teams***

You can develop strategies for new products by placing new product development in the hands of special teams. Continuous new product development requires permanent team structures whose members change as the required disciplines evolve. A particular product may require special design or engineering expertise, and you can transfer the corresponding employees to the team responsible for that product. Later, it may need marketing input, and an employee with marketing knowledge can join the team. As the team gets input from different areas of the business, it can develop strategies that work for the whole company.

b) ***Develop a New Product as a Project***

Companies that only develop new products occasionally can set up a project organization to develop a new product and a corresponding strategy. The project manager receives overall goals for the new product development and assembles the staff he needs to carry out the work. The project has a fixed budget, a schedule and representatives from design, engineering, production and marketing to develop an integrated approach. A project structure combines the interdisciplinary expertise required with a higher degree of control than the permanent team structure.

c) ***Product Strategies in a Matrix Organization***

Instead of adding specific structures such as teams or project groups to a traditional organization, organize the company around interdisciplinary work groups with flexible boundaries. Such a structure features the multiple reporting paths of a matrix organization, where an employee may report to one manager for organizational or disciplinary issues and another manager for work-related matters. The group developing new product strategies combines the different areas of expertise with links to groups responsible for technical and design work, manufacturing and marketing. A consensus-based process lets your company develop new product strategies with input from all areas of the business.

d) ***New Product Development in a Traditional Organization***

A traditional hierarchical organization can include product development functions as part of the product organization. Separate staff or departments carry out marketing, product management and product development functions. The marketing function focuses on market development and promotion of the company, product management deals with existing products, and product development designs new products and releases them for production. Each determines the strategies relevant for their functions, with marketing implementing sales strategies, product management focusing on how the consumer uses the product and product development deciding on strategic directions for new products.

8.14. Pricing Strategy for New Product

There are three main approaches a business takes to setting price:

a) Cost-based pricing

Price is determined by adding a profit element on top of the cost of making the product.

b) Customer-based pricing

Where prices are determined by what a firm believes customers will be prepared to pay Competitor-based pricing: where competitor prices are the main influence on the price set. Let's take a brief look at each of these approaches.

c) Cost based pricing

This involves setting a price by adding a fixed amount or percentage to the cost of making or buying the product. In some ways this is quite an old-fashioned and somewhat discredited pricing strategy, although it is still widely used. After all, customers are not too bothered what it cost to make the product they are interested in what value the product provides them.

d) Cost-plus (or "mark-up") pricing

It is widely used in retailing, where the retailer wants to know with some certainty what the gross profit margin of each sale will be. An advantage of this approach is that the business will know that its costs are being covered. The main disadvantage is that cost-plus pricing may lead to products that are priced un-competitively. Here is an example of cost-plus pricing, where a business wishes to ensure that it makes an additional Rs.50 of profit on top of the unit cost of production.

Unit cost:	₹100
Mark-up:	50%
Selling price:	₹150

How high should the mark-up percentage be? That largely depends on the normal competitive practice in a market and also whether the resulting price is acceptable to customers. In the UK a standard retail mark-up is 2.4 times the cost the retailer pays to its supplier (normally a wholesaler). So, if the wholesale cost of a product is £10 per unit, the retailer will look to sell it for 2.4x 10 = Rs.24. This is equal to a total mark-up of Rs.14 (i.e. the selling price of Rs.24 less the bought cost of Rs.10). The main advantage of cost-based pricing is that selling prices are relatively easy to calculate. If the mark-up percentage is applied consistently across product ranges, then the business can also predict more reliably what the overall profit margin will be.

e) Penetration Pricing

You often see the tagline "special introductory offer" the classic sign of penetration pricing. The aim of penetration pricing is usually to increase market share of a product, providing the opportunity to increase price once this objective has been achieved. Penetration pricing is the pricing technique of setting a relatively low initial entry price, usually lower than the intended established price, to attract new customers. The strategy aims to encourage customers to switch to the new product because of the lower price. Penetration pricing is most commonly associated with a marketing objective of increasing market share or sales volume. In the short term, penetration pricing is likely to result in lower profits than would be the case if price were set higher. However, there are some significant benefits to long-term profitability of having a higher market share, so the pricing strategy can often be justified. Penetration pricing is often used to support the launch of a new product, and works best when a product enters a market with relatively little product differentiation and where demand is price elastic – so a lower price than rival products is a competitive weapon.

f) Price skimming

Skimming involves setting a high price before other competitors come into the market. This is often used for the launch of a new product which faces little or no competition – usually due to some technological features. Such products are often bought by "early adopters" who are prepared to pay a higher price to have the latest or best product in the market.

Good examples of price skimming include innovative electronic products, such as the Apple iPad and Sony PlayStation. There are some other problems and challenges with this approach: Price skimming as a strategy cannot last for long, as competitors soon launch rival products which put pressure on the price (e.g. the launch of rival products to the iPhone or iPod). Distribution (place) can also be a challenge for an innovative new product. It may be necessary to give retailers higher margins to convince them to stock the product, reducing the improved margins that can be delivered by price skimming. A final problem is that by price skimming, a firm may slow down the volume growth of demand for the product. This can give competitors more time to develop alternative products ready for the time when market demand (measured in volume) is strongest.

g) *Loss leaders*

The use of loss leaders is a method of sales promotion. A loss leader is a product priced below cost-price in order to attract consumers into a shop or online store. The purpose of making a product a loss leader is to encourage customers to make further purchases of profitable goods while they are in the shop. But does this strategy work? Pricing is a key competitive weapon and a very flexible part of the marketing mix. If a business undercuts its competitors on price, new customers may be attracted and existing customers may become more loyal. So, using a loss leader can help drive customer loyalty. One risk of using a loss leader is that customers may take the opportunity to "bulk-buy". If the price discount is sufficiently deep, then it makes sense for customers to buy as much as they can (assuming the product is not perishable). Using a loss leader is essentially a short-term pricing tactic for any one product. Customers will soon get used to the tactic, so it makes sense to change the loss leader or its merchandising every so often.

h) Predatory pricing (note: this is illegal)

With predatory pricing, prices are deliberately set very low by a dominant competitor in the market in order to restrict or prevent competition. The price set might even be free, or lead to losses by the predator. Whatever the approach, predatory pricing is illegal under competition law.

i) Psychological pricing

Sometimes prices are set at what seem to be unusual price points. For example, why are DVD's priced at Rs.12.99 or Rs.14.99? The answer is the perceived price barriers that customers may have. They will buy something for Rs.9.99, but think that Rs.10 is a little too much. So a price that is one pence lower can make the difference between closing the sale, or not! The aim of psychological pricing is to make the customer believe the product is cheaper than it really is. Pricing in this way is intended to attract customers who are looking for "value".

j) Competitor-based pricing

If there is strong competition in a market, customers are faced with a wide choice of who to buy from. They may buy from the cheapest provider or perhaps from the one which offers the best customer service. But customers will certainly be mindful of what is a reasonable or normal price in the market. Most firms in a competitive market do not have sufficient power to be able to set prices above their competitors. They tend to use "going-rate" pricing – i.e. setting a price that is in line with the prices charged by direct competitors. In effect such businesses are "price-takers" – they must accept the going market price as determined by the forces of demand and supply. An advantage of using competitive pricing is that selling prices should be line with rivals, so price should not be a competitive disadvantage. The main problem is that the business needs some other way to attract customers. It has to use non-price methods to compete – e.g. providing distinct customer service or better availability. The marketing mix, which is the means by which an organisation reaches its target market, is made up of product, pricing, distribution, promotion and people decisions. These are usually shortened to the acronym "5P's". Product decisions revolve around decisions regarding the physical product (size, style, specification, etc.) and product line management. Product decisions are based on how much the organisation has to adjust the product on the standardisation - adaptation continuum to differing market conditions. This results in the evolution of five basic strategic alternatives - extension; extension, adaptation; adaptation, extension; adaptation and invention. Extension is the nearest to a standardised product, communications strategy and Invention at the other end of the continuum, that is, an adaptation strategy. The more adaptive the policy the more costly it will be for the organisation.

9

PRODUCT RELATED DECISION AND STRATEGIES

9.1. Brand – Meaning and Definition

The marketing practice of creating a name, symbol or design that identifies and differentiates a product from other products. An effective brand strategy gives you a major edge in increasingly competitive markets. But what exactly does "branding" mean? Simply put, your brand is your promise to your customer. It tells them what they can expect from your products and services, and it differentiates your offering from that of your competitors. Your brand is derived from who you are, who you want to be and who people perceive you to be. Are you the innovative maverick in your industry? Or the experienced, reliable one? Is your product the high-cost, high-quality option, or the low-cost, high-value option? You can't be both, and you can't be all things to all people. Who you are should be based to some extent on which your target customers want and need you to be. The foundation of your brand is your logo. Your website, packaging and promotional materials all of which should integrate your logo communicate your brand. Your brand strategy is how, what, where, when and to whom you plan on communicating and delivering on your brand messages. Where you advertise is part of your brand strategy. Your distribution channels are also part of your brand strategy. And what you communicate visually and verbally is part of your brand strategy, too. Consistent, strategic branding leads to a strong brand equity, which means the added value brought to your company's products or services that allows you to charge more for your brand than what identical, unbranded products command. The most obvious example of this is Coke vs. a generic soda. Because Coca-Cola has built powerful brand equity, it can charge more for its product and customers will pay that higher price. The added value intrinsic to brand equity frequently comes in the form of perceived quality or emotional attachment. For example, Nike associates its products with star athletes;

hoping customers will transfer their emotional attachment from the athlete to the product. For Nike, it's not just the shoe's features that sell the shoe. Defining your brand is like a journey of business self-discovery. It can be difficult, time-consuming and uncomfortable. It requires, at the very least, that you answer the questions below:

a) What is your company's mission?

b) What are the benefits and features of your products or services?

c) What do your customers and prospects already think of your company?

d) What qualities do you want them to associate with your company?

Do your research. Learn the needs, habits and desires of your current and prospective customers. And don't rely on what you think they think. Know what they think. Once you've defined your brand, how do you get the word out? Here are a few simple, time-tested tips

a) *Get a great logo*: Place it everywhere.

b) *Write down your brand messaging*: What are the key messages you want to communicate about your brand? Every employee should be aware of your brand attributes.

c) *Integrate your brand*: Branding extends to every aspect of your business how you answer your phones, what you or your salespeople wear on sales calls, your e-mail signature, everything.

d) *Create a "voice" for your company that reflects your brand*: This voice should be applied to all written communication and incorporated in the visual imagery of all materials, online and off. Is your brand friendly? Be conversational. Is it ritzy? Be more formal. You get the gist.

e) *Develop a tagline*: Write a memorable, meaningful and concise statement that captures the essence of your brand.

f) *Design templates and create brand standards for your marketing materials*: Use the same colour scheme, logo placement, look and feel throughout. You don't need to be fancy, just consistent.

g) *Be true to your brand*: Customers won't return to you or refer you to someone else if you don't deliver on your brand promise.

h) *Be consistent*: This tip involves all the above and is the most important tip on this list. If you can't do this, your attempts at establishing a brand will fail.

9.2. Need for Branding

You know that branding is the key to any company, whether they sell coffee or industrial parts or clothing. But convincing your organization or clients that branding is necessary for all components of their business to succeed can be a bit more difficult than deciding exactly what colours best represent their brand mission.

How would you explain the process of branding to your clients? If you're not sure how you'd break down your approach, you may be doing it wrong.

Dave Holston, author of The Strategic Designer, will walk you through the brand development process from conducting research to developing brand values to communicating it all through your designs in his Brand Strategy Course. Here, he shares 4 reasons why companies brand:

I. *Branding provides a competitive advantage*

Whether you're a non-profit or a for-profit, your organization needs to compete for resources, funding and talent, and audience attention. To win your category, organizations plan and implement strategy: a roadmap that outlines specific actions and measures for reaching their goals and out manoeuvring their peers for needed resources. When done correctly the organization's brand mirrors their strategic plan, and helps promote strategic areas and initiatives that will move the organization forward.

II. *Brands provide a stable asset*

Products might fail, companies are bought and sold, technologies change on a daily basis, but strong brands carry on through all these changes. Brands are the most sustainable asset of any organization, and when aligned with the overall strategy of the organization they can function as the central organizing principle for the organization's decision making. Consider that the Coca-Cola brand has been around for more than 120 years, while most of the world's other valued brands have existed for just 50 years, and most corporations only last 25 years.

III. ***Brands provide economic value***

The value of organizations is divided into two areas: intangible and tangible assets brands being intangible assets. A study of organizations in the S&P 500 index showed that over a 30-year period between 1975 and 2003 the overall corporate value of intangible assets increased from 17% to 80%. The magazine Business Week has concluded that brands account for more than one-third of shareholder value. This leaves us with the conclusion that the value of most businesses comes from intangible assets, brands being the most prominent of these assets. Consider that the Coca-Cola brand name alone is worth $67 million and accounts for over 54% of the stock market value of the organization. Or consider the value of brand to a non-profit like the Red Cross and the importance of their brand in attracting donations and volunteers. Because of their financial impact, brands are a unique organizational asset. Brands play a key role in attracting employees, partners and most importantly audiences to an organization. Brands help cut through the clutter of the marketplace, creating awareness for organizations and helping them attract and develop the mutually beneficial relationships with customers, suppliers and the public that they need to reach their goals.

IV. ***Brands set expectations***

We live in a world based on promises. The airline mechanic promises to do a thorough job, checking and rechecking the aircraft to make sure it's safe. Restaurants promise to provide fresh food made in clean environments. Our teachers promise to educate and protect our children during the school day. Often there are legal repercussions that bind people to fulfill these promises, but more often than not promises and vows are maintained based on the individual's own moral and ethical code. We have an unspoken contract with the people we live and work with, that they will do what they say they'll do. We have similar agreements with companies, products and services. At the heart of branding is the promise that is made by the organization to the audience. The brand promise tells the audiences who you are, what you believe in, and what unique value you provide. The ability to fulfil your promises at every stage of the relationship is the defining factor for most organizations success or failure. When promises are broken the reputation of the organization is called into question, and the brand suffers. When brand promises are kept, audiences respond with loyalty and affection.

We encounter brand promises on a daily basis. The simple act of getting a soda out of a vending machine is an exercise in brand promise. The vending machine offers many drink options to choose from, but more than likely our drink selection will be based on prior experiences with a specific product. We have an expectation of an experience when we make our selection, much of which has been established through the decision-making steps of awareness, interest, desire, and satisfaction. Interestingly, the things that influence our decision-making process have little to do with the product or service. Much of our experience with a product or service is created through the associations that we've made with the product through advertising, brand identity and the environment in which the product is experienced.

9.3. Purpose of Branding

We often hear about branding, whether it's about branding yourself, your products or your services. Branding can be applied personally and is the way that a person builds their reputation, or digitally, via web, search engine optimisation or social media.

There are so many different definitions of what branding is, but in this case I'll use this definition. Branding is ultimately the strategic and disciplined process of building awareness and creating customer loyalty. Branding is about making sure that your brand is visible at every opportunity and expressing why your chosen market should choose your brand over another. As entrepreneurs there should be an innate desire to lead and outpace the competition. As we know 'victory belongs to the most persevering' (Napoleon Bonaparte).

I. *Identification: Who are you? Who needs you? Why should they care?*

With a myriad of brands selling either the same or similar products or services, what makes a particular market make that choice to choose you? Think about when you walk down an aisle in the supermarket. How do you quickly decide which can of beans to buy? You decide by the communication style, the logo and the colours. Not only will visual styling help you to navigate your way through the aisles and grab your attention, there is also a psychological process that, as consumers, we all go through and subconsciously encourages us to buy. Consumers identify with the brand in a meaningful way, by connecting to a set of values that the brands communicate and the consumer also holds.

II. *Confidence*

This confidence is created by effectively communicating their brand promise, giving the customer confidence that they have made the right choice. Think of your brand as a promise… a promise you make to your customers and all other touch points. Before you make that promise, it is imperative that you are able to back it up. You cannot build a successful, long-term brand on promises that you can't support.

III. *Community*

Whether done deliberately or not segmentation occurs, bringing together a passionate community of fans who engage and relate to your brand and become your best brand advocates. They will talk about you, and have that brand love that happens on and offline. It will come in the form of referrals, likes, retweets and favourites. Your best opportunity to build a brand community is by giving back or providing value to the people. Remember that your brand doesn't live in a vacuum. Begin to create a narrative for your brand. Be clear about what your values are and strategically position your brand in the marketplace and you will begin to see organic growth of your brand and leverage, Identification, Confidence and Community to build brand influence and customer loyalty. Now that you are fully aware of the purpose of branding and how it will dramatically elevate your business.

9.4. Essentials of Good Branding

Good branding is essential to building a successful business, because the brand is the first part of a company that other people see. Business Betties is a company that knows all about the importance of branding. They started about three years ago and are located in East Longmeadow, Mass. The company is run by graphic designer Allison Biggs, 33, and photographer Suzanne Larocque, 43. They provide female entrepreneurs and women-run businesses with the visual branding tips they need to help their businesses take off. Their company works with local clients out of their home office, as well as clients across the country via online means. Their number one goal in the business is to help women entrepreneurs create the best branding possible. They said that entrepreneurs should keep the following five things in mind when working toward better branding:

I. ***Consistency***

Once a decision on colours, fonts or other visuals has been made, it needs to be stuck with for everything; changing the look on different things is a big blunder in branding. "Making sure that you're not sending mixed messages with your branding is really important," Larocque said. It can hurt you to change your look because people won't recognize you and your business, and you want them to recognize you.

II. ***Prioritize***

The Betties suggest taking things in segments and focusing on one thing at a time to strengthen a brand little by little. They want to remind entrepreneurs that things do not have to be done all at once; sometimes starting with focusing on a logo and then moving on to other aspects is the best option.

III. ***Know the Difference between a Brand and a Logo***

"A brand extends far beyond what your logo is," Biggs said. A brand consists of everything visual as well as a consistent writing style, and the Business Betties don't want people to limit their idea of a brand. "Really understanding the personality of what your brand is and who your audience is, and really speaking to that" is also essential to better branding, Larocque added.

IV. *Be Yourself*

"We really want to promote being authentic" is how they both put it. Entrepreneurs can use their brand to reveal themselves; they do not have to adhere to the certain images that others or media say they have to be to be professional.

V. *Quality*

Even with a small budget, a lot can be done without having to skimp. They suggest spending a little extra in some places, such as with business cards, to make sure that you have the best looking product you can get for your budget. "Make sure that you get those things a little bit higher quality, because you want to make a good impression," Biggs said.

9.5. Merits and Demerits of Branding

Merits and demerits of branding are discussed in the following.

***Merits*:**

From the perspective of the consumer

- It helps in identifying the product.
- It helps in differentiating the product from rival's product.
- It ensures a good quality product to the customers.
- Easy recognition of the product is possible through branding in stores and outlets.
- Purchase of a branded product provides psychological satisfaction to the customers.

From the perspective of the producer

- It provides the product a distinct identity.
- A seller gets a competitive advantage over other rival products.
- A smart brand name helps in introducing a brand new product within the market.
- Brand loyalty amongst the customers helps the corporate to cut down its marketing cost.
- A seller gets a better price because the brand includes a higher perceived worth.

Demerits:

From the perspective of the consumer

- Brand development expensive process and therefore branded products are costly.
- Too many branded products, persistently confuse the customers.
- Once the brand is established, a marketer could bring down the quality and standard of the product.

From the perspective of the producer:

- Seller is forced to maintain the quality and standard of the branded product otherwise buyers will switch to other brands.
- It is important for the producer to invest sufficient resources in promoting the brand name.

9.6. Classification of Brands

We often talk about "brand" as if it is one thing. It's not of course, in fact, the meaning and the use of the term differs, quite markedly, depending on the context. Brand is categorized in at least 21 different ways as discussed in the following.

i. *Product brand* – Elevating the perceptions of commodities/goods so that they are associated with ideas and emotions that exceed functional capability. Consumer packaged goods brands (CPG), otherwise known as fast moving consumer goods brands (FMCG), are a specific application.

ii. *Personal brand* – Otherwise known as individual brand. The brand a person builds around themselves, normally to enhance their career opportunities. Often associated with how people portray and market themselves via media. The jury's out on whether this should be called a form of brand because whilst it may be a way to add value, it often lacks a business model to commercialize the strategy.

iii. *Service brand* – Similar to product brands, but involves adding perceived value to services. More difficult in some ways than developing a product brand, because the offering itself is less tangible. Useful in areas like professional services. Enables marketers to avoid competing skill vs skill (which is hard to prove and often devolves to a price argument) by associating their brand with emotions. New online models, such as subscription brands, where people pay small amounts for ongoing access to products/services, are rapidly changing the loyalty and technology expectations for both product and service brands – for example, increasingly products come with apps that are integral to the experience and the perceived value.

iv. *Corporate brand* – Otherwise known as the organizational brand. David Aaker puts it very well: "The corporate brand defines the firm that will deliver and stand behind the offering that the customer will buy and use." The reassurance that provides for customers comes from the fact that "a corporate brand will potentially have a rich heritage, assets and capabilities, people, values and priorities, a local or global frame of reference, citizenship programs, and a performance record".

v. *Investor brand* – Normally applied to publicly listed brands and to the investor relations function. Positions the listed entity as an investment and as a performance stock, blending financials and strategy with aspects such as value proposition, purpose and, increasingly, wider reputation via CSR. As Mike Tisdall will tell you, done well, a strong investor brand delivers share price resilience and an informed understanding of value.

vi. *NGO (Non Governmental Organization) or Non Profit brand* – An area of transition, as the sector shifts gear looking for value models beyond just fundraising to drive social missions. Not accepted by some in the non profit community because it's seen as selling out. Necessary in my view because of the sheer volume of competition for the philanthropic dollar.

vii. *Public brand* – Otherwise known as government branding. Contentious. Many, including myself, would argue that you can't brand something that doesn't have consumer choice and a competitive model attached to it. That's not to say that you can't use the disciplines and methodologies of brand strategy to add to stakeholders' understanding and trust of government entities. That's why I talk about the need for public entities to develop trustmarks rather than brands. Jill Caldwell takes this idea of how we consider and discuss infrastructure further and says we now have private-sector brands that are so much a part of our lives that we assume their presence in much the same way as we assume public services. Caldwell refers to brands like Google and Facebook as "embedded brands".

viii. *Activist brand* – Also known as a purpose brand. The brand is synonymous with a cause or purpose to the point where that alignment defines its distinctiveness in the minds of consumers. Classic examples: Body Shop, which has been heavily defined by its anti-animal-cruelty stance; and Benetton, which confronts bigotry and global issues with a vehemence that has made it both hated and admired.

ix. *Place brand* – Also known as destination or city brands. This is the brand that a region or city builds around itself in order to associate its location with ideas rather than facilities. Often used to attract tourists, investors, businesses and residents. Recognizes that these groups all have significant choices as to where they choose to locate. A critical success factor is getting both citizens and service providers on board, since they in effect become responsible for the experiences delivered. Most famous example is probably "What happens in Vegas stays in Vegas".

x. *Nation brand* – Whereas place brands are about specific areas, nation brands relate, as per their name, to the perceptions and reputations of countries. Simon Anholt is a pioneer in this area.

xi. *Ethical brand* – Used in two ways. The first is as a description of how brands work, specifically the practices they use and the commitments they demonstrate in areas such as worker safety, CSR and more – i.e. a brand is ethical or it is not?. Secondly, denotes the quality marquees that consumers look for in terms of reassurance that the brands they choose are responsible. Perhaps the most successful and well known example of such a brand is Fairtrade. These types of ethical brands are often run by NGOs – e.g. WWF's Global Forest and Trade Network.

xii. *Celebrity brand* – How the famous commercialize their high profile using combinations of social media delivered content, appearances, products and gossip/notoriety to retain interest and followers. The business model for this has evolved from appearances in ads and now takes a range of forms: licensing; endorsements; brand ambassador roles; and increasingly brand association through placement (think red carpet).

xiii. *Ingredient brand* – The component brand that adds to the value of another brand because of what it brings. Well known examples include Intel, Gore-Tex and Teflon. Compared with OEM offerings in manufacturing, where component is white label and simply forms part of the supply chain, ingredient brands are the featured elements that add to the overall value proposition. A key reason for this is that they market themselves to consumers as elements to look for and consider when purchasing. In this interesting piece, Jason Cieslak wonders though whether the days of the ingredient brand are drawing to a close. His reasons? Increased fragmentation in the manufacturing sector, lack of space as devices shrink, stronger need for integration and lack of interest amongst consumers in what goes into what they buy.

xiv. *Global brand* – The behemoths. These brands are easily recognized and widely dispersed. They epitomize "household names". Their business model is based on familiarity, availability and stability – although the consistency that once characterized their offerings, and ruled their operating models, is increasingly under threat as they find themselves making changes, subtle and otherwise, to meet the cultural tastes and expectations of people in different regions.

xv. *Challenger brand* – The change makers, the brands that are determined to upset the dominant player. While these brands tend to face off against the incumbents and to do so in specific markets, "Being a challenger is not about a state of market; being number two or three or four doesn't in itself make you a challenger," says Adam Morgan of Eat Big Fish. "It is a brand, and a group of people behind that brand, whose business ambitions exceed its conventional marketing resources, and needs to change the category decision making criteria in its favour to close the implications of that gap."

xvi. *Generic brand* – The brand you become when you lose distinctiveness. Takes three forms. The first is specific to healthcare and alludes to those brands that have fallen out of patent protection and now face competition from a raft of same-ingredient imitators known as generics. The second form of generic brand is the brand where the name has become ubiquitous and in so doing has passed into common language as a verb – Google, Xerox, Sellotape. The third form is the unbranded, unlabelled product that has a functional description for a name but no brand value at all. This last form is the ultimate in commoditization.

xvii. *Luxury brand* – Prestige brands that deliver social status and endorsement to the consumer. Luxury brands must negotiate the fine line between exclusivity and reality. They do this through quality, association and story. These brands have perfected the delivery of image and aspiration to their markets, yet they remain vulnerable to shifts in perception and consumer confidence and they are under increasing pressure from "affordable luxury" brands. Coach for example struggled with revenues in 2014 because of declining sales growth in China and Japan, two of the world's key luxury markets.

xviii. *Cult brand* – The brands that revolve around communities of fierce advocates. Like the challenger brands, these brands often pick fights with "enemies" that can range from other companies to ideas, but pure-play cult brands take their cues from their own passions and obsessions rather than the market or their rivals. They tend to have followers rather than customers, set the rules and ask people to comply and, if they market at all, do so in ways where people come to them rather than the other way around.

xix. *Clean slate brand* – The pop-ups of brand. Fast moving, unproven, even unknown brands that don't rely on the heritage and history that are so much a part of mainstream brand strategy. These brands feed consumers' wish for the new and the timely.

xx. *Private brand* – Otherwise known as private label. Traditionally, these are value-based, OEM-sourced retail offerings that seek to under-cut the asking price of name brands. They focus on price. There is significant potential though in my view for these brands to become more valuable and to play a more significant role at the 'affordable premium' end of the market. For that to happen, private brands will need to broaden their appeal and loyalty through a wider range of consideration factors.

xxi. *Employer brand* – The ability of a company to attract high quality staff in much-touted competitive markets. Often tied to an Employee Value Proposition. Focuses on the recruiting process though it is sometimes expanded to include the development of a healthy and productive culture. Sadly, given the process obsession of too many HR staff and the lack of interest from a lot of marketing people to venture into people-issues, this tends to be a brand in name rather than a brand by nature. Great potential but, given the very low satisfaction rates across corporate cultures globally, a lot more work is needed to realize the full potential of this idea.

It's no wonder, on review, that so many people outside marketing struggle to understand what a brand is. And we haven't even talked about brand in reference to structure (brand architecture models such as endorsed brands, house of brands and power brands) or the different types of brand audiences (B2B, B2C, B2T, B2G, H2H). A brand can of course function across a number of these roles simultaneously – a product brand can be a challenger brand or a global brand, for example. That in itself is an important reminder that we often encounter the same brand in different ways in different contexts – and the criteria for whether a brand is successful or not can shift markedly depending on which categorization is being applied. The challenge for marketers given these dissipated meanings of brand is to somehow ensure that the emotions that a brand generates are valuable, relevant and differentiated in each context in which it is judged while, at the same time, aligning with the brand strategy overall. I don't see much evidence of that yet.

9.7. Brand Testing

The brand name is a "bucket" that, over time, you hope to fill with goodwill and positive feelings about your product. The brand name is memory linkage to your product and is an identifier that distinguishes your brand from all other brands. Needless to say, the brand name is a critical marketing variable in virtually all product categories. It is most important to avoid a bad brand name, such as a name no one can remember, or a name that does not fit the product, or a name that reminds consumers of some other product. That's why research is so vital.

Qualitative Investigations

The starting point for developing a new brand name is qualitative research. What is the most important consumer motivations related to the product category? What motives and perceptions drive the brand-decision process? How are each of the major competitive brand names perceived? What do competitive brand names communicate? Based on this qualitative understanding, what should be the communication objectives for the new brand name? Qualitative research is somewhat useful in screening large numbers of possible brand names and helpful in refining and developing new brand-name possibilities.

Innovation Services

One approach is to let consumers help develop brand-name possibilities. Once basic consumer motivations and perceptions are understood via qualitative research, consumers can be used to help generate hundreds of brand-name possibilities. Not just any consumers will do, however. Highly creative individuals are the key. They can help create new brand names that fulfill the communication objectives. Decision Analyst maintains a panel of more than 2,000 highly creative people (called Imaginators®) who work in small groups, online or offline, to generate hundreds, or even thousands, of brand-name possibilities. Decision Analyst's Insights & Innovation Team then uses these brand-name suggestions as starter ideas to create even more brand names. At this point, the number of brand names is generally whittled down to 50 or 100, based on human judgment and the communication objectives. The final steps involve quantitative testing.

NameScreen®

The product-naming process typically begins with the creation of a large number of potential names. NameScreen® is our online system to identify the best names. Respondents review, sort, and rate the 50 to 100 brand-name candidates. The 5 to 10 highest-rated names are recommended for further development and testing, usually in the context of a product test, package test, or concept test.

Brand Name Testing

The final testing would typically involve placing the new product with its new brand name in a shelf-set display to measure which of several brand names is most effective in stimulating interest in buying and using the new product. This can also be accomplished through concept testing, or product testing, where the only difference among different sample cells is the brand name. By holding all of the other variables constant, the effect of the name itself can be measured.

9.8. Trademark

A device (as a word) pointing distinctly to the origin or ownership of merchandise to which it is applied and legally reserved to the exclusive use of the owner as maker or seller A distinguishing characteristic or feature firmly associated with a person or thing.

9.9. Packaging

Definition of Packaging

a) The action or process of packing something; also: a method of packing

b) The processing of food and especially meat for future sale.

c) Material (as a covering or stuffing) used to protect packed goods (as for shipping); also: material used for making airtight or watertight.

9.10. Merits and Demerits of Packaging

Merits

a) Gives identity to the product

b) Makes it distinguishable from the other products.

c) Creates customer loyalty.

d) Creates and maintains organisation goodwill.

Demerits

a) High investment required.

b) May create negative image, if the brand fails in the market.

c) Unwillingness on part of the customers to pay extra amount for branded goods.

9.11. Packaging Strategies

One of the most critical roles for packaging is promoting products. Indeed, just as ease-of-use and readability are elements of the strategic packaging mix, packaging is an important part of a company's strategic marketing mix. Most packages for consumer products are designed for one of three purposes:

i. To improve the packaging of an existing product

ii. To add a new product to an existing product line

iii. To contain an entirely new product

Redesign of packaging for existing products may be prompted by several factors. Many times, a company may simply want to breathe new life into a maturing product by updating its image or adding a new feature to the package, such as an easy-pour spout. Or, a company may redesign the package to respond to a competitive threat, such as a new product that is more visible on the shelf. Other strategic reasons for package redesign are: changes in the product; economics, which may require less or more expensive packaging; product line restructuring; alterations in market strategy, such as aiming the product at a different age group; trying to promote new uses for a product; or legal or environmental factors that lead to new materials or technology. Even small packaging changes for established brands and products typically require careful consideration, since a great deal of money is often at risk if a company alienates or confuses customers. A second reason for package redesign is to extend a product or brand line. In these instances, the packaging strategy usually reflects an effort to closely mimic the established brand or product, but to integrate the benefits of the new feature into the existing package in such a way that customers will be able to easily differentiate it from other products in the line. The chief risks inherent in packaging for extensions are that the new package will confuse customers or frustrate retailers. The third impetus for package design is the need to generate housing for an entirely new product. This is the most difficult type of packaging to create because it often requires the designer to instil consumer confidence in an unknown product or brand, and to inform the buyer about the product's uses and benefits. Packaging for products and brands that are entirely new to the marketplace are the most challenging to develop. In contrast, packaging for goods that are entering established product categories require less education, but they must overcome established competition. A common packaging strategy for such products entails mimicking the packaging of leading products, which helps to assure the buyer that the product is "normal."

9.12. Labelling

A label is a carrier of information about the product. The attached label provides customers with information to aid their purchase decision or help improve the experience of using the product. Labels can include:

- Care and use of the product
- Recipes or suggestions
- Ingredients or nutritional information
- Product guarantees
- Manufacturer name and address
- Weight statements
- Sell by date and expiration dates

- Warnings

9.13. Purpose of Labelling

(i) *Describe the Product and Specify its Contents*

A label provides complete information regarding the product. It mainly includes ingredients of the product, its usage, and caution in use, cares to be taken while using it, date of manufacturing, batch number, etc.

(ii) *Identification of the Product or Brand*

It is easier to identify a particular product among many with the help of labelling. For example, you as a consumer want to select CINTHOL SOAP. The task of finding the desired soap from a heap of various branded soaps becomes easier with the help of labelling.

(iii) *Grading of Product*

When a product has different qualities, labeling helps to find out which pack contains what type of quality. For example, Hindustan Unilever Ltd., manufactures three types of tea and to differentiate the each type of tea, the company uses Green, Red and Yellow coloured labels.

(iv) *Help in Promotion of Products*

The fourth function of labelling is to promote sales. Sometimes a consumer gets encouraged to buy a product simply due to attractive label. Nowadays labelling is used as an effective sales promoting tool.

(v) *Providing information required by Law*

Another important function performed by labelling is to provide statutory warning required by law. To put 'smoking is injurious to health' on the package of cigarette and 'Chewing Tobacco is Injurious to Health' on the package of Pan Masala are the examples of statutory warning? Similarly, in case of hazardous or poisonous products, appropriate statutory warning need to be put on the label.

9.14. After Sale Services

Most people end meetings with familiar sentiments like, "Keep in touch," "Let's do this again sometime," and "Give me a call sometime next week." A sale should follow a similar progression. Marketers should never be content with a no-strings-attached, have-a-nice-day handshake at the end of the sale. Why? Because today's best marketers don't just sell; they build relationships with customers. Contrary to popular belief, staying in touch with your customers isn't just for your sake – it's also for your customer's sake. There are many ways to serve your customers well after a sale by helping them to continually get the most out of your service or product.

The small business owners create post-transaction touch points and after-sales service practices that ensure they're offering the best experience they can to their customers, all while keeping their brand top of mind. These marketing habits boost both loyalty and up selling ability. They also add to the value of the originally purchased product or service. There was a reason that your customers bought, and there's a way to "wow" them after the sale is complete with excellent follow-up services and products. By doing so, you give them more proverbial bang for their buck. Engaging customers in this way mutually benefits both of you in the long run. While customers get extra value with after sales services and products, your company gets a leg up in its quest to recruit an army of brand ambassadors and trusted voices who can provide feedback on new products, services, initiatives and more.

Examples of 8 different types of service to offer after sales:

I. *Cards*

A piece of physical correspondence is always a strong marketing tool. Not only does it get your brand into the hands and home of your customer, but it also serves as a physical reminder of your company while sitting on their kitchen counter for a day or two. Carefully craft the card's message, pick a meaningful post-sale arrival day and always reinforce that you're available. This process can even be automated with services like Zen Direct or Send out Cards.

II. *Quality and Unique Packaging*

Today's retailers are capitalizing on the modern customer's recycling habits, shifting their shopping bags to reusable ones that customers use for a variety of reasons. This is very intentional. Investing in quality, good-looking, distinct packaging is a great way to provide after sales service. It benefits both the customer and your brand.

III. *Coupons*

Did you just complete a sale? Why not catalyze another? Depending on your product or service offering, extending a coupon to a recently converted customer as a token of gratitude could do just that. If a secondary purchase doesn't make sense for your customers, consider prodding customers toward buying your product or service as a gift with the coupon you're presenting. Or consider providing a coupon that encourages the recipient to give it to a friend, family member or next-door neighbour. Both options provide tangible post-sale value.

IV. *Personal Phone Call*

If applicable, call your customers within thirty days of a sale. Don't call to upsell or ask for referrals, but instead simply to ask how your product or service is working for them and if there's anything they need. This simple human touch can solidify a customer's loyalty. And if they don't pick up or don't have time to talk, don't sweat it. Just leave them a simple message letting them know that you appreciate their business and are available for any questions they have.

V. *Tutorials*

Maybe your product is nuanced and difficult to use. Maybe it has some often underused features. Consider creating or hosting a tutorial, something that adds tangible value to the product. A tutorial not only puts your brand back on the radar screen of your customers but also provides unique, interactive after-sales service and maintains engagement.

VI. *Periodic Surveys*

Customers of certain business types may really appreciate being included in the feedback loop via periodic surveys. Some businesses attach a coupon to survey completion, boosting the value that comes with allowing a customer to feel that their voice is heard.

VII. *Birthday Email or Gift*

Birthday recognition through a timely email or a thoughtful gift can be very powerful. This is especially true if you are reaching customers' months after a sale, at a time when their memory of your brand is fading or gone. Consider pairing a coupon with a birthday email and craft the language to be fully genuine free of a sales-y tone and what the recipient may perceive to be ulterior motive. Simply wish them a happy birthday.

VIII. *Holiday Announcements*

Holidays are great excuses for re-engaging past customers with your brand. Even if your message simply announces a closure during a holiday season, wishing the customer an enjoyable holiday, it's a reminder that your brand exists. Holidays are also a common time to run promotions and sales. The kind of after-sales service that grows customer value. Surely the primary goal of after-sales service, first and foremost, is to best take care of your customers. Secondarily, after-sales service is meant to build loyalty and trust, which leads to even more valuable customers. If you're able to create an experience that "wows" or impresses customers, you've put your sales team in a prime position to grow the value of those customers. What do we mean by that? Well, wowed customers are very much on deck for any or all of the following sales strategies:

- ***Product and service pairings:*** Companies with multiple product or service offerings probably see common pairings or combinations. When someone buys a new smartphone, for example, they often pair it with a case, headphones or a number of other accessories to enhance their experience with the product. What can you pair with a sale to enrich your customer's experience with the product or service you offer?

- ***Upsell (plus warranties and special services):*** Upselling may carry a negative connotation. But, as seen with product and service pairings, selling an accompaniment to a product or service is meant mainly to ensure that a customer's experience is positive. Salespeople and customers alike should be cognizant of higher-priced offerings and the advantages of those offerings, as it may not be the ground-floor offering that's best for their particular vertical. Also, consider matching products with extended warranties, special maintenance services and other programs which, again, create a better overall experience for the customer.

- ***New products and services:*** Past and current customers should be the first to know about new product and service rollouts. That group, after all, is your ambassadorship and a more than capable vehicle for reaching new business. Honor them by breaking the news to them and watch as they engage with your brand.

- ***Customer loyalty program:*** Do you have perks or rewards for your customers? Customer loyalty programs aren't new, but they're awfully effective at maintaining engagement between brand and buyer, all while encouraging sales. If you don't already have one in place, brainstorm ways you could start and how it could aid both your customers and your bottom line.

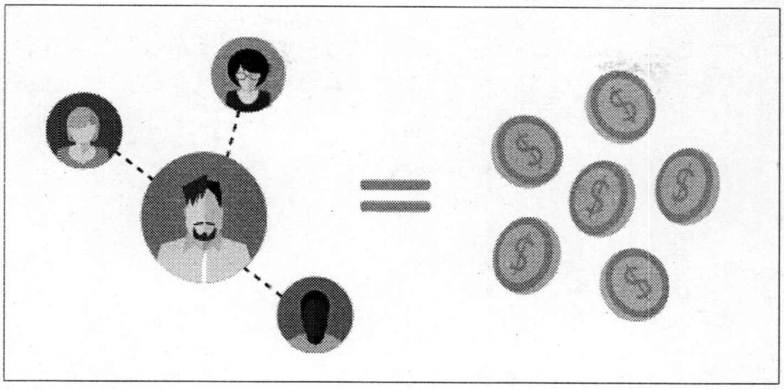

Figure: Referrals

Asking for referrals and rewarding customers who refer your business to their friends and networks is the final stage of after-sales service. Effective referral programs are a big win for small businesses because they help customers develop habits that include your company. Consider establishing a referral program with rewards that are low-hanging fruit. Providing gift cards in small increments, discounts or movie tickets for referrals shows your company's appreciation while bolstering customer loyalty.

Keep the following in mind when chasing referrals:

- You don't want to come off pushy or needy. So when asking for the referral, focus not on the referral itself but instead the value of your product or service offering and how it could benefit such a referral.
- Remember, customers generally follow instructions. If you appeal to them and ask them to review your business or share it with friends or family or co-workers, expect a lot of them to do that. That puts pressure on you to make sure you offer clear, easy-to-follow instructions that don't require dog tricks from the customer.
- Don't copycat. Come up with creative, strategic ways that your particular business can reward customers for their referrals. There's no universal reward suggestion, so make sure it fits your customer's needs and desires, along with your sales strategy.

10

PRICING DECISIONS

10.1. Price and Pricing – Meaning and Definition

In general terms price is a component of an exchange or transaction that takes place between two parties and refers to what must be given up by one party (i.e., buyer) in order to obtain something offered by another party (i.e., seller). Yet this view of price provides a somewhat limited explanation of what price means to participants in the transaction. In fact, price means different things to different participants in an exchange:

Buyers' View – For those making a purchase, such as final customers, price refers to what must be given up to obtain benefits. In most cases what is given up is financial consideration (e.g., money) in exchange for acquiring access to a good or service. But financial consideration is not always what the buyer gives up. Sometimes in a barter situation a buyer may acquire a product by giving up their own product. For instance, two farmers may exchange cattle for crops. Also, as we will discuss below, buyers may also give up other things to acquire the benefits of a product that are not direct financial payments (e.g., time to learn to use the product).

Sellers' View - To sellers in a transaction, price reflects the revenue generated for each product sold and, thus, is an important factor in determining profit. For marketing organizations price also serves as a marketing tool and is a key element in marketing promotions. For example, most retailers highlight product pricing in their advertising campaigns. Price is commonly confused with the notion of cost as in "I paid a high cost for buying my new plasma television." Technically, though, these are different concepts. Price is what a buyer pays to acquire products from a seller. Cost concerns the seller's investment (e.g., manufacturing expense) in the product being exchanged with a buyer. For marketing organizations seeking to make a profit the hope is that price will exceed cost so the organization can see financial gain from the transaction. Finally, while product pricing is a main topic for discussion when a company is examining its overall profitability, pricing decisions are not limited to for-profit companies. Not-for-profit organizations, such as charities, educational institutions and industry trade groups, also set prices, though it is often not as apparent. For instance, charities seeking to raise money may set different "target" levels for donations that reward donors with increases in status (e.g., name in newsletter), gifts or other benefits. While a charitable organization may not call it a price in their promotional material, in reality these donations are equivalent to price setting since donors are required to give a contribution in order to obtain something of value.

10.2. Importance of Pricing

There is often a tendency for marketers to focus more on activities like promotion, product development, and market research while prioritizing their responsibilities. These are often perceived as the more interesting aspects of the product and marketing mix. However, pricing needs to be given its due attention since it has great impact on the rest of the activities and the company. Pricing is of vital importance because of the following reasons.

Pricing as a Flexible Variable

Pricing changes can be made quickly and with almost no lead time if the business needs to make some product positioning changes or to counter a competitor's activities. In comparison, a change to the product or to a distribution channel can take months and sometimes significant cost inputs. Similarly any promotion decisions will also require additional financial input. Though it is important to plan for pricing changes and their impact on the brand and product perception, this can still be accomplished much faster than any other changes.

Define the Right Pricing

Any pricing decisions for a product need to be made through proper research, analysis and an eye on strategic objectives for the organization and the product. A decision made too quickly with superficial assessment can result in a loss of revenue. A price below the perceived value can lead to both a loss in potential additional revenue and a target audience that judges the quality of the brand through price points. If this price is raised later on, the existing customers may feel like they are being unfairly burdened. A price set too high can result in potential buyers staying away altogether. Pricing is often done by a team of experts who spend time conducting research that considers all variables of the market and brand.

Pricing as a Trigger for First impressions

In some product categories, a consumer will form a perception about its quality and relevance as soon as they see the price. Eventually, the decision to buy or not may be based on the perceived value of the entire product or marketing mix offering. But there is always a danger that the first impression triggered by the price point will either make the rest of the offering irrelevant or it will be a biased assessment.

Pricing as a Key to Sales Promotions

Sales promotions are often a short time price based offering such as a percentage reduction or a two in one type offer. These are meant to generate interest in the product or make use of a special occasion or event. Used wisely, this can be a useful method of increasing sales but the company must avoid the temptation to offer these special prices too often. In this scenario, buyers will put off purchasing the product till the next sales promotion of price reduction.

10.3. Factors Influencing Pricing Decisions

There are number of factors affecting the **pricing decisions** and price is not determined simply, there are many factors affecting pricing decisions. The reason is that the price is a very sensitive issue for the customers in their purchasing behaviour. Following are the two main factors affecting pricing decisions.

i. Internal Factors

ii. External Factors

i) Internal Factors

Internal factors are those factors that are related to the internal environment of the business. This means that the issues that prevail within the business organization and upon which the organization has control are included in this category. Internal factors further include the following.

- Marketing Objectives & Marketing Mix Strategies
- Costs
- Organizational Considerations

Each of these is discussed one by one.

Marketing Objectives & Marketing Mix Strategies

The objectives of the business serve as a basis for the development of proper marketing mix strategy that also includes in the price determination process. Those businesses that have kept clear objectives feel convenience in setting an effective price for their products or services, because their prices are built on the ground of stated objectives. Following are some of important objectives that are covered by most businesses.

Survival

In this objective the main purpose of the business is survival in the market. The profit maximization purpose becomes secondary importance for such business, because its survival is at stake due to unfavourable market conditions like tough competition, changes in tastes of customers etc. In this case the business tries to keep its price low, so that a sufficient proportion of its product or service should be sold.

Profit Maximization

Another important objective is the profit maximization that is employed by many businesses. Such businesses count the costs and demand of their products or services and set different prices. From these price combinations, a business chooses the price that can give maximum profit, return on investment or cash flow. This objective is beneficial for the short run and it neglects the long term future of the business. Some businesses try to increase their market share for the purpose of getting highest profit, because their management believed that higher market share lead to lower cost and hence higher profits. Businesses adopting such strategy also keep their prices low.

Product Quality Leadership

A business can set its basic objective as the product quality leadership in the market. For this purpose, such business keeps its price higher in order to cover the higher performance of its product along with the costs incurred on research and development. Price can be used to accomplish other objectives for a business. Example include lowering of price to avoid increasing competition, keep prices competitive to make market stable and avoid government intervention, to increase demand by lowering prices etc. In short the decisions taken in respect of price affect other marketing mix variable decisions and so all of these decisions should be consistent with one another to make a marketing program effective. The business should also keep its product as differentiated and set relatively high price for the uniqueness of its product. In this way price is based on many non-pricing factors.

b) Costs

Cost is the fundamental element in setting prices for a product or service. The simple rule is that the business charges such price that should not only cover all of the costs incurred in manufacturing, distribution and promotion of the product or service, but also provide a fair return on the invested money. If a business has low costs, then it can increase its sales and profit by lowering the price of its product or service.

Kinds of Costs:

Generally there are two major types of costs which are as follow.

a) Fixed Cost

b) Variable Cost

a) Fixed Cost

The fixed cost is such cost that remains fixed and does not change with the changing level of production or sales. The total fixed cost remains same but fixed cost per unit may change. The example includes rent paid for the building, interest paid on loan, salaries to employee staff etc.

b) Variable Cost

The variable cost is that kind of cost which changes with the change in the level of production and sales. Although the total variable cost change but the unit variable cost remains the same. For example, each car produced includes the variable cost of tires, metal sheets, Misc items etc that change with the increase or decrease in the quantity of production and sales. The management of the business should ascertain different level of costs with respect to different levels of production and sales so that the lowest cost can be attained for the determination of effective prices for the manufactured products or services.

Organizational Considerations

This factor includes the fact that who should be given the responsibility to set the price within the organization. There many ways to deal with such an issue. In smaller businesses, top management is responsible for setting the price of the product. On the other hand, in large organizations product line managers or divisional manager has the authority to set price for the product or service. In case of industrial markets, salespersons handle the pricing of product by negotiating with the customers within the pre-specified range of prices. In certain price sensitive industries (Oil Companies, Aerospace etc) have a separate pricing department that can either directly determine the best price or facilitates the pricing process of the business. In some firms, top management like the proposed prices of the lower level employees like salespersons etc.

ii) External Factors

External Factors include factors that are related to the external environment of the business. The business has less control over these variables of the external environment. The following are included in this category.

a) The Market and Demand

b) Costs, Prices and Offering of Competitors

a) The Market and Demand

We have already discussed that the lower limits of price are determined by the costs incurred. On the other hand the upper limits are determined by the demand and market elements. Price is balanced by the benefits of owning the relative product or service by consumer and industrial customers. For this purpose the price and demand relationship for a product is essential to be understood before setting its price.

Pricing in different Markets

Different market conditions require different sets of pricing strategies. Generally there are following four types of markets.

a) Pure Competition

b) Monopolistic Competition

c) Oligopolistic Competition

d) Monopoly

e) Consumer perception about value and price

f) Price Demand Relationship

a) Pure Competition

In case of pure competition in the market, there are many buyers and sellers in the markets dealing with uniform commodities like wheat etc. There is one ongoing price in the whole market and no single buyer or seller can affect this price. Because the customers can easily obtain their required quantity at the ongoing price of the market, so no seller can charge higher prices. Similarly, no seller can charge a lower price because he can sell all his offered quantity to a lot of customers on the market. In case of the rise of the price or profit in the market, new sellers are attracted to enter in the market. In pure competition, pricing, sales promotion, new product development and marketing research are not supported. In other words the sellers on the market do involve in preparation of marketing strategies.

b) Monopolistic Competition

In case of monopolistic competition there are many sellers and buyers who offer their products not at a single price but at a range of prices. The difference in the price range is due to the differentiated product or service offering by the sellers. Customers can feel the difference between the products and hence pay different price for them. These differences can be in shape of features, quality or style etc. So in this kind of market businesses spend more time and money on differentiating their product or services in the shape of sales promotion, advertising etc. A single business is not affected by the marketing strategies of its competitors because there are many competitors in the market.

c) Oligopolistic Competition

Another factor affecting pricing decisions is oligopolistic. In oligopolistic market, there are few sellers and buyers which are conscious about the pricing and other marketing strategies of competitors. The offered products are either uniform or differentiated. It is difficult for new seller to enter in the market. A certain change in the price of single firm affects its own soil in a negative way even if a seller lowers its price; its competitors also decrease their price. This means that the benefits are only for a short while.

d) Monopoly

Another market condition is monopoly in which there is only a single seller who can offer its products or services at different rates. As the seller is single and the buyers are much more, therefore the seller charges a relatively higher price because there is no fear of competition. In case of regulated monopoly, the seller can charge only a fair price, but in case of unregulated monopoly the seller has freedom to charge extra for its offering. But mostly the monopoly firm keeps its price low for a number of reasons like quick penetration in the market, government intervention etc.

e) Consumer Perception about Value & Price

The bottom reality in the pricing decision is that the customers are the final authority who determines the price of a product or service. It is obvious that the consumers pay the price for the exchange of the benefits that they avail by using the relative product or service. So businesses should focus on the pricing that is consumer oriented in which they try to determine that how much would be the consumer willing to pay for how much benefit of a certain product or service.

f) Price Demand Relationship

Businesses should also consider the important relationship between the price of a product or service and its demand. Generally price and demand is inversely related which means that the increase in the price would lead to the decrease in the demand for that product and vice versa. The reason behind this inverse relationship is that the customers have limited resources for the fulfilment of their demands. In some case the price and demand show the direct relationship which means that the increase in the price would lead to the increase in the demand of that product in the market. But this only happens with the prestigious products where increased price means increased quality. The business management should also consider the elasticity of the demand of their offering product while setting its price.

ii) Costs, Prices & Offering of Competitors

One of external factors affecting pricing decisions of the business is the costs, price and offering of the competitors as compared to its own cost, price & offering. This means that the management of the business should take into account the change in the price and offering of the competitors and take steps accordingly.

There are also some other external factors affecting pricing decisions and are important to be considered in determining a price for a product or service, like economic conditions of the country, government rules and regulations etc.

10.4. Pricing Objectives

Pricing can be defined as the process of determining an appropriate price for the product, or it is an act of setting price for the product. Pricing involves a number of decisions related to setting price of product. Pricing policies are aimed at achieving various objectives. Company has several objectives to be achieved by the sound pricing policies and strategies. Pricing decisions are based on the objectives to be achieved. Objectives are related to sales volume, profitability, market shares, or competition. Objectives of pricing can be classified in five groups as shown in the following figure.

a) Profits-related Objectives

Profit has remained a dominant objective of business activities.

Company's pricing policies and strategies are aimed at following profits-related objectives:

i. Maximum Current Profit

One of the objectives of pricing is to maximize current profits. This objective is aimed at making as much money as possible. Company tries to set its price in a way that more current profits can be earned. However, company cannot set its price beyond the limit. But, it concentrates on maximum profits.

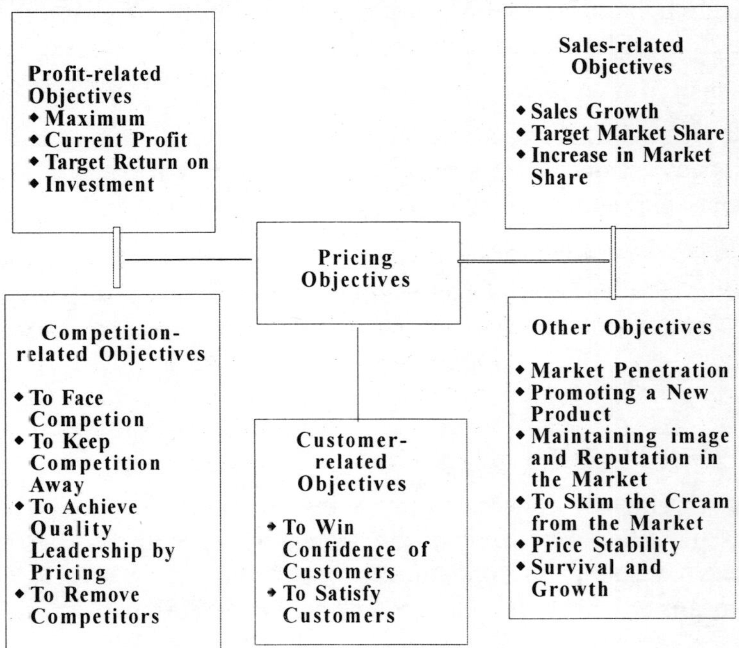

Figure. Pricing Objectives

ii. Target Return on Investment

Most companies want to earn reasonable rate of return on investment.

Target return may be:

a) Fixed percentage of sales

b) Return on investment (ROI)

c) A fixed rupee amount.

Company sets its pricing policies and strategies in a way that sales revenue ultimately yields average return on total investment. For example, company decides to earn 20% return on total investment of 3 crore rupees. It must set price of product in a way that it can earn 60 lakh rupees.

b. Sales-related Objectives

The main sales-related objectives of pricing may include:

i. Sales Growth:

Company's objective is to increase sales volume. It sets its price in such a way that more and more sales can be achieved. It is assumed that sales growth has direct positive impact on the profits. So, pricing decisions are taken in way that sales volume can be raised. Setting price, altering in price, and modifying pricing policies are targeted to improve sales.

ii. Target Market Share:

A company aims its pricing policies at achieving or maintaining the target market share. Pricing decisions are taken in such a manner that enables the company to achieve targeted market share. Market share is a specific volume of sales determined in light of total sales in an industry. For example, company may try to achieve 25% market shares in the relevant industry.

iii. Increase in Market Share:

Sometimes, price and pricing are taken as the tool to increase its market share. When company assumes that its market share is below than expected, it can raise it by appropriate pricing; pricing is aimed at improving market share.

c) Competition-related Objectives

Competition is a powerful factor affecting marketing performance. Every company tries to react to the competitors by appropriate business strategies.

With reference to price, following competition-related objectives may be discussed.

i). To Face Competition

Pricing is primarily concerns with facing competition. Today's market is characterized by the severe competition. Company sets and modifies its pricing policies so as to respond the competitors strongly. Many companies use price as a powerful means to react to level and intensity of competition.

ii). To Keep Competitors Away

To prevent the entry of competitors can be one of the main objectives of pricing. The phase 'prevention is better than cure' is equally applicable here. If competitors are kept away, no need to fight with them. To achieve the objective, a company keeps its price as low as possible to minimize profit attractiveness of products. In some cases, a company reacts offensively to prevent entry of competitors by selling product even at a loss.

iii). To Achieve Quality Leadership by Pricing

Pricing is also aimed at achieving the quality leadership. The quality leadership is the image in mind of buyers that high price is related to high quality product. In order to create a positive image that company's product is standard or superior than offered by the close competitors; the company designs its pricing policies accordingly.

iv). To Remove Competitors from the Market

The pricing policies and practices are directed to remove the competitors away from the market. This can be done by forgoing the current profits by keeping price as low as possible in order to maximize the future profits by charging a high price after removing competitors from the market. Price competition can remove weak competitors.

d) Customer-related Objectives

Customers are in centre of every marketing decision. Company wants to achieve following objectives by the suitable pricing policies and practices:

i) To Win Confidence of Customers

Customers are the target to serve. Company sets and practices its pricing policies to win the confidence of the target market. Company, by appropriate pricing policies, can establish, maintain or even strengthen the confidence of customers that price charged for the product is reasonable one. Customers are made feel that they are not being cheated.

ii) To Satisfy Customers

To satisfy customers is the prime objective of the entire range of marketing efforts. And, pricing is no exception. Company sets, adjusts, and readjusts its pricing to satisfy its target customers. In short, a company should design pricing in such a way that result into maximum consumer satisfaction.

e) Other Objectives

Over and above the objectives discussed so far, there are certain objectives that company wants to achieve by pricing.

They are as under:

i. Market Penetration

This objective concerns with entering the deep into the market to attract maximum number of customers. This objective calls for charging the lowest possible price to win price-sensitive buyers.

ii. Promoting a New Product

To promote a new product successfully, the company sets low price for its products in the initial stage to encourage for trial and repeat buying. The sound pricing can help the company introduce a new product successfully.

iii. Maintaining Image and Reputation in the Market

Company's effective pricing policies have positive impact on its image and reputation in the market. Company, by charging reasonable price, stabilizing price, or keeping fixed price can create a good image and reputation in the mind of the target customers.

iv. To Skim the Cream from the Market

This objective concerns with skimming maximum profit in initial stage of product life cycle. Because a product is new, offering new and superior advantages, the company can charge relatively high price. Some segments will buy product even at a premium price.

v. Price Stability

Company with stable price is ranked high in the market. Company formulates pricing policies and strategies to eliminate seasonal and cyclical fluctuations. Stability in price has a good impression on the buyers. Frequent changes in pricing affect adversely the prestige of company.

vi. Survival and Growth

Finally, pricing is aimed at survival and growth of company's business activities and operations. It is a fundamental pricing objective. Pricing policies are set in a way that company's existence is not threatened.

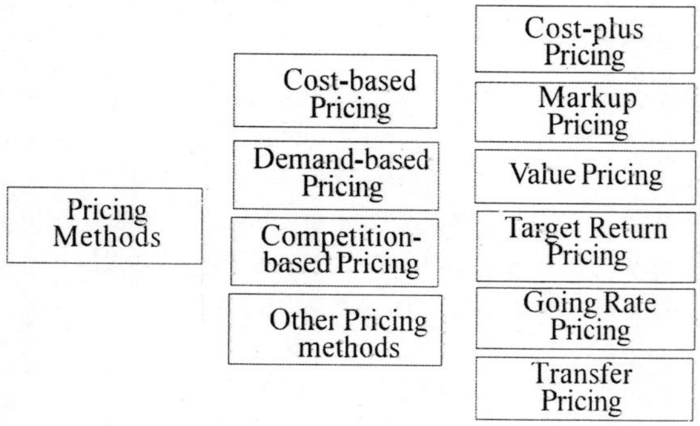

Figure: Various Pricing Methods

10.5. Methods of Pricing Determination

An organization has various options for selecting a pricing method. Prices are based on three dimensions that are cost, demand, and competition. The organization can use any of the dimensions or combination of dimensions to set the price of a product. The following figure shows different pricing methods:

The different pricing methods are discussed below:

Cost-based Pricing

Cost-based pricing refers to a pricing method in which some percentage of desired profit margins is added to the cost of the product to obtain the final price. In other words, cost-based pricing can be defined as a pricing method in which a certain percentage of the total cost of production is added to the cost of the product to determine its selling price. Cost-based pricing can be of two types, namely, cost-plus pricing and mark-up pricing.

These two types of cost-based pricing are as follows:

i) Cost-plus Pricing

Refers to the simplest method of determining the price of a product. In cost-plus pricing method, a fixed percentage, also called mark-up percentage, of the total cost (as a profit) is added to the total cost to set the price. For example, XYZ organization bears the total cost of Rs. 100 per unit for producing a product. It adds Rs. 50 per unit to the price of product as' profit. In such a case, the final price of a product of the organization would be Rs. 150. Cost-plus pricing is also known as average cost pricing. This is the most commonly used method in manufacturing organizations. In economics, the general formula given for setting price in case of cost-plus pricing is as follows:

P = AVC + AVC (M)

AVC= Average Variable Cost

M = Mark-up percentage

AVC (m) = Gross profit margin

Mark-up percentage (M) is fixed in which AFC and net profit margin (NPM) are covered.

AVC (m) = AFC+ NPM

ii. For determining average variable cost, the first step is to fix prices. This is done by estimating the volume of the output for a given period of time. The planned output or normal level of production is taken into account to estimate the output. The second step is to calculate Total Variable Cost (TVC) of the output. TVC includes direct costs, such as cost incurred in labor, electricity, and transportation. Once TVC is calculated, AVC is obtained by dividing TVC by output, Q. [AVC= TVC/Q]. The price is then fixed by adding the mark-up of some percentage of AVC to the profit [P = AVC + AVC (m)].

iii. The advantages of cost-plus pricing method are as follows:

a. Requires minimum information

b. Involves simplicity of calculation

c. Insures sellers against the unexpected changes in costs

The disadvantages of cost-plus pricing method are as follows:

a. Ignores price strategies of competitors

b. Ignores the role of customers

ii) Mark-up Pricing

Refers to a pricing method in which the fixed amount or the percentage of cost of the product is added to product's price to get the selling price of the product. Markup pricing is more common in retailing in which a retailer sells the product to earn profit. For example, if a retailer has taken a product from the wholesaler for Rs. 100, then he/she might add up a mark-up of Rs. 20 to gain profit. It is mostly expressed by the following formulae:

a. Markup as the percentage of cost= (Markup/Cost) *100

b. Markup as the percentage of selling price= (Markup/ Selling Price)*100

c. For example, the product is sold for Rs. 500 whose cost was Rs. 400. The mark up as a percentage to cost is equal to (100/400)*100 =25. The mark up as a percentage of the selling price equals (100/500)*100= 20.

iii) Demand-based Pricing

Demand-based pricing refers to a pricing method in which the price of a product is finalized according to its demand. If the demand of a product is more, an organization prefers to set high prices for products to gain profit; whereas, if the demand of a product is less, the low prices are charged to attract the customers. The success of demand-based pricing depends on the ability of marketers to analyze the demand. This type of pricing can be seen in the hospitality and travel industries. For instance, airlines during the period of low demand charge less rates as compared to the period of high demand. Demand-based pricing helps the organization to earn more profit if the customers accept the product at the price more than its cost.

iv) Competition-based Pricing

Competition-based pricing refers to a method in which an organization considers the prices of competitors' products to set the prices of its own products. The organization may charge higher, lower, or equal prices as compared to the prices of its competitors. The aviation industry is the best example of competition-based pricing where airlines charge the same or fewer prices for same routes as charged by their competitors. In addition, the introductory prices charged by publishing organizations for textbooks are determined according to the competitors' prices.

v) Other Pricing Methods

In addition to the pricing methods, there are other methods that are discussed as follows:

a) Value Pricing

Implies a method in which an organization tries to win loyal customers by charging low prices for their high- quality products. The organization aims to become a low cost producer without sacrificing the quality. It can deliver high-quality products at low prices by improving its research and development process. Value pricing is also called value-optimized pricing.

b) Target Return Pricing

Helps in achieving the required rate of return on investment done for a product. In other words, the price of a product is fixed on the basis of expected profit.

c) Going Rate Pricing

Implies a method in which an organization sets the price of a product according to the prevailing price trends in the market. Thus, the pricing strategy adopted by the organization can be same or similar to other organizations. However, in this type of pricing, the prices set by the market leaders are followed by all the organizations in the industry.

d) Transfer Pricing

Involves selling of goods and services within the departments of the organization. It is done to manage the profit and loss ratios of different departments within the organization. One department of an organization can sell its products to other departments at low prices. Sometimes, transfer pricing is used to show higher profits in the organization by showing fake sales of products within departments.

11

CHANNELS OF DISTRIBUTION DECISION

11.1. Channels of Distribution – Meaning and Definition

A set of interdependent organizations (intermediaries) involved in the process of making a product or service available for use or consumption. The distribution channel is made up of various kinds of intermediaries such as retailers, distributors, wholesalers, and agents. These intermediaries fulfil a variety of functions. The structure of the distribution channel has to be decided first and foremost. Example of a Channel is shown in the following.

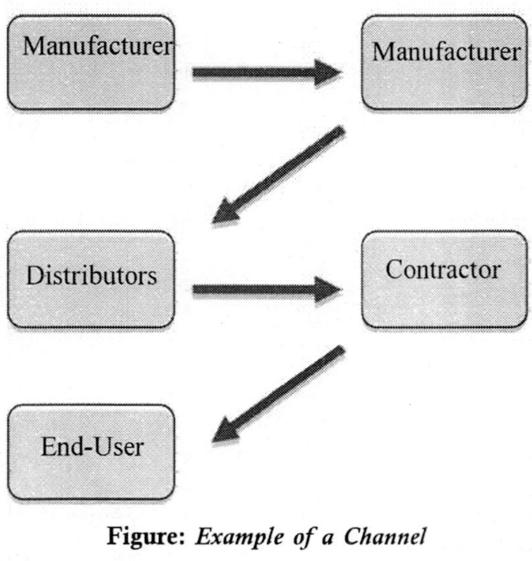

Figure: *Example of a Channel*

11.2. Channel Objectives

A distribution channel is a network of firms that are interconnected in their quest to provide sellers a means of infusing the marketplace with goods and buyers a means of purchasing those goods, doing all as efficiently and profitably as possible. The channels of distribution are designed to achieve following objectives:

a) Movement of goods

a. The main objective of distribution is to make flow of goods from production place to consumption place. For this, the role of the distribution channel system and its members becomes very important.

b. Availability of goods

The objective of distribution function is to make or supply necessary goods to the large masses of customers living indifferent geographical areas.

c.Protection of goods

The objective of distribution is also to properly storing, handling and protecting the goods and supplying them to the consumers in good condition.

d.Cost reduction

The objective of distribution is also to reduce cost of product by bringing effectiveness in distribution process.

e.Customer satisfaction

The other objective of distribution function is to help consumers feel satisfied through effective distribution.

11.3. Role of Distribution Channels

Distribution is one of the important mixes among marketing mixes. The role of distribution in marketing and in the whole economy can be discussed as follows:

a. Delivery of satisfaction

Marketing concept emphasizes on earning profit through satisfaction of the customers. Besides market research for the development and sales of goods according to need and wants of consumers, the participants of distribution channel also help producers in production of new goods.

b. Standard of living

Distribution function helps to improve living standard of the consumers in the society. Proper distribution of necessary goods and services to the consumers easily at right time does not only satisfy them but also brings change in their living standard. Distribution brings improvement in living standard of consumers through generation of employment, increase in income and transfer of ownership. Hence, it brings positive effect in the society.

c. Value addition

The functions of distribution such as transportation, warehousing, inventory management etc. increase the importance of products by creating place utility, time utility and quantity utility. Distribution mix plays an important role to increase the value of the products through delivery of goods in right quantity, at right place and right time.

d. Communication

Distribution serves as link between producers and consumers. Producers can make flow of information and messages to consumers about their products, price, promotion etc. through channel members. Similarly, they receive information about customers, competitors and environmental changes from channel members.

e. Employment

The function of distribution creates employment opportunities in society. Market intermediaries work as direct and indirect sources of employment. Different producers need to supply their innumerable products to consumers. Thousands of distributors, agents, wholesalers, retailers, brokers etc. involve in supplying the products to the consumers. Similarly, many persons of the society can get job in the transport and warehouses sectors, etc.

f. Efficiency

Producers produce limited types of goods in mass quantity. but the consumers demand different types of goods in small quantity. When goods are produced in a mass quantity, they can be obtained at lower price. Distribution helps to satisfy the needs of consumers by supplying assortment of different products of different producers. From this, efficiency can be achieved in both production and distribution.

g. Financing

Intermediaries themselves make arrangement to keep reserve and stock of goods. The producers need not make arrangement and management of distribution centers and warehouse. The producers need not do anything except remaining busy in production, the timely payment by intermediaries and financial helps become more important for smooth operation of production. Similarly, the role of finance is also decisive in mobilizing other means of production.

11.4. Factors Influencing Distribution Channels

Dominant factors affecting channel selection are discussed below:

a. Factors Related to Products

Product is a prime factor in channel selection. Product-related factors are among most relevant and powerful factors affecting channel decision. Channel must be fit the type and nature of company's products. Such factors include the following.

Perishability of Product

Perishable products must be sold and consumed immediately after production. So, for perishable products, normally, direct or short channel is advisable. For durable products, indirect or multilevel channel is preferable. However, due to availability of rapid means of transportation and advanced cold storage facilities, the perishable product can also be sold by long-indirect channels.

Technical Aspects

Technical products cannot be used without sufficient information and direct supervision. Even, they need more frequent services. It is advisable to adopt indirect and multilevel channels to assist consumers to use the technical product properly and safely. For simple products, direct channels can be used.

New v/s Existing Product

Consumers need more information and attention for new products. More efforts and time are required to convince consumers. As a result, a company may opt for indirect channel to take help of middlemen in this task. For existing products, the company can use direct and/or indirect channels.

Complexity and Risk Related to Use of Product

Complex and risky products are sold via middlemen as consumers expect more direct supervision and assistance.

Size of Product

In case of heavy and bulky products, direct or short channel is more suitable. This is due to difficulties related to physical movement of the product.

Divisibility of Product

Mostly, indivisible products are distributed directly to customers. Divisible products can be conveniently distributed by middlemen.

Unit Price of Product

Precious products, like gold, jewellery, certain chemicals, software, etc., are distributed using direct or short channels of distribution. Use of direct and short channel can minimize risk of theft or robbery.

Legal Aspect

Quite obviously, permitted (legal) products can be distributed by any convenient channel of distribution. But, illegal products are distributed by direct channels for secrecy purpose.

b. Factors Related to Company

Company's internal situations have direct impact on choice of marketing channel. Manager has to analyze company-related factors to decide the best fit channel(s). Company-related factors include the following.

Company's Financial Position

Financially sound companies can maintain separate and well-equipped departments for distribution of products. Such companies can open and manage own retail outlets and can hire salesmen to manage distribution effectively. They do not require services of middlemen and, hence, can distribute the product directly. But, financially weak companies have to opt for indirect channels to share resources and expertise of channel members.

Product Mix of Company

A company's product mix consists of product lines and product items in each product line. Many product lines and several product items/ varieties in each of the product lines can enable the firm to offer multiple choices to a large number of consumers. Even, the firm can take benefit of the scale of economy. In such case, direct channels are more advisable. Small companies with limited product lines and/or product items should distribute products via wholesalers and retailers, who sell products of many companies.

Desire for Control

If a company desires to have direct and close control over production and selling activities, direct channels are preferred and vice-versa.

Experience and Expertise

Successful distribution needs considerable experience and expertise. If a company possesses necessary experience, expertise, and staff, it can manage selling activities by its own. When a company lacks such experience and skills, it has to involve middlemen, and prefers indirect channels.

Facilities and Staff

Sufficient facilities and capable staff are essential for effective distribution of products. If a company manages for needed facilities and staff, direct channels are used, otherwise indirect channels are used.

Company's Past Experience

A company's past experience can also affect channel decision. When a company has favorable and satisfactory experience to work with middlemen, it may continue working with them. In case, if it is not satisfied with terms and services of middlemen, it would shorten its channel of distribution.

c) Factors Related to Middlemen

Companies consider several middlemen-related factors while deciding on channels. Most common factors include the following.

Creditworthiness of Middlemen

Middlemen's credibility is an important criterion to decide on the channel. If middlemen have good reputation and creditworthiness, a company can multiply its gain and, as a result, prefers to involve them in their distribution activities. Creditworthiness is a critical aspect while offering dealership or franchise for definite area.

Attitudes of Middlemen

Positive attitudes of middlemen make companies to involve them in distribution activities. Companies like to select indirect channel with one or more levels. Opposite situation leads companies to select direct channels.

Services Rendered by Middlemen

Channel decisions depend on number and quality of services offered by middlemen to customers. When the channel members are ready to provide several services to customers, like home delivery, free repairing, credit facility, installment payment schemes, and other post-sales services, the manufacturers like to involve them in distribution to avail such services to their customers. When middlemen do not provide the useful services to customers, companies prefer direct channels.

Financial Capacity of Middlemen

Strong financial capacity of middlemen attracts manufacturers. This is due to the fact that strong financial position benefits both manufacturers and customers. Strong financial position results into speedy recovery of bills receivable, less chances of bad debts, immediate payment, credit facility to customers, and also advanced payment.

Terms and Conditions

When terms and conditions laid down by middlemen are not favorable, the manufacturers don't like to involve them in distribution activities. They prefer direct distribution channels.

d. Factors Related to Market

Market (consumer behavior) is a crucial factor in channel selection. Main factors related to market include the following.

Size of Market

In case of a large and concentrated market, it is economically affordable for a company to manage its own distribution setup. When market is small, it is advisable to assign distribution task to middlemen.

Geographical Concentration

When firm's customers are highly concentrated (living in nearby area) in particular region, it can directly deal with customers by using any of the direct channels. But, when customers are scattered in several regions, it is not convenient to use direct channels. Middlemen can do better job with less costs.

Services Expected by Market

Number and types of services expected by the target market, and company's capacity and readiness to meet them are important issues to be considered in this connection. For example, if the market expects a lot of services and the company is unable and/or unwilling to satisfy them, indirect channels are preferred to avail the services from middlemen.

Habits of Consumers

Distribution channels must be fit with habits of consumers. Manager should find out why, how, when, where and from whom the consumers like to buy. For example, if consumers are habituated to buy a little quantity frequently from nearby retailer on credit, a company must involve retailers (along with wholesalers) to avail products at all the places where consumers reside.

Current Market Trend

Firm's distribution system must be compatible with the recent market trend. Trend includes a number of variables like policies and practices of giant national and multinational companies, functioning of departmental stores and corporate retailers, cyber marketing and network marketing, business partnering with banking, insurance, and other service providers, customers' awareness, and so on. Manager must observe these reforms and innovative practices minutely and accordingly a suitable channel should be selected.

e. Factors Related to Competition

Current and anticipated competition affects company's decision on marketing channel. Relevant competition-related aspects must be analyzed while selecting the channel. Competition-related factors include the following.

Intensity of Competition

When there exists a severe competition in the market, a company must consider competitors distribution strategies and practices while selecting marketing channels. In case of less competition, a company choice will be independent of competition.

Response and Reactions of Competitors

Reactions and response of the close competitors must be taken into account while deciding on distribution channel. A company must select such channels that can help availing competitive advantages.

Company's Competitive Position in Market

A leader company can design its own distribution network. It can select a specific channel of distribution as per its requirements. But, the follower companies have to follow market leader. Their choice depends on leader's practice.

f. Factors Related to Environment

Marketer has to consider overall business environment while deciding on marketing channel. Domestic and global environmental forces have direct or indirect impact on company's activities and operations. Main environmental forces that affect channel decision include the following.

Economic Condition of Country

Country's economic condition affects firm's operations. In economically poor countries, short or direct channels are used to sell product at low price. In developing and developed countries, normally, indirect channels are used to distribute products.

Phases of Trade Cycle

Phases of trade cycle, like recession, recovery, prosperity, etc., indicate the country's economic condition. Normally, in prosperity stage, long and indirect channels are used due to need for mass distribution and willingness of people to pay high price for the product. Direct and short channels are more suitable when the economy is passing through recession phase as direct and short channels keep the selling price low.

Legal Provision

Government policies and legal provisions have direct or indirect implication on firm's distribution activities. Manager must identify relevant provisions affecting distribution activities and, accordingly, an appropriate channel(s) should be selected. Taxes, charges, administrative procedures, restrictions, and other issues are worth noted in this regard.

Availability of Facilities

Availability, costs, and quality necessary facilities play decisive role in channel selection. Facilities like transportation, communication, warehousing, banking, insurance, supporting government agencies at national and international level, degree of harmony among states of the country, and relations among nations at large affect firm's channel decisions.

11.5. Functions of Distribution Channels

The functions of distribution channels are discussed in the following.

- The primary function of a distribution channel is to bridge the gap between production and consumption.
- A close study of the market is extremely essential. A sound marketing plan depends upon thorough market study.
- The distribution channel is also responsible for promoting the product. Awareness regarding products and other offers should be created among the consumers.
- Creating contacts or prospective buyers and maintaining liaison with existing ones.
- Understanding the customer's needs and adjusting the offer accordingly.
- Negotiate price and other offers related to the product as per the customer demand.
- Storage and distribution of goods.
- Catering to the financial requirements for the smooth working of the distribution chain.
- Risk taking for example by stock holding.

11.6. Types of Distribution Channels

Different types of channel of distribution are as follows:

Manufacturers and consumers are two major components of the market. Intermediaries perform the duty of eliminating the distance between the two. There is no standardized level which proves that the distance between the two is eliminated.

(A) Direct Channel or Zero Level Channels

When the manufacturer instead of selling the goods to the intermediary sells it directly to the consumer then this is known as Zero Level Channel. Retail outlets, mail order selling, internet selling and selling.

(B) Indirect Channels

When a manufacturer gets the help of one or more middlemen to move goods from the production place to the place of consumption, the distribution channel is called indirect channel. Following are the main types of it.

i) *One Level Channel*

In this method an intermediary is used. Here a manufacturer sells the goods directly to the retailer instead of selling it to agents or wholesalers. This method is used for expensive watches and other like products. This method is also useful for selling FMCG (Fast Moving Consumer Goods).

ii) *Two Level Channel*

In this method a manufacturer sells the material to a wholesaler, the wholesaler to the retailer and then the retailer to the consumer. Here, the wholesaler after purchasing the material in large quantity from the manufacturer sells it in small quantity to the retailer. Then the retailers make the products available to the consumers. This medium is mainly used to sell soap, tea, salt, cigarette, sugar, ghee etc.

iii) *Three Level Channel*

Under this one more level is added to Two Level Channel in the form of agent. An agent facilitates to reduce the distance between the manufacturer and the wholesaler. Some big companies who cannot directly contact the wholesaler, they take the help of agents. Such companies appoint their agents in every region and sell the material to them. Then the agents sell the material to the wholesalers, the wholesaler to the retailer and in the end the retailer sells the material to the consumers.

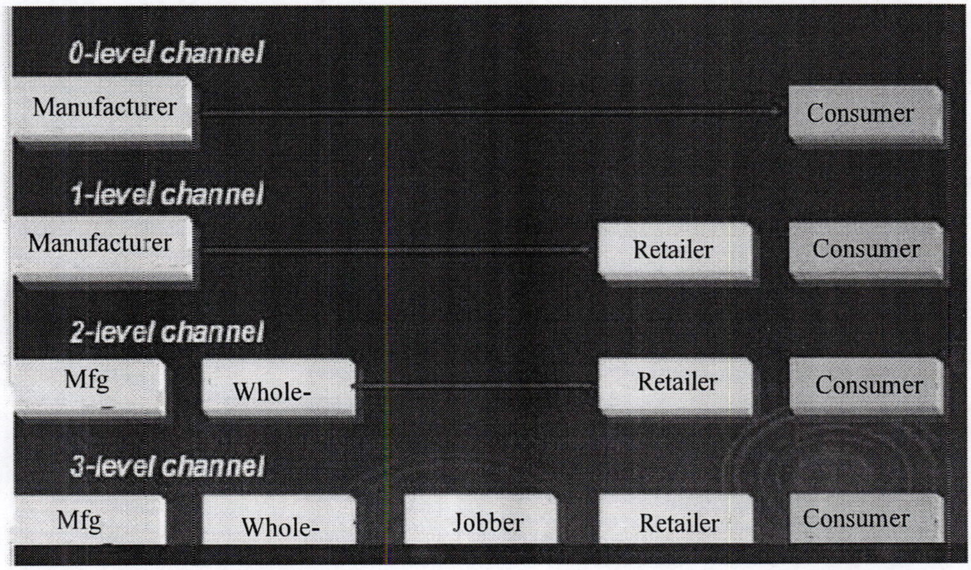

Figure: ***Different types of channels***

11.7. Role of Intermediaries

The products or services are transferred from manufacturer to the customers through marketing intermediaries. The place, time and possession gaps are overcome by the marketing intermediaries that separate the products or services from their users. Following are the important functions of marketing intermediaries.

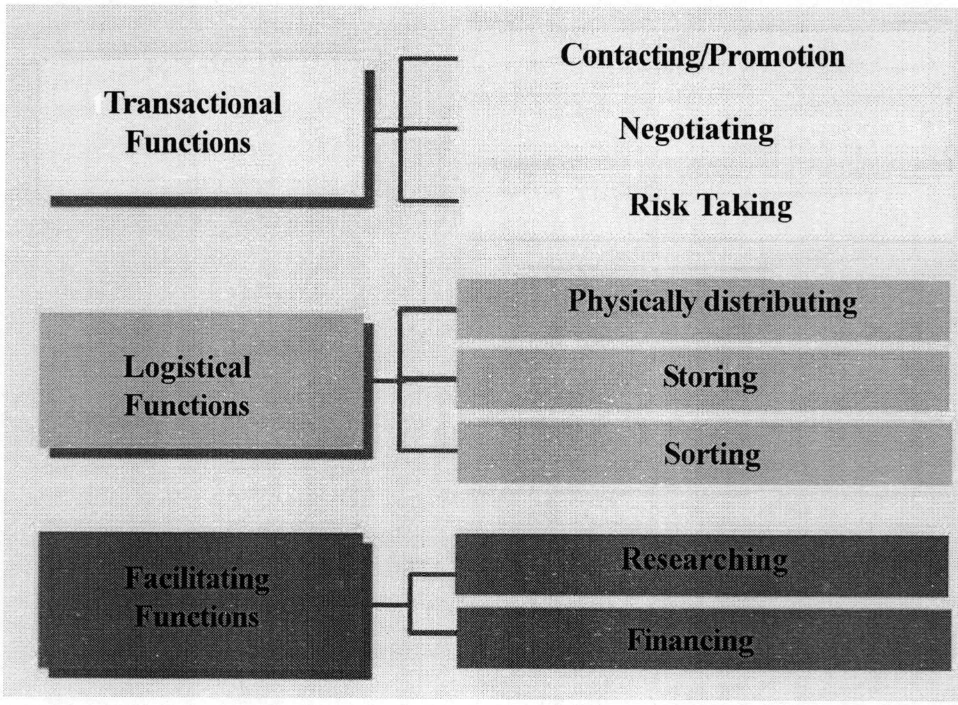

Figure: ***Channel functions performed by the intermediaries***

Functions of marketing intermediaries are discussed in the following.

a) *Information:* One big function of marketing intermediaries is that they are helpful in provision of useful information about the forces and actors in the markets in the management and marketing research teams.

b) *Promotion*: They also communicate with the customers about the new offering of the businesses.

c) *Contact*: Prospective customers are found by the marketing intermediaries and then they are effectively communicated by these intermediaries.

d) *Matching*: Marketing intermediaries also match the various diversified needs and wants of customers to the different supplies of the manufacturers including the assembling, grading and packaging of products.

e) *Negotiation*: This is an important function in which the intermediaries negotiate with the customers in order to reach at a certain price so that the ownership of the product is shifted.

f) *Physical Distribution*: The physical distribution of products is also done by them.

g) *Financing*: Intermediaries also provide some funding to the businesses which are properly used by the businesses to cover some of their distribution costs.

h) *Risk Taking*: These intermediaries also take some risk in acquiring different old and new products or services from various businesses.

11.8. Wholesalers

The word" wholesaler" is derived from the word "Wholesale" that means sell good in large quantity or in bulk. According to **S.E Thomas** "A wholesaler is a trader who purchases goods in large quantities from manufacturer and resells them to retailers in small quantities". Wholesalers **can be defined** as the wholesaler as the one who buys goods in large quantities from manufacturer and sells them in small quantities with the object of earning profit. He therefore, is neither a manufacturer nor a retailer but acts as a link between the two parties.

11.9. Functions of Wholesalers

The most important functions of a wholesaler in the marketing of goods are as under:-

a) Assembling

The wholesaler buys good from different manufacturer producing the same streak of goods. He assembles them in his warehouse for the purpose of sale to the retailers.

b) Storage

A wholesaler stores the goods in his warehouse. He makes them available in appropriate and requisite quantities as and when they are required by retailers.

c) Grading and Packing

A wholesaler sorts out the goods according to their quality, size, shape, content etc and then packs them carefully to sell them to the retailers.

d) Transplantation

Wholesaler buys goods in bulk from the producers and transports them in his own godown. The wholesaler also provides the facility of transportation to the retailer shop, which is one of the important functions of wholesale trading.

e) Financing

This is an important function of wholesaler. A wholesaler usually buys goods on cash from the producers and sells on credit to the retailer. In this way, he provides financing facilities to trade transactions.

f) Risk bearing

The wholesaler bears all the trade and financial risks of the business. Since he buys goods in bulk for making them available to retailer in small quantities, he takes all the risk involved in marketing of goods. He not only assumes the risk of loss arising from a unexpected fall in the prices of goods but also the risks of damage, deterioration in quality, spoilage etc in his warehouse.

g) Market Information

One of the most important functions of wholesaler is that it provides important market information to retailer and manufacturer, which help the retailers about the demand of consumer and manufacturer, so that he produces the goods according to the changes in the tastes and fashions of the consumer.

h) Dispersing and selling

The wholesaler keeps the goods in warehouse. He sells them to the retailers who are often scattered over a large area. The retailers contact the wholesaler when goods are sold and this process continues over the years. The wholesaler thus helps in the dispersion process of marketing.

11.10. Services of Wholesalers

Services of wholesalers are discussed in the following.

- Wholesaler helps the manufacturer to concentrate on the manufacturing operations.
- The wholesaler buys in large quantities. Thus, he enables the manufacturer to get the benefit of economies of large scale production.
- The wholesalers collect orders from a large number of retailers and supply them from the stock of goods supplied in bulk by the manufacturer.
- By stocking products of seasonal nature, he makes it possible for the manufacturer of such products to continue production.
- The wholesaler helps the manufacturer to regulate his production in accordance with the changing requirements of the market.
- The wholesaler enables the manufacturer to make better use of his capital for production by relieving him of the necessity of carrying large stocks.

- Wholesalers help in price stabilization. They stock goods during the slack season and sell them during the period of peak demand.

Services to Retailers

The wholesaler renders the following services to the retailers:

- The retailer need not carry stock of large variety of products to meet the demand of his customers.
- Wholesalers relieve the retailers of the necessity of placing orders to different manufacturers. Thus, the number of the sources of supply for the variety of goods is reduced to the minimum; hence buying problem is considerably simplified.
- Wholesalers enable retailers to obtain supplies more quickly than they could by placing orders directly to different manufacturers.
- The wholesaler provides a greater opportunity for a retailer to order a number of products at the same time so that transport and packing costs are incurred in respect of a single consignment in place of a number of consignments. This leads to savings in transport and packing costs.
- Wholesalers specialize in a particular line of products. Therefore, he has an expert knowledge of the market conditions relating to such products. He passes on his knowledge to the retailer who cannot posses such knowledge as he deals in a large number of products of different varieties.
- Wholesalers help retailers to take advantage of favorable fluctuations in prices.
- By enabling retailers to replenish their stocks in smaller quantities, wholesalers enable them to operate their business with lesser amount of capital and derive the benefits of economy in space, and more economical sue of capital.
- Wholesalers provide financial assistance of material significance to retailers. This is done by allowing credit to the retailers purchasing goods from them. This in effect helps the retailer to manage his business with smaller amount of working capital.

11.11. Classification of Wholesalers

There are 7 types of wholesalers which are discussed in the following.

Merchant Wholesalers: *These wholesale suppliers own and produce a product or service and resell their products to resellers, retailers, distributors and other wholesalers. If you can buy the products you require direct from the supplier you will usually be able to obtain the best prices and profit margins.*

General Wholesalers: Wholesalers that fall into this category will usually buy large quantities of products from one or more suppliers and will be intending to add value to them by reselling in smaller quantities to distributors, retailers and resellers. This type of wholesale supplier will often have multiple suppliers adding diversity to their product range and choice for their customers. This type of wholesaler may resell products from a number of different industries and in several different categories.

Speciality Wholesalers: This type of wholesaler will resell products in a specific industry or product category, but may have products from multiple suppliers. Because specialty wholesalers specialize in a specific industry or product type they tend to have good product knowledge and good pricing.

Specific Product Wholesalers: These are wholesalers who only supply 1 type of product for example footwear or computers. They may supply several brands but only within one product category. Manufacturers often use this type of wholesaler to distribute one or more of their products.

Discount Wholesalers: This type of wholesaler will supply significantly discounted stock. Generally the stock is discounted because the products are discontinued lines, returned goods or refurbished goods.

Drop Ship Wholesalers: This type of wholesaler will complete the sale of a product but will have it dispatched from their supplier directly to their customer without actually handling the goods.

On-line Wholesaler: Wholesalers who sell their products on-line offer discounted prices as they can reduce their overheads such as rent and rates of physical premises. This type of wholesaler is therefore able to add a lower percentage to their purchase price and still make margin.

A business or person that sells goods to the consumer, as opposed to a wholesaler or supplier, who normally sell their goods to another business.

11.12. Services Rendered by Retailers

Retailers provide important services to both the wholesalers and the consumers. These can be explained as under:

(I) Services To Wholesalers

a) They supply invaluable information with regard to tastes, preferences, fashions and demands of the customers to the wholesalers who in turn transmit the same to the producers which is of immense utility to them.

b) By taking over the function of retailing from the wholesalers and manufacturers, retailer's relive them from selling goods in small quantities to the consumers.

c) Many retailers usually place orders in advance with the wholesalers which is very helpful in planning the purchases of the wholesalers.

d) Sometimes retailers make advance payments for the goods to be received from the wholesalers. In this manner, they help in financing the wholesale trade.

e) Without the services of the retailers a new product cannot be introduced in the market supplied to him by the wholesalers.

(II) Services to Consumers

a) The retailers assemble variety to produces from the wholesaler and place them at the doorstep of the consumers and provide them a convenience of choice.

b) They provide credit facilities to the consumers thereby helping them in times of difficulty.

c) They extend personalized service to the consumers and try to give them maximum satisfaction.

d) They introduce new products to the consumers and also guide them as to their uses.

e) They extend free home delivery and after sales service to the consumers.

f) They allow cash discount to the consumers on the products sold.

g) They buy and stock products best suited to the consumers.

h) They give valuable advice regarding the use and maintenance of the products delivered by them.

i) They cater to the needs of every type of consumer by keeping in view their paying capacity.

j) They supply fresh products to the consumers.

k) They usually take back the goods which do not suit to the consumers and replace them.

11.13. Physical Distribution

Physical distribution is the group of activities associated with the supply of finished product from the production line to the consumers. The physical distribution considers many sales distribution channels, such as wholesale and retail, and includes critical decision areas like customer service, inventory, materials, packaging, order processing, and transportation and logistics. You often will hear these processes be referred to as distribution, which is used to describe the marketing and movement of products. Accounting for nearly half of the entire marketing budget of products, the physical distribution process typically garnishes a lot of attention from business managers and owners. As a result, these activities are often the focus of process improvement and cost-saving initiatives in many companies.

11.14. Objectives of Physical Distribution

The principal objectives of physical distribution are to deliver the right goods to the right customer at the right time and place. In other words, efficiency and satisfactory service are key goals of physical distribution, although there might be some conflicts with each other.

(i) To Give Better Customer Service

By improving the physical distribution system, the company's promotional efforts are strengthened.

(ii) To Enhance Sales

By making sure that basic products in regular demand are always available, and having contingency plans for quick order processing of items.

(iii) To Decrease Cost

By intelligently organizing the physical distribution system and determining the optimum number and location of warehouses, improving materials handling, increasing stock turnover, and using sealed containers to ship products.

11.15. Importance of Physical Distribution System

The importance of physical distribution to a company can vary and is typically associated with the type of product and the necessity it has to customer satisfaction. Strategically staging products in locations to support order shipments and coming up with a rapid and consistent manner to move the product enables companies to be successful in dynamic markets. Physical distribution is managed with a systems approach and considers key interrelated functions to provide efficient movement of products. The functions are interrelated because any time a decision is made in one area it has an effect on the others. For example, a business that is providing custom handbags would consider shipping finished products via air freight versus rail or truck in order to expedite shipment time. The importance of this decision would offset the cost of inventory control, which could be much more costly. Managing physical distribution from a systems approach can provide benefit in controlling costs and meeting customer service demands.

12

MARKETING COMMUNICATION

12.1. Marketing Communication – Meaning and Definition

Marketing communication is a fundamental and complex part of a company's marketing efforts. Marketing communication includes advertising, direct marketing, branding, packaging, your online presence, printed materials, PR activities, sales presentations, sponsorships, trade show appearances and more. Marketing communications is essentially a part of the marketing mix. The marketing mix defines the 4Ps of marketing and Promotion is what marketing communications is all about. It is the message your organization is going to convey to your market. You need to be very particular about different messages you are going to convey through different mediums. Traditionally printed marketing was the whole sole method of conveying the messages to the consumers. However, in recent times, emails, sms, blogs, television and company websites have become the trendy way of conveying the organization's message to the consumers. It is important though that the message you give in one medium should tally with the message provided in other medium. For example, you should use the same logo in on your website as the one you use in your email messages. Similarly, your television messages should convey the same message as your blogs and websites.

12.2. Communication Process

There are certain steps that should be involved in the effective marketing communication process. The marketing and promotional activities should focus on these steps in order to attract a huge portion of long run customers. Following are the steps that make communication process effective.

a) Identification of the Target audience

b) Determination of the communication objectives

c) Designing of Message

d) Message Content

e) Message Structure & Format

f) Choosing Media

g) Collecting Feedback

Each of these is now explained below.

a) Identification of the Target Audience

The first step in the effective marketing communication process is to identify the target audience. These audiences may be potential customers or other people that can influence the decisions of these customers. The audience may include the individuals, groups, general public or special public. The audience has a direct effect on the decisions of the communication, like what to say? How to say? And when to say? Etc.

b) Determination of the Communication Objectives

In this step the marketing communicator should clear the objectives of the Communication Process. In most of the situations, the purchase is required by the marketing communicator, but purchase is made after a prominent customer decision making process. The communicators should also understand the standing position of the customer. Generally there are six. Stages of Customer Readiness through which a customer pass to make a purchase which are as follow.

- Awareness
- Knowledge
- Liking
- Preference
- Conviction
- Purchase

The target group of the marketing communicator is not much familiar with the new product or its silent features. So the marketing communicator should create the awareness and knowledge of its new product and features. But this is not the surety to the success; the new product should also provide superior customer value too.

c) Designing of the Message

In this step the marketing communication, communicator focuses upon the design of the message. Any message that can attract the attention, develop the interest, arousal of desire and stimulate the action is the effectively designed message. This procedure is best known as AIDA model that can make any message effective and potential. Besides this the marketing communicator also decides about the content and structure of the message.

d) Message Content

In this step of the marketing communication process the content of the message is decided. The theme or an appeal is suggested that can bring the desired response from the audience or receiver. Following are the three appeals that should be used in this regard.

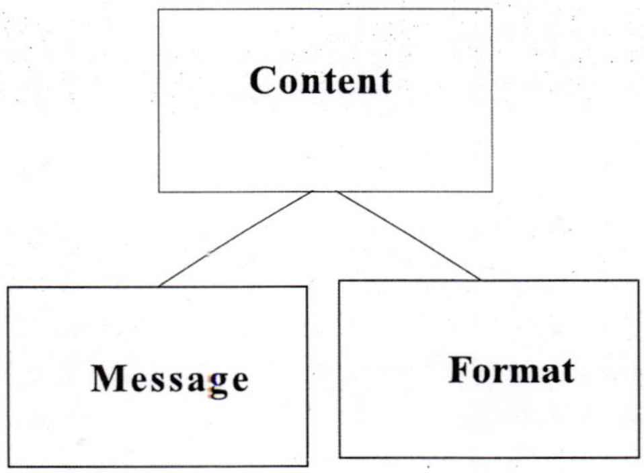

Rational appeal

The self interest of the audience is focused on the rational appeal in which the benefits availed by the usage of the products or services.

Emotional Appeal

In this case positive or negative emotions are stimulated to encourage the purchase of the product.

Moral Appeal

In this situation the morality is included in the message to influence the targeted customers.

e. Message Structure & Format

In this step the important issues of the message structure together with the message format is analyzed. In marketing communication of a product, it must be decided that the message must include the conclusion or may keep to the audience to get a conclusion from them. Or the massage presents either only the strengths of the product or both the strengths and weaknesses. Moreover the format of the message is also focused on which the size and shape use, eye-catching colors, and headlines etc are decided in the most effective manner.

f. Choosing Media

The channels of communication are decided in this step of a marketing communication process, which may take the following two forms.

Personal

In this channel of communication two or more persons directly communicate with each other like face to face, through the mail, on the telephone, or through a chat on the internet. Personal Addressing and feedback is allowed in the personal communication.

Non Personal

Non personal messages are spread through these channels which also excludes the option of feedback. Such channels include print media, display media, broadcast media, online media etc.

g. Collecting Feedback

This is the last step of the marketing communication process in which the feedback from the target customers. This can help the marker to alter the promotion program or other marketing activities. For this purpose the buying behavior of targeted customers is analyzed in the light of the New Product. Questions may also be asked to the customers to collect their views about the positive and negative aspects of the new product.

12.3. Objectives of Communication

Marketing communication is how you stay in touch with and convey important information about your company to your customers. Communication vehicles can include newsletters, websites, e-mail correspondence and other written materials. The content and design of these pieces of communication must meet the objectives of educating, encouraging action or building brand awareness.

Sales

Communicating with your customers keeps them apprised of new happenings in your business and fulfills the objective of promoting your products and services. This can include new product launches, sales, expansion or introduction of new offerings. The objective of this form of marketing communication is to encourage customers to act or to keep them involved with your business. One example of sales marketing communication is an e-mail blast that informs consumers about an upcoming, limited-time sale and provides a link to the company's online product catalog where they can immediately take advantage of the savings opportunity.

Education

Many effective forms of marketing communication provide customers or potential customers with information about your product, service, business or industry. For example, an accountant that publishes and distributes a newsletter on tax tips is establishing himself as a expert in the industry by way of educating the public about basic accounting practices. The objective of this form of marketing communication is to establish the knowledge of the business and its expertise, while encouraging people to use more in-depth services.

Retention

An objective of effective marketing communication is to retain your existing customers and increase their investment in your business. Establishing customer reward programs that are presented through marketing mediums like direct mail help achieve this. Letting your customers know you appreciate their business and presenting them with opportunities to save money, while at the same time up selling them to new, more or better products, results in increased income for your small business.

Referral

Bringing in new business by way of existing customers is an objective of marketing communication practices. Communicating with existing customers via social media, email and your website and encouraging them to refer you to others creates an independent sales team that works on your behalf. Rewarding customers for their referrals further solidifies your relationship with them at the same time.

Brand Awareness

Every communication message you share should reinforce your brand image in the mind of consumers. This can be accomplished through consistent messaging and a commonly-used color scheme, logo and graphic design on all marketing materials. Consumers will associate your message and image with your product, creating a strong brand identity.

12.4. Importance of Communication in Marketing

Effective communication is a building block of successful organizations". In other words, communication acts as organizational blood.

- Communication promotes motivation by informing and clarifying the employees about the task to be done, the manner they are performing the task, and how to improve their performance if it is not up to the mark.
- Communication is a source of information to the organizational members for decision-making process as it helps identifying and assessing alternative course of actions.
- Communication also plays a crucial role in altering individual's attitudes, i.e., a well informed individual will have better attitude than a less-informed individual. Organizational magazines, journals, meetings and various other

forms of oral and written communication help in moulding employee's attitudes.

- Communication also helps in socializing. In today's life the only presence of another individual fosters communication. It is also said that one cannot survive without communication.
- As discussed earlier, communication also assists in controlling process. It helps controlling organizational member's behavior in various ways. There are various levels of hierarchy and certain principles and guidelines that employees must follow in an organization. They must comply with organizational policies, perform their job role efficiently and communicate any work problem and grievance to their superiors. Thus, communication helps in controlling function of management.

12.5. Barriers to Communication

Common Barriers to Effective Communication are discussed in the following:

The use of jargon. Over-complicated, unfamiliar and/or technical terms.

Emotional barriers and taboos. Some people may find it difficult to express their emotions and some topics may be completely 'off-limits' or taboo.

Lack of attention, interest, distractions, or irrelevance to the receiver.

Differences in perception and viewpoint.

Physical disabilities such as hearing problems or speech difficulties.

Physical barriers to non-verbal communication. Not being able to see the non-verbal cues, gestures, posture and general body language can make communication less effective.

Language differences and the difficulty in understanding unfamiliar accents.

Expectations and prejudices which may lead to false assumptions or stereotyping. People often hear what they expect to hear rather than what is actually said and jump to incorrect conclusions.

Cultural differences: The norms of social interaction vary greatly in different cultures, as do the way in which emotions are expressed. For example, the concept of personal space varies between cultures and between different social settings.

12.6. Marketing Communication and Four Ps

The four Ps are the categories that are involved in the marketing of a good or service, and they include product, price, place and promotion. Often referred to as the marketing mix, the four Ps are constrained by internal and external factors in the overall business environment, and they interact significantly with one another.

12.7. Product

Product refers to a good or service being offered by a company. Ideally, a product should meet a certain consumer demand, or it should be so compelling that consumers believe they need it. To be successful, marketers should understand the life cycle of a product, and business executives should have a plan for dealing with products at every stage of their life cycles. The type of product also partially dictates how much businesses can charge for it, where they should place it, and how they should promote it.

12.8. Place

Place decisions outline where the product is sold and how it is delivered to the market. The goal of business executives is to get their products in front of the consumers who are most likely to buy them. In some cases, this may refer to placing a product in certain stores, but it also refers to the placement of the product on a store's display or where a product is showcased on a web page. In some cases, placement may refer to the act of placing a product on TV shows, films or blogs in order to garner attention for the product, but this type of placement overlaps with promotion.

12.9. Price

Price is the cost consumers pay for a product. Marketers must link the price to the real and perceived value of the product, but they also must take into account supply costs, seasonal discounts, and prices used by competitors. In some cases, business executives may manipulate a price to make a product seem more like a luxury, or they may lower a price so that more consumers can try the product.

12.10. Promotion

Promotion includes advertising, public relations and promotional strategy. This ties into the other three Ps of the marketing mix, as promoting a product shows consumers why they need it and why they should be willing to pay a certain price for it. In addition, marketers tend to tie promotion and placement elements together so they can reach their core audiences.

13

PROMOTION DECISION – I

13.1. Promotion – Meaning and Definition

Promotions refer to the entire set of activities, which communicate the product, brand or service to the user. The idea is to make people aware, attract and induce to buy the product, in preference over others. Market promotion can help company realize various objectives. Company can increase sales, improve its image, and maintain close and live contact with the market by suitable promotional efforts. A company's survival, growth, and development are based on how effectively it communicates with the market. Promotion is one of the marketing mix elements among a system of five in a promotional plan (often known as the five Ps). These elements are personal selling, advertising, sales promotion, direct marketing, and publicity. A promotional mix specifies how much attention to pay to each of the five subcategories, and how much money to budget for each. A promotional plan can have a wide range of objectives, including: sales increases, new product acceptance, creation of brand equity, positioning, competitive retaliations, or creating a corporate image. Fundamentally, however, there are three basic objectives of promotion:

- To present information to consumers as well as others
- To increase demand
- To differentiate a product from others in the marketplace

There are different ways to promote a product in different areas of media. Promoters use Internet advertisement, special events, endorsements, and newspapers or magazines to advertise their product. Many times with the purchase of a product there are incentives like discounts, free items, or contests. These methods are used to increase the sales of a given product. Marketing strategy is a process that can allow an organization to concentrate its limited resources on the greatest opportunities to increase sales and achieve a sustainable, competitive advantage. Marketing strategy includes all basic and long-term activities in the field of marketing that deal with the analysis of the strategic situation of a company and the formulation, evaluation and selection of market-oriented strategies and therefore contribute to the goals of the company and its marketing objectives. Marketing strategies may differ depending on the unique situation of the individual business or product. However, there are a number of ways to categorize some generic strategies.

13.2. Objectives of Promotion

Main objectives of market promotion can be described with reference to below stated points.

To Stimulate Demand

It is the primary objective of market promotion. Through the use of appropriate means of market promotion, such as advertising, sales promotion, personal selling, and so forth, the company can stimulate demand for the product. Market promotion efforts convert potential buyers into actual buyers. Company, by highlighting product benefits, tries to match the product with needs, wants, and expectations of buyers. As per need, various means of market promotion are used to establish the information link with the target customers.

To Inform Consumers

Promotion is aimed at informing consumers about features, qualities, performance, price, and availability of firm's products. Market promotion is also a valuable means to inform consumers the changes made in the existing products and introduction of new products. In the same way, market promotion, by various tools of market communication, is used for communicating the special offers, price concession, utility of products, and incentives offered by the company.

To Persuade Consumers

Market promotion is an effective way to persuade consumers the superiority of product over competitors. A firm can communicate competitive advantages the product offers to distinguish it from competitors' products. Obviously, market promotion can assist the firm to convince buyers that the firm's product is the best solution to their unmet needs and wants. Advertising is one of the most effective tools to distinguish the product from competitors' products.

To Promote a New Product

In a large and decentralized market, market promotion is an inevitable medium to promote a new product. By suitable promotional strategies, a company can successfully introduce a new product in the market as against existing products.

Company can inform about availability, distinct features, and price of newly launched product. In every stage of consumer adoption of a new product, market promotion has critical role to play.

To Face Competition

Market promotion enables the firm to face competition effectively. In today's market situation, it is difficult to stand without the suitable promotional efforts. In short, it can be said that marketer can fight with competitors effectively, can prevent their entry, or can throw the competitor away from the market by formulating and implementing effective market promotion strategies.

To Create or Improve Image

Advertising, personal selling, and publicity and public relations all promotional tools are capable to create or improve image and reputation of the firm. Many companies have become popular in the market due to effective market promotion. Company can reach the customers at every corner of the world through market promotion. Brand image is purely an outcome of promotional efforts. For example, Hindustan Unilever, Colgate Palmolive, Sony, Philips, Hero Honda, Ambuja Cement, and many national and multinational companies have made their permanent place in the market due to successfully launching of market promotion programmes.

13.3. Methods of Promotion

Promotions is the part of marketing that specifically involves communicating company or product information to targeted customers. This is a key component of the broader marketing system, because it is what usually makes customers aware of you, attracted to your brand, interested in buying and ultimately, loyal customers. Advertising, public relations and personal selling are three staple methods of promotion, though some new techniques have emerged in the early 21st century.

Advertising

Advertising takes up a significant portion of a company's budget allocated toward marketing and promotion. It includes the development and paid delivery of brand or product messages through media. Companies usually have internal advertising departments that design and develop ads, or they work with advertising firms who specialize in the advertising process. Since you pay for ad placement in media such as television, radio, newspapers and magazines, you generally have more control over the message than you do through some other promotional methods.

Public Relations

Maintaining goodwill with the public is an important long-term strategy for both small and large companies. A variety of public relations tactics are used to reach out to customers through unpaid-for media messages. Press releases are one of the most common and routine PR tactics. This is when a company sends an overview of a major change or event, product launch or other news to various media outlets. Press conferences, features news reports and newsletters are other common PR tools. A general objective of PR is to keep your brand in front of people even beyond paid ads. The challenge is you can't always control the way your PR messages are delivered or received.

Selling

While business typically engages in some level of advertising and public relations, the use of personal selling tactics varies considerably. Some small businesses don't employ active sales associates based on the small-scale products or services they sell. Companies with big-ticket items, such as electronics or appliances, more often use sales associates to stress the benefits of products to customers and to overcome their concerns. Selling is one of the most interactive forms of promotion.

Digital/Interactive

The evolution of the Internet and related technologies has given rise to digital and interactive promotional methods. Email marketing, online advertising and mobile advertising have all become common components of promotional campaigns. These methods are often relatively affordable for small businesses and offer direct connections to tech-savvy consumers who spend significant time online. Social media portals such as Twitter, Facebook and YouTube also provide inexpensive ways to interact with customers in real time.

13.4. Factors Determining of Promotion–Mix

The factors which are responsible for determining the promotion-mix are discussed in the following.

Nature of Product: The different type of product requires different promotional tools. Such as, for the industrial products Viz. Machinery, equipment or land personal selling is more appropriate as a great deal of pre-sale and after-sale services is required to sell and install such products. On the other hand, advertising and publicity are more suitable for the consumer goods, especially the convenience goods.

Nature of Market: The number and location of customers greatly influence the promotion mix. In case the groups of potential customers is small and are concentrated in a particular locality, then personal selling is more likely to be effective. Whereas, if the customer base is large and widespread, then the blend of advertising, personal selling, and the sales promotion is required to sell the product. Also, the type of customers influences the managerial decisions of the promotion mix. The type of promotion for the urban, educated and institutional customers would be different as compared to the rural, illiterate and household customers.

Stage of Product's Life: The promotion mix changes as the product moves along its life cycle. During the introduction stage, the principal objective of the promotion is to create the primary demand by emphasizing the product's features, utility, etc. therefore, the blend of advertising and publicity is required. As the product reaches its maturity stage the advertising and personal selling is required to maintain the demand of the customers. And finally, during the decline stage the expenses on other promotional activities are cut, and more emphasis is laid on sales promotion with the intent to push up the declining sales.

Availability of Funds: The marketing budget also decides the promotion mix. If the funds available for the promotion are large, then the blend of promotional tools can be used, whereas in the case the funds are limited then the management must choose the promotional tool wisely.

Nature of Technique: Each element of the promotional mix has unique features that significantly influence the purpose of promotion. Such as, the advertising is an impersonal mode of communication that reaches a large group of customers. Its expression can be amplified with the use of colors and sound that helps in developing the long lasting brand image in the minds of the customer. The Personal selling involves face to face interaction that helps in developing cordial and personal relations with the customers. Likewise, the sales promotion is short-term incentives given to the customers with the intent to boost sales for a shorter period of time.

Promotional Strategy: The promotion mix largely depends on the company's promotional strategy, i.e. whether it accepts the Push Strategy or a Pull Strategy. In a Push strategy, the manufacturer forces the dealers to carry the product and promote it to the customer, i.e. convince the potential buyers to buy it. Here, personal selling and trade promotion are likely to be more effective. In the case of a Pull Strategy, the consumers ask the dealers to carry the product, i.e. customers themselves purchase the product. Here, advertising and consumer promotion are more appropriate.

Readiness of Buyer: Different promotional tools are required at different stages of buyer readiness. Such as, at the comprehension stage, the blend of advertising and personal selling plays a vital role. Whereas at the conviction stage, personal selling is more effective. At the time of sales closure, the blend of sales promotion and personal selling is likely to be more effective. Hence, the advertising and publicity are more effective at the early stages of buying decision process while the sales promotion and personal selling are more effective during the later stages.

13.5. Personal Selling

Personal selling is a promotional method in which one party (e.g., salesperson) uses skills and techniques for building personal relationships with another party (e.g., those involved in a purchase decision) that results in both parties obtaining value. In most cases the "value" for the salesperson is realized through the financial rewards of the sale while the customer's "value" is realized from the benefits obtained by consuming the product. However, getting a customer to purchase a product is not always the objective of personal selling. For instance, selling may be used for the purpose of simply delivering information.

13.6. Features of Personal Selling

Main features of personal selling are:

- *Personal Form*: Under personal selling a personal contact is established between the buyers and the salesman. In other words, both the parties face each other.
- *Development of Relationship*: Personal selling results in the development of personal relationship between the sales person and the possible buyer. Such a relationship has an important place in sales.
- *Oral Conversation*: There is oral conversation between the sales person and the buyer regarding the features of the product, i.e., price, colour, shape, design, method of using, etc.
- *Quick solution of Queries*: The prospective buyer can make inquiries regarding the product. Salesman answers these queries quickly and removes any doubts in the mind of the buyer.
- *Receipt of Additional Information*: Normally, before introducing its product, a company is aware of the preferences of the probable buyers. Nevertheless, during the course of personal selling, when the sales person is in direct contact with the buyers he/she gathers additional information regarding their tastes and likings.
- *Real Sale*: Under personal selling, the buyers are not only informed about the product but the goods are actually sold to them.

13.7. Importance of Personal Selling

Following points explain the importance or benefits of personal selling:

- *Two-Way Communication*: It is the best tool for two-way communication. Salesman can provide necessary information to customer about company's offer, and also can collect information from customer. Customer can actively involve with salesman to solve his doubts and objections. It is not possible in any other methods of market promotion.

- *Personal Attention*: Advertising and publicity are among mass communication tools. They do not cater individual needs. Personal selling focuses on personal problems of customers. It is comparatively more effective and result-oriented.
- *Detail Demonstration*: Except television advertisements, demonstration is not possible. However, television demonstration is much limited. Salesman can provide a detail demonstration and can supervise when customer is making the actual use of products. For technical products, it has more relevance.
- *Complementary to other Promotional Tools*: Personal selling can support advertising, sales promotion, and publicity. It removes the drawbacks of advertising and sales promotion. Advertising increases awareness while personal selling reinforces the advertising message. Similarly, it can make sales promotion tools more effective by personal guidance or conviction.
- *Immediate Feedback*: This is the only market promotion technique that provides an immediate feedback. At the end of every call/visit, a salesman can easily judge whether the customer is interested or indented to buy.
- *Individual Services*: Salesmanship offers individual services. It can meet personal expectations of buyers. It leads to customer satisfaction.
- *Flexibility*: Sales talks and presentation can be adjusted according to situation to suit individual nature, motives, and problems.
- *Customer Confidence*: By systematic sales talk and presentation, a capable salesman can remove all doubts, quarries, objections and misunderstandings, and can win customer's confidence. It increases customers' faith in company and its offers.
- *Triple Rewards*: Salesmanship offers triple rewards. It benefits all parties, including customer, salesman, and company. Customer is satisfied with products and services; salesman can achieve his targets; and company can improve its market share and profits.
- *Improving Image*: Note that salesmanship can remove bad image or misunderstanding by highlighting company's achievements and offers. The detailed explanation about company and its products removes all doubts and misunderstandings. It helps in restoring company image and reputation in market.

13.8. Merits of Personal Selling

Some of the merits of personal selling are discussed in the following.

- Flexibility and Adaptability
- Minimum Wastage
- It creates Impinging and Lasting Impressions
- It generates Gainful Employment Opportunities
- Improving the Living Standards of Teeming Millions
- Salesmanship makes the Economic System more Stable

13.9. Demerits Personal Selling

Some of the demerits of personal selling are discussed in the following.

- It is Expensive
- Problem of Getting Gifted Salesman
- High Stake in Consumer Loyalty
- More Administrative Problems
- It is not an easy Profession
- As a Profession has Little Respect
- Mark of Fraud
- Bad Pay-masters

13.10. Salesmanship: Meaning and Definition

Practice of investigating and satisfying customer needs through a process that is efficient, fair, sincere, mutually beneficial, and aimed at long-term productive relationship.

13.11. Features of Salesmanship

The important features of Salesmanship are:

- Personal Selling is Oral Presentation
- Personal Selling is the Ability to Persuade
- Personal Selling creates and retains Customers
- Service First to anything Else

- Personal Selling works for Mutual Gain
- Personal Selling is an Educative Process
- Personal Selling is a Creative Process
- Sales Person is the Ambassador of the Firm

13.12. Qualities of Successful Salesman

Some of the qualities which are highly required to become a successful sales professional are discussed in the following.

Conscientiousness

This trait is found in people who take great pride in their work, are organized and efficient. But, if you are not organized and efficient, you can learn to be. Conscientious also means you keep going in your job, no matter what.

Respectful

- Part of doing this is making sure that they have time and you schedule time for work. People want the bottom line. Old tactics don't work. People are busy, respect their time above all.
- You have to make sure that your customers and potential customers are treated like gold."

Initiative

Sales reps don't wait for orders. They're go-getters and take matters into their own hands. Being disciplined like this helps salesmen to stay on track.

They listen

When you listen to your clients/customers, you find out what they want and need, and how to make that happen. If you don't know exactly how to make happen what your client has asked for, be absolutely sure that*there is a way.* You just haven't found it, yet.

Persistent

You have to have thick-skin to be a salesperson. Why? Because you're going to become very familiar with the word "no." You have to be confident and persistent if you want to remain involved with sales.

Coachable

Being energetic, willing to learn and having the ability to adapt are all a part of being "coachable." Coachable means an early adopter of the suggestion.

Positive

Having a positive attitude and being cheerful makes it easier to approach customers and keep their attention until after you've made the sale. This positive attitude exudes from a person.

Resourceful

The true salesmen are able to shift gears if a sale isn't going the way that they envisioned. Instead of just taking "no" as an answer, they will attempt a different approach by using their creativity and imagination.

Passionate

A top-notch salesperson actually enjoys their job. If you hate it, change or get out. Most importantly, the salesman will be passionate about the products or services that they're selling. If they're on board with a brand' message, they can excitedly share that vision with prospective clients and customers. Happy, positive, love it, passionate.

Ask questions

Searcy states that there is data that has discovered "that the higher-performing sales representatives ask more questions often more than twice as many." But, these salespeople don't ask questions that focus solely on data.

Independent

The salesman is a self-motivator. The independent salesperson can build themselves up to do more. They can pat themselves on the back and appreciate their own greatness. Most independent salespeople do not have to be thanked for each call or sales, they know how to say, "Good job, me!"

Time managers

Here's a simple equation: more selling time increases sales and compensation. The best salespeople manage their time effectively, such as finding the best routes from location to location, so that they have more opportunities and time to spend securing a sale. If one place or person takes too long, or longer than expected, the time manager makes up for it somewhere else.

Overachieve

Author and sales expert Grant Cardone informed Open Forum that salespeople should "over commit and over-deliver." You have to go above and beyond. True salespeople don't know when to stop and typically are pushing for more. More people, more clients, more work, more money, just more. The quality more.

Personable

A great salesperson has no problem getting along with others. And, most importantly, they enjoy meeting new people and realize the power of networking. It's not surprising to see salespeople involved with so many local events and organizations. Most sales people love people, and it shows. They are energized by people. They go home and can hardly sleep after an event.

Alertness

Salespeople are always prepared. They have to be ready for any situation that they're thrown into and know how to successfully break free. The salesperson is aware of herself and her body. If she is not alert, she has felt it coming on and taken care of it. Caffeine up, run up and down the block or eat less, they do whatever it takes. Alertness is key to so many of the principles of being a great salesperson.

13.13. Kinds of Salesman

Main categories that a salesman's are generally divided are as follows:

- Manufacturer's salesman
- Wholesaler's salesman
- Retail salesman
- Specialty salesman
- Industrial salesman
- The exporter's salesman

13.14. Selling Process

The selling process is generally divided into seven steps that, once you understand them, will empower you to sell virtually anything you want and satisfy your customers:

- Prospect and qualify
- Preapproach
- Approach
- Presentation
- Overcome objections

- Close the sale
- Follow-up

Each step of the seven-step process is covered thoroughly in this and the next six chapters so that you can learn the details of each step and how to apply them in various selling situations.

14

PROMOTION DECISION –II

14.1. Advertising – Meaning and Definition

Advertising is bringing a product (or service) to the attention of potential and current customers. Advertising is focused on one particular product or service. Thus, an advertising plan for one product might be very different than that for another product. Advertising is typically done with signs, brochures, commercials, direct mailings or e-mail messages, personal contact, etc.

14.2. Objectives of Advertising

Main Objectives of advertising are mentioned in the following.

- Trial
- Continuity
- Brand switch
- Switching back

Let's take a look on these various types of objectives.

Trial: the companies which are in their introduction stage generally work for this objective. The trial objective is the one which involves convincing the customers to buy the new product introduced in the market. Here, the advertisers use flashy and attractive ads to make customers take a look on the products and purchase for trials.

Continuity: this objective is concerned about keeping the existing customers to stick on to the product. The advertisers here generally keep on bringing something new in the product and the advertisement so that the existing customers keep buying their products.

Brand switch: this objective is basically for those companies who want to attract the customers of the competitors. Here, the advertisers try to convince the customers to switch from the existing brand they are using to their product.

Switching back: this objective is for the companies who want their previous customers back, who have switched to their competitors. The advertisers use different ways to attract the customers back like discount sale, new advertise, some reworking done on packaging, etc.

Basically, advertising is a very artistic way of communicating with the customers. The main characteristics one should have to get on their objectives are great communication skills and very good convincing power.

14.3. Functions of Advertising

Advertising has become an essential marketing activity in the modern era of large-scale production and severe competition in the market.

It performs the following functions:

(i) Promotion of Sales

Advertising promotes the sale of goods and services by informing and persuading the people to buy them. A good advertising campaign helps in winning customers and generating revenues.

(ii) Introduction of New Products

Advertising helps in the introduction of new products in the market. A business enterprise can introduce itself and its products to the public through advertising. Advertising enables quick publicity in the market.

(iii) Support to Production System

Advertising facilitates large-scale production. The business firm knows that it will be able to sell on a large-scale with the help of advertising. Mass production will reduce the cost of production per unit by making possible the economical use of various factors of production.

(iv) Increasing Standard of Living

Advertising educates the people about the products and their uses. It is advertising which has helped people in adopting new ways of life and giving up old habits. It has contributed a lot towards the betterment of the standard of living of the society.

(v) Public Image

Advertising builds up the reputation of the advertiser. Advertising enables a business firm to communicate its achievements and its efforts to satisfy the customers' needs to the public. This increases the goodwill and reputation of the firm.(vi) Support to Media: Advertising sustains press. Advertising provides an important source of revenue to the publishers of newspapers and magazines and the producers of T.V. programmes.

14.4. Role of Advertising

The role of advertising is discussed in the following.

I. Manufacturers and Advertising

Manufacturers and producers, who intend to make available goods to the people at profit, do take full advantage of advertising as a major weapon to popularize their products and services. The specific benefits that accrue to the manufacturers are:

a) It increases and stabilizes the sales turnover

Even the best product cannot be sold on its own, though it is said "good wine needs no bush". People should know that the product is the best. In a highly sensitive and competitive mechanism, profits of the firm cannot be maximized by mere reducing the costs but by multiplying the sales-turnover. Advertising does this, by changing the consumer attitude favorably. Further, the sales turnover rate so attained should be maximized and maintained at any rate. Advertising does this by repeat sales. A regular, effective and frequent advertising helps in building more loyal class of customers at all times.

b) It maintains the existing market and explores the new

A forward looking company always has its eyes on the future business prospects though it cannot lose sight of the current position. A company's success is reflected not only in creating market but its maintenance and extension. It is a natural feeling that when advertising campaign decreases, the products are not measured up to, the consumer expectations. Further, current business situations warrant a forceful entry into new markets. In such newly exposed markets, advertising does spade-work for the sponsor to sow the seeds of prosperity.

c) It controls product prices

Through advertising, it is possible to control the product prices with profit, particularly the retail prices. Very often the greedy retailers exploit the needy consumers by charging higher prices. If this consumer exploitation is not bridled, both the producers and consumers are to suffer for no fault of theirs. The manufacturer can help him and help consumers by printing the consumer prices on the product packages. In current context, product package protects not only the contents of it but also the consumer interest.

II. Middlemen and Advertising

In the chain of distribution, middlemen act as the essential links between the producers and the consumers. Their existence is justified by the functions they perform and the services they render. Here, benefits of advertising are seen from angle of retailer a last link in the chain of distribution.

a) It guarantees quick sales

Every retailer holding the stocks of different producers is interested in quick turnover. Advertising, by bringing these whole ranges of products to the notice of consumers, quickens the pace of sales. Faster sales imply the specific advantages such as reduced capital lock-up, loss of stock, and increased profits. Advertising gives him much leeway and freedom to better serve the needs of consumers. Therefore, he earns better by serving better.

b) It acts as salesman

Advertising has been rightly described as salesmanship in print. What a travelling salesman does for the selling house is done by advertising at least cost. That is why; most retail organizations do not employ large army of travelling salesmen.

Instead, they are willing to spend on advertising which attracts consumers to the stores where the counter salesmen cater to their needs. In fact, advertising has been heralded as a boon to retailers who are freed from the problems of sales management. In fact, goods are sold in advance by advertising.

c) It makes retail price maintenance possible

The consumers are very keen on getting quality products at stable price over a longer period of time. Each consumer has his or her own family budget which he or she strives hard to match the expenditure to the disposable income for a socially acceptable decent living. If the prices go on changing abruptly, those individual budgets are likely to be distorted to such an extent that the consumers have to think of substitutes for the products they are enjoying at present. The budget tally may involve even the shift in the brand preference. Consumers behave a sigh of relief because; the advertised products publish the retail prices that are likely to be in force at least for three to six months and in some cases over a year.

III. Sales-Force and Advertising

Sales of the selling house are the result of the efforts put in by both direct and indirect approached. Personal selling is the direct method of selling, while advertising is indirect. Both are important in the scheme of successful marketing. Both are to be dovetailed for the best results. The sales-force stands benefitted as under:

a) It creates colourful background

A good salesman is nothing less than an actor who by his skill in selling wins the hearts of consumers and sells the company products and services. All such sales acumen has value and the glamour only when he has a matching back-drop.

He may be agile, tactful, versatile salesman but the extent of his success is resting heavily on the colourful back-ground created by the advertising. Salesmanship without advertising is like a song without music or a whisky without water. Advertising creates stage for him for his acting to stage effects to magnify his performance.

b) It reduces his burden of job

In case salesman alone is called upon to accept the challenge of selling, it goes much difficult. In absence of advertising, he is forced to play a double role the role of advertising and that of salesmanship both rolled into one. Advertising provokes public interest, wins the confidence, and promotes conviction. With such ready back-ground, salesman can capitalize easily to sell well. As advertising sells between the calls, the work of salesman is rendered easier and cozier.

c) It instills self-confidence

The victory of a selling house is conditioned by the nature or quality of sales-force rather than its quantity or number. A sales-force that is self-confident and drive-packed is an asset than the army needing a big push without self-start. Advertising, by educating sales-force, acts a creative force as it instills self-confidence, initiative and drive in them. Advertising gears the salesmen to the top by making them self- confident and self-starting.

d) Consumers and Advertising

The final aim of all marketing efforts is to satisfy the needs of consumers by transmitting the benefits of productive efficiency to the final users. Advertising is an essential concomitant of modern marketing mechanism that helps consumers in three ways:

i) It is a driving-force in decision-making

The present-day complex world of industry has been able to provide with the largest possible varieties of products to such an extent that the consumers are at loss to decide. Further, each producer claims that his own products are the best. In such situation, it is advertising that comes to the rescue of a consumer to select the best by providing him with comparative account of each in terms of features, prices, utility, quality, durability, convenience and the like, the consumer finds it easy to decide with such ready information.

ii) It ensures better quality products at reasonable prices

Advertising stimulates the sales of a good product and accelerates the destruction of bad product or products by imprinting the image of the product on the minds of the consumers and earn a long standing reputation for the manufacturing house. It is the work of branding to build the image because; every brand stands for quality, value, guarantee, price and service. This means that a rupee paid has definite value received. Maintenance of quality and price of a product is important not only as an objective but as a bench-mark for quality improvement and price reduction.

iii) It saves good deal of time

The modern gracious living has made the members of the family to put forth their best to make both the ends to meet. In the past, the things were cheaper and the requirements were limited. Hence, it was enough for a single member to earn the bread for the entire family. However, today's crazes for too many things and the mounting inflation have made more members of the family to contribute to the family income. Each one has joined the rat race of earning more where he is racing against the limited time. Today, the people are so busy that they pant for the arrival of Sunday to have badly needed rest. For such people, advertising is a great time- saver. Advertising saves time in the sense that it sells the goods and services well in advance. That is, through the ads, people know about products and services they are to only contact the selling outlets to get them.

iv. Society and Advertising

Advertising is both a business and social force and institution. As a business and social process, it affects every-one in the society. The society stands to benefit as under:

i) It uplifts the living standards

Advertising nourishes the consumer power and creates wants for better standard of living. Standard of living depends on the national income and its distribution on one hand and the consumption pattern on the other hand with relevance to disposable income. Advertising gives kick to the consumption pattern making them to buy more and more; this results in more, better and cheaper production; increased production means more employment and more earnings and, therefore, more spending. Thus, more, better and cheaper production will be in the easy reach of people with low income packets even enabling them to enjoy higher standard of living.

ii) It generates gainful employment opportunities

Advertising is capable of generating gainful employment opportunities directly and indirectly for those who have talent and courage. Direct employment opportunities are wide open in the varied branches of the every growing field of advertising. It is highly specialized and challenging area requiring the services of talented people like artists, painters, photographers, message writers, singers, campers, musicians, carpenters, press men, actors and actresses, technicians, agents and executives too. It is these persons who handle the meticulous and delicate tasks. Indirectly, it has given employment by supporting all those industries that supply input to these advertising activities such as paper paints, colours and dyes, electric, electronic, steel and other metal industries. This employment generation is of special importance to the developing countries like India.

iii) It provides new horizons of knowledge

Advertising is a great educator. It is a form of education. Every advertiser has something to share with the society. Thus, employer speaks of job vacancies and an idle candidate solicits job; parents hunt brides and bride-grooms; some announces the arrival of a baby while others the departure of old; producers speak of their products, service or the idea that they propose to sell.Each ad is a piece of information and has a theme behind. To convey the theme, the advertising copy tells a story, gives a statistical profile, narrates a history, gives enchanting illustrations that we have never heard and seen. Thus, it is educator and entertainer.

iv)It up-holds the culture of a nation

Culture is man-made environment in which he lives along with others. It stands for the values of life and living. These values are subject to change and are guided by the dynamics of social, political, economic and ethical dimensions. The cultural function of advertising is to understand, reflex and accept the value structure of society well before it vanishes. Advertising, within the limits, set by the culture, is to create new expectation for the consumers.

14.5. Advertising vs. .Personal Selling

Advertising is one of the widely used techniques of promotion, wherein modes like television, radio, newspapers, internet, etc. are used for creating demand or interest of the customers towards the product or services offered by the company. On the other hand, personal selling is the verbal communication of the message, to one or more customers, so as to create sales. Both advertising and personal selling are two major elements of promotion mix, which is employed by the organization to reach communication objectives. Advertising differs from personal selling, in the fact that the former is a monolog activity, but the latter is dialogue. To further comprehend the difference between advertising and personal selling, take a read of the article given below. There are hundreds of advertisements, that we go through almost every day that are used for commercial or social purposes. These are messages, which reach us through various mediums; though we do not recognize them they are present. Personal selling involves direct contact between the seller and buyer. It is one of the best techniques used for business customers.

The comparison between advertising and personal selling is showing in the following chart.

Basis For Comparison	Advertising	Personal Selling
Meaning	Advertising is a means of communication, which calls customer's attention towards the product or service, through mass media.	Personal selling refers to a form of promotion, wherein the sales representative sells the product to customers, by directly visiting them.
Communication	One-way communication	Two-way communication
Form	Impersonal form of communication	Personal form of communication
Strategy	Pull strategy	Push strategy
Message	Standardised	Customised
Channel	Mass media	Sales personnel
Time	Conveys message to end number of individual in less time.	Conveys message to a few customers only in relatively high time.
Feedback	Lacks direct feedback	Facilitates direct and instant feedback

Definition of Advertising

Advertising can be defined as the act of drawing the attention of the target audience, towards a product or service. It is an impersonal, paid message, delivered to the general public with the sole aim of creating demand for the product and thus increasing sales. It has a great role to play in marketing, to make people aware of the product. The sponsors of the advertisement have full control over it. The advertising message is aired through various channels like radio, television, magazines, newspapers, posters, billboards, websites, blogs, apps, text messages, social networks, e-mail, etc. Advertising aims at creating such an image in the minds of the audience, that they are instigated to purchase that product. The greatest advantage of advertising is its range, i.e. it reaches a large number of people in one go.

Definition of Personal Selling

Personal Selling, as the name signifies, is a promotional tool, where companies use sales force, to increase sales of product and services. Under personal selling, there is a face to face meeting between the clients or customers and the sales representative, wherein the representatives visit customers personally, so as to transact a sale, by offering and inducing them to make a purchase. Personal Selling involves developing a strong relationship with customers, discovering their needs and providing them such products, which satisfy their needs. The process requires huge workforce to cover the entire market. Moreover, proper training is also an important requirement of this process, to deal with different types of customers and instigating them to buy the product.

Key Differences between Advertising and Personal Selling

The fundamental difference between advertising and personal selling, are as follows:

a) Advertising alludes to paid form of communication, which commercializes product or service, offered by an identified sponsor, to increase sales. On the other hand, a form of promotion, wherein the sales personnel sells the product to customers, by directly visiting them, is known as personal selling.

b) While advertising is a one-way communication, wherein the message is transmitted to the customers, personal selling is a two-way communication, wherein the message is transmitted to customers, as well as feedback is provided simultaneously.

c) Advertising is a non-personal form of communication the message reaches the target audience after it is being aired. On the contrary, personal selling, as the name suggest involves salesman visit to customer's place individually, which is a personal form of communication.

d) Advertising uses pull strategy, which draws public attention and persuades them to buy the product. As against, personal selling uses push strategy, which induces them to buy the product.

e) In advertising, the flexibility is missing, as the message is standardized and cannot be changed according to customers. In contrast, personal selling uses customized messages.

f) Advertising uses mass media, like radio, television, hoardings, the internet, blogs, apps, newspaper, etc. On the flip side, in personal selling, salesman delivers the message, personally to the target audience.

g) Advertising conveys a message to end number of individual in less time. As against this, personal selling conveys the message to a few customers only in relatively high time.

h) There is a lack of feedback in advertising, whereas, in personal selling, feedback is always present.

14.6. Types of Advertising

The different types of advertising are discussed in the following.

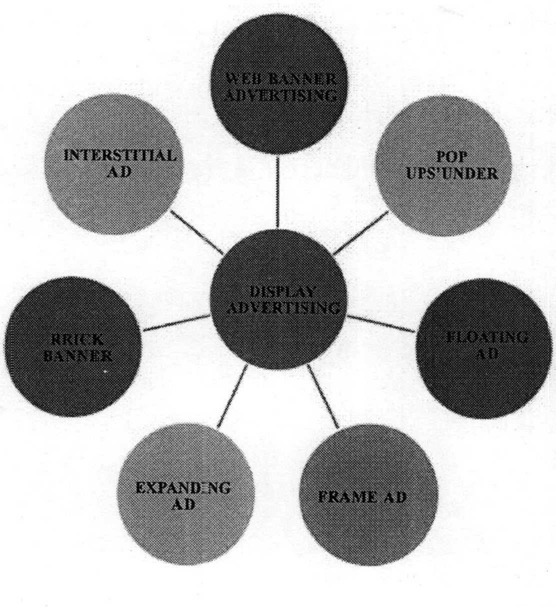

- Newspaper. Newspaper advertising can promote your business to a wide range of customers.
- Magazine. Advertising in a specialist magazine can reach your target market quickly and easily.

- Radio.
- Television.
- Directories.
- Outdoor and transit.
- Direct mail catalogues and leaflets.
- Online

14.7. Institutional Advertising

Institutional advertising focuses on touting the benefits, ideas, or philosophies of your business, or its entire industry, to enhance or repair its reputation rather than selling a product or service. Since institutional advertising attempts to build a positive image, it's closely related to public relations. In fact, it's a form of advertising that may be used in a public relations campaign. Institutional advertising relating to an entire industry is usually funded and developed by industrial, trade or professional associations rather than individual businesses.

14.8. Advertisement Media

This means through which advertisements is delivered to the target audience. Media include broadcast media, print media, cinema, hoardings and outdoor media.

14.9. Different Advertisement Media

The types of different advertisement media are discussed in the following.

- Television
- Radio
- Print Publications
- Internet
- Direct Mail
- Signage
- Product Placement
- Mobile Devices
- Sponsorships
- Other Media Outlets

14.10. Factors Determining Choice of Advertisement Media

Selection of a suitable medium for advertising is really a complex problem to the advertiser. There are a number of kinds and classes of media in the modern advertising. Hence, the advertising media selection means not only the choice of the right classes of media out also the individual medium within the class or classes. Besides there is no single medium that is best suited for all advertisers. In reality, a medium which is best suited for one may be almost useless for another. The medium once employed for advertising a particular product itself may be found unsuited subsequently. Therefore, the right choice of a medium calls for a careful analysis. If the medium is unsuited the whole amount of money spent on the advertising campaign shall turn to be a waste. The advertiser, therefore, while selecting the media, should consider the following factors:

Class of the audience: Firstly, the advertiser must note the class of the audience to be influenced by the medium. The audience can be classified into different groups by their social status, age, income, educational standard, religion, cultural interests. They may also be divided into men and women.

Extent of coverage: Secondly, the advertiser must consider the number of audience to be covered by the medium. Every media has a general as well as an effective circulation. The general circulation is made up of the total number of people who read or subscribe to the media. The effective circulation is the number prospective customers who read it and the number of those who influences sales, though they may not buy for themselves. Effective circulation must be considered while estimating the number of people to be covered. The extent to which the medium reaches the same audience as that covered by some other media i.e., the percentage of over-lapping must also be taken into account.

Nature of the product: Nature of the product itself is a principal factor governing the selection of the medium. Products can be classified into various kinds consumer's products and manufacturer's products etc.

Nature of the competition: The nature of the competition exerts greater influence of the selection of the media. If the competition is stiff utmost care is needed in the selection of medium and a larger advertising budget is also required. In many cases where the advertising copy is similar or the choice of the media solely determines the effectiveness of the campaign as compared with that of the other competitors.

Reputation of the medium: Newspapers and magazines can offer a beautiful illustration for the reputation of the media. There are a few newspapers and magazines which have international reputation with a high readership. Advertisements in such magazines and newspapers are generally recognized and believed as true. Such advertisements also add prestige to the product.

Cost of the media: Cost of the medium in most cases, is an important factor in the selection of the medium. Advertisements in certain media are expensive. For instance, TV and Radio advertisements. Magazines and newspaper advertisements are generally considered as less expensive. Yet, certain magazines and newspapers, having larger circulation and high reputation charge higher rates. The rates also differ depending upon the space occupied and the preferential positions. The first page of a newspaper is rarely missed by the reader. Hence they have more attention value, than the advertisements presented anywhere inside the newspaper.

Time and location of buying decisions: The location of the audience and the time by which it should reach them must also be looked into. This consideration also enables the advertiser to keep his retail outlets in the proximity of the customers.

14.11. Limitation of Advertising

The following are the main limitations of advertising:

a) Less Forceful

Absence of personal touch makes advertising less forceful. Paying attention to the message is not compulsory for the customers.

b) Lack of Feedback

It is very difficult to judge the effectiveness of an advertising message as there is no accurate feedback regarding its impact.

c) Inflexibility

Advertising message is standardized and hence cannot be changed according to the requirements of different customers.

d) Low Effectiveness

An increase in the volume of advertising has made it difficult to make any advertising message in general to be received properly by the target customers. Many messages don'ts really get even noticed, not to speak of being effective etc.

14.12. Advertising Budget

An advertising budget is an estimation of a company's promotional expenditures over a period of time. An advertising budget is the money a company is willing to set aside to accomplish its marketing objectives. When creating the advertising budget, a company must weigh the trade-offs between spending one additional advertising dollar with the amount of revenue that dollar will bring in as revenue.

14.13. Factor Governing Size of Advertising Budget

Before finalizing the advertising budget of an organization or a company, one has to take a look on the favorable and unfavorable market conditions which will have an impact on the advertising budget. The market conditions to watch out for are as follows:

- Frequency of the advertisement
- Competition and Clutter
- Market Share of the Product
- Product Life Cycle Stage

Frequency of the Advertisement

This means the number of times advertise has been shown with the description of the product or service, in the granted time slots. So here, if any company needs more advertising frequency for its product, then the company will have to increase its advertising budget.

Competition and Clutter

The companies may have many competitors for its product. And also there are plenty of advertisements shown which is called clutter. The company has to then increase their advertising budget.

Market Share

To get a good market share in comparison to their competitors, the company should have a better product in terms of quality, uniqueness, demand and catchy advertisements with resultant response of the customers. All this is possible if the advertisement budget is high.

Product Life Cycle (PLC) Stage

If the company is a newcomer or if the product is on its introduction stage, then the company has to keep the budget high to make place in the market with the existing players and to have frequent advertisements. As the time goes on and product becomes older, the advertising budget can come down as then the product doesn't need frequent advertising. When the market conditions are studied thoroughly, then the company has to set up its advertising budget accordingly. For setting advertising budget, there are four methods: They are as follows.

Percentage of Sales: In this method, the budget is decided on the basis of the sales of the product from previous year records or from the predicted future sales. This is a pure prediction based method and best applicable to the companies which have fixed annual sales. But if in case there is a requirement for more promotional activities then this method has a disadvantage because there will be decrease in advertisements as the budget is fixed.

Affordability: this method is generally used by the small companies. Only the companies which have funds and can afford advertising opt for this method. The companies can go for advertising at any time in whole year whenever they have money to spend. The amount spent also varies from time to time as per the advertisements takes place.

Best guess: This method is basically for newcomers who have just entered the market and they have no knowledge or say they are not aware of how the market is and how much to spend on advertising. Thus, this method is applied by the higher level executives of the company as they are the only experienced people.

14.14. Methods of Framing Advertising Budget

There are different types of methods which are used for framing the advertising budget. Some of the methods used widely for framing advertising budget are discussed in the following one after another.

I) Affordable method

This is a very simple method of budget allocation. After the budget has been allocated in all the areas i.e. all the other expenses have been taken care of the company then allocates the left over money for the advertisements. This method is also called "All you can afford". Those companies, which follow this method, consider advertisement as expenditure and no expectations on returns are associated with this method. These firms believe that advertising is tactical and not strategic and hence does not need much attention. Companies use this method, at the level of their affordability. Small businesses often use this method with the logic that the company cannot spend more on advertising than the amount it has left after the other expenses. Another logic is that the products should be good in itself and then it will sell automatically without much of advertisements. This method is clearly an outcome of no sound decision making. The company could be overspending or under spending a well. The fact that some firms follow this method is a clear indication of their lack of knowledge and poor understanding of the role of advertisements.

II) Arbitrary Allocation

This method seems to be a weaker method than the affordable method for setting a budget. The arbitrary allocation method is completely dependent on the management's discretion and hence has no theoretical basis. The budget is determined by management solely. They on the basis of what they feel to be necessary. So ultimately the decision depends on the psychological and economical build up of the people in the management and not on the market requirements.

The arbitrary allocation approach has no obvious advantages because of the following factors.

i. There has been no systematic thinking

ii. No objectives have been budgeted for

iii. The concept and purpose of advertising and promotion have been largely ignored.

It is thus understood that that the manager believes some money must be spent on advertising and promotion and that is why he picks up an amount, which has no logical explanation. Amazingly there are many companies both large and small, profit making and non-profit making who continue to set their budgets this way. It is now upon the readers to decide whether this method should be used or not.

III) Percentage of Sales method

This is the most commonly used method for budget setting. Large firms generally go by this method. According to this method, advertising and promotions budget is based on sales of the product. Management determines the amount by either.

- By taking a percentage of the sales revenue.
- Assigning a fixed amount of the unit product cost to promotion and multiplying this amount by the number of units sold.

Some companies instead of considering the past sales consider the percentage-of-projected future sales as a base. This method also uses either a straight percentage of projected sales or a unit cost projection. In the straight-percentage method, the marketing manager estimates projected sales for the coming year. The budget is a percentage of these sales, often an industry standard percentage. In its simplest application, a fixed percentage of last year's sales figure is allocated as the budget.

For example, suppose the total sales of a company ABC Pvt. Ltd. in 2005-2006 were Rs 20,00,000. Now according to this method the simplest calculation for advertisement budget is say 10% of the last year's sales. So the advertisement budget for the year 2006-2007 is 10% of Rs 20, 00,000 i.e. Rs 20,00,00. In case the ad budget is to be decided on the basis of sales units, let us assume that the manufacturing cost per unit of table fan for ABC Pvt. Ltd. is Rs 500 and the advertising money allocated per unit is Rs 30. The projected sales figure is 1,00,000 fans for the coming year 2007-2008, then the total advertising budget can be calculated as Rs 1,00, 000 x 30 = 30,00,000). The percentage figure selected is definitely not a standard percentage across any industry. This figure varies from one industry to the other and also among different firms in the same industry. It depends on the company policy. Actual money spent varies considerably depending on the individual company's total sales figure. As shown in the example the budget for a current year depends on the sales of the last year. Now if a company keeps the percentage fixed and then sales this year decreases then advertisement budget for next year is also less. But marketing says that if the sales are less in a year one way out of many to increase it in the next year could be an increase in the advertisement and promotional budget. Thus one advantage of using future sales as a base is that the budget is not based on last year s sales. As the market changes, management should consider the effect of these changes on sales into next year's forecast rather than relying on past data. There are a number of advantages associated with this method. It is somewhat financially safe and helps a company keep advertisement spending within limits irrespective of the fact whether the base is past year's sales or what the firm expects to sell in the upcoming year. This method is simple, straightforward, and easy to implement. Regardless of which basis-past or future sales-is employed, the calculations used to arrive at a budget are not difficult. This budgeting approach is generally stable when competing firms spend approximately the same percentage of their sales on promotion. Promotion expenditures vary with what company is aiming for in terms of sales. It encourages management to think of the relationship among promotion cost, selling price and profit per unit. This method is suitable for the companies whose ad budget is small relative to sales however the percentage-of-sales method has some disadvantages as well. The basic premise on which the budget is established is sales. As just discussed if the level of sales determines the amount of advertising and promotions to be spent then the cause-and-effect relationship between advertising and sales is reversed. It treats advertising as an expense associated with making a sale rather than an investment. Companies that consider promotional expenditures an investment and reap the rewards. In explaining the advantages it was just mentioned that since it is a percentage of sales, either past or future expected, the method is stable. Now this can happen when all firms in the industry uses a similar percentage, but then what happens if one firm varies from this standard percentage? The problem is that this method does not allow for changes in strategy either internally or from competitors. But this is a highly impractical proposition because there are many kinds of market structures and in any time the leader can choose to divert from the standard. The percentage-of-sales method of budgeting may result in severe misappropriation of funds i.e. over budgeting or under budgeting. When sales decrease we may need more budget in advertisement as decrease in budget might lead to further decrease in incremental sales. The percentage-of-sales method is also difficult to employ for new product introductions because in this case there is no sales history available. Also projections of future sales may be difficult, if the product is highly innovative and absolutely new in the market.

Caselet: Marlboro

Marlboro cigarettes were introduced in the 1920s. The brand share was only one per cent in the early 1950s. The company invested heavily in building brand image in 1954 (cowboy country) and now the brand share among young smokers is in excess of 60% in the USA.

Caselet: Glaxo

When Glaxo introduced Zantac (Zinetac in India), the medication for gastric ulcer, it was forecasted to gain no more than 10% share against the well-entrenched Tagamet. Glaxo's investment-driven campaign helped Zantac achieve more than 50% share and became the leading brand.

IV) Percentage of Profits method

In this method, companies set their budget at a certain percentage of their current or forecasted profits. The problems and advantages of this method is more or less in line with the previous method. Moreover the cost factor is also there which has an effect on profit. Now due to changes in macro environmental factors like, political, social, demographic, economic (inflation) and legal the cost component might change over time and across geography in the same industry. This in turn will affect the stability of this method of budget setting.

V) Unit of Sale Method

Consumer durable firms make use of this method as a variant on sales percentage. While it mostly works out same as a sales percentage, here the firm puts an amount of advertising expenses on the unit as add on. This method may also be referred to as the fixed-sum-per-unit-of product method. It is based on the premise that a specific amount of advertising is required for marketing each unit. This method proves more useful especially in the case of advertising of speciality goods with higher prices, however this method might not prove efficient for consumer goods of lower price bracket because the market situations are very volatile and change frequently. This method is further undependable in case of fashion products as the market is even more dynamic.

VI) Historical Method

In this method last year's advertising budget is adopted for the year with a view that practically no change has taken place in the market and market growth is slow, which does not justify any addition to the budget. Last year's budget could be multiplied by a factor to cover media rate increase.

VII) Competitive Parity Method

This method involves setting budgets to match competitors' outlays and funds. In this method, the company monitors competitors' advertising and follows it. This method is generally used in markets in which advertising is heavier and it is felt absolutely important to the companies not to be left behind the competitors. Normally, it is felt that the brand leader needs to spend proportionately less as a share of total advertising to maintain its market share, while conversely a brand trying to improve its market share will have to spend proportionately more. But such a type of budgeting plan fails to reflect the firms' own advertising needs or marketing requirements. None of the marketing managers in practice ever will accept the fact that they set their advertising and promotions budgets on the basis of what their competitors allocate. But a close examination of their advertising expenditures, both as a percentage of sales and in respect to the media where they are allocated, will show little variation in the percentage-of-sales figures for firms within a given industry. The rationale for setting the budget this way is that the collective wisdom of the industry is involved. Some are of the opinion that since it takes the competition into consideration, marketplace is more stable and marketing warfare is minimized in turn minimizing the unusual or unrealistic ad expenditures. However there are a number of disadvantages with this method which are listed in the following.

- It ignores the fact that advertising and promotions are designed to accomplish specific objectives and not merely to face competition.
- It assumes that the ad campaigns will be equally effective because firms have done similar expenditures. This highly ignores the contributions of creative executions and/or media allocations.
- It ignores a very natural possibility that some companies simply make better products than others.
- There is no guarantee that competitors will not increase or decrease its own expenditures, regardless of what other companies do because competition cannot be fully assessed at the beginning of a financial year.
- Finally there is no reason why competitive parity should avoid promotional wars. We are a witness to the Coke versus Pepsi wars.

Nevertheless companies employ the competitive parity method. But a wiser decision is not to ignore the competition but use this method in conjunction with the percentage-of-sales or other methods. Marketing never suggests to always keep parity with competitors however it suggests a very meticulous vigilant on them.

VIII) Return on Investment (ROI)

In the percentage-of-sales method, advertising budget depends on the level of sales. But advertising causes sales. In the marginal analysis and S-shaped curve approaches increase in advertisement budgets may lead to increases in sales. In other words the advertisement budget can be considered as an investment. In the ROI budgeting method, advertising and promotions are considered investments, like plant and equipment. In other words investments in advertisements lead to certain returns. Like other aspects of the firm's efforts, advertising and promotion are expected to earn a certain return. To many the ROI method is an ideal method of setting advertisement budget. But in reality it is rarely possible to assess the returns provided by the promotional effort-at least as long as sales continue to be the basis for evaluation.

IX) Vidale and Wolfe's model

This model calls for a larger advertising budget, as it believes that higher the sales response rate, higher the sales decay rates i.e. the rate at which customers forget the advertising and brand, and higher the untapped sales potential. This model leaves out other important factors, such as the rate of competitive advertising and the effectiveness of company's ads.

X) The compromise model

In actual practice, marketing executives usually blend some well-accepted methods and arrive at a compromise budget. The compromise however does not mean a senseless averaging of the different methods; instead it is a logical and practical approach. The marketing men know that they will have to find answer to certain basic questions described below in order to arrive at the compromise budget.

- Who are the target audience?
- What is the size of audience and location?
- What are the media available for advertising?
- Which media combination is suitable?
- What kind of campaign is required?
- What frequency of advertisement is required?

XI) John little model

This method is an adaptive control method for setting the advertising budget. According to this, suppose the company has set an advertising expenditure rate based on its most current information. It spends this rate in all markets except in a subset of 2n markets randomly drawn. In n test markets, the company spends at a lower rate and in the other n markets it spends at a higher rate. This procedure will yield information on the average sales created by low, medium and high rates of advertising that can be used to update the parameters of the sales response function. The updated function can be used to determine the best advertising rate for the next period. If this experiment is conducted each period, advertising expenditure will closely track optimal advertising expenditure.

XII) Total Group Budget

In case of multi location and multi product line firms, a total amount is decided as advertising and each strategic business unit receives a share according to their needs. This method helps the group to segregate some amount for corporate group advertising for building the image of the organization.

XIII) Operational Modeling

Market research gives advertising expenses, market response and sales per advertising figures and the modeling is done to explain the budget.

XIV) Composite Method

This method takes in to consideration several factors in formulating the advertising budget which include indices like firm's past sales, future sales projection, production capacity, market environment, sales problems, efficiency level of sales personnel, seasonality of the market, regional considerations, changing media scenario and changing media impact on the target market segment, market trends and results of advertising and marketing.

XV) Incremental Concept Approach to Advertisement Budgeting

According to Managerial Economics a business maximizes its profits at that point where the incremental cost is equal to the incremental revenue. Businessmen are fully aware that as long as the cost of producing one extra unit is less than the revenue generated by it, the business is a profitable one. Any further production after the level at which the additional per unit cost equals the per-unit additional revenue will be unprofitable. Some of the key areas with respect to this method are discussed in the following.

- A similar approach can be applied for advertisement as well. Advertisers can keep on increasing the advertisement budget to the extent where the last unit spent on advertising is equal to the net profit contribution by the additional sales generated from the promotion.
- From managerial economics viewpoint, this is the optimum advertisement expenditure giving maximum profit. This is also referred to as the concept of marginality. In other words the advertisement expenditure should be carried on to that point where there is no further scope of increasing the incremental revenue from the incremental expenditure on advertising. Also the total advertisement budget should be apportioned among various media and product lines until marginal returns are equal.
- In spite of being theoretically sound, this model is very difficult to be implemented because it is very difficult to measure the additional profit generated by additional expenditure on advertisement.

14.15. Advertising Agency

Firm that (a) creates new promotional ideas, (b) designs print, radio, television, and internet advertisements, (c) books advertisement space and time, (d) plans and conducts advertising campaigns, (e) commissions research and surveys, and (f) provides other such services that help a client in entering and succeeding in a chosen market. In general, advertising agencies are not deemed agents of the advertisers, because they act as principals for the services they buy on behalf of their clients.

14.16. Function of an Advertising Agency

The functions of an advertising agency are illustrated below with the help of a visual representation.

14.17. Factors Affecting Selection of Advertising Agency

Businesses come to the conclusion of hiring an external ad agency, only when they are certified of the fact that the agency will help them execute their advertising and promotional campaigns more effectively. This is because the individuals working in an agency are not just passionate about advertising, but are also knowledgeable experts in their own field and thrive on the values of unity and dedication for the project at hand. Most advertisers work in collaboration with the hired agency, in order to ensure that the work is carried out smoothly and also adheres to industry standards. With their immense experience and technical know-how of the industry, ad agencies can work wonders for the promotional activities of any business. But before you decide to hire the services of an ad agency for your advertising efforts, you must conduct thorough research on the background of the agency. Few relevant points in this regard are discussed in the following.

Total extent of the Agency

In most cases, the larger the agency, the better quality of services offered by the same. When an agency operates on a larger scale, it is pretty obvious that it has the financial prowess to hire a good amount of ad professionals. Also, smaller agencies do not have the skill to provide a wide range of services. With the advent of large agencies, it is always preferable to consult a huge ad agency.

Number of clients under the Agencies' belt

Most agencies have their own website or brochure. You must log on to their website and view the existing clients being handled by the agency, before hiring them to carry out your own work. If the agency has a client on board that deals in the same line of products as yours, it is recommended to avoid the agency in order to avoid the occurrence of repetitive work and exchange of crucial business information with the competitor.

Types of services on offer

It is essential to view the types of ad and non-ad based services offered by the agency. Depending on your promotional needs and size or extent, you can hire a small or a large ad agency accordingly. Moreover, certain types of agencies specialise in a particular field such as FMCG advertising while other agencies may specialise in industrial marketing.

Creative talent possessed by the Agency

You must always calculate the number and amount of creative personnel owned by the ad agency, as it forms the basic criteria for selection. Creativity can be calculated on the basis of factors such as quality of personnel, experience, diversity, and specialisation and so on.

Media Contacts possessed by the Agency

With the help of adequate media contacts, the agency will be able to accommodate the desired place, date and time required for the promotion of your business. Agencies that closely work with most communication channels such as radio channels, TV channels, publishers, printers and so on are the ones to consider.

Agency location and Proximity

It is important to calculate the location of the agency for better communication and contact with the agency. The closer the proximity to the agency, the better convenience, control and involvement with its activities.

Methods of payment and compensation

It is good to compare the ad rates demanded by different agencies before zeroing in on the perfect one. This is because different agencies charge different amounts and promotional activities are always bound by tight budgets.

Total amount of involvement

An agency must show complete respect for the client and allow it to take part in the activities, give its feedback and work with the same form time-to-time. Moreover, monthly reports and expenses should be shown by the advertiser on an alternate basis.

Endorsement of the Agency

Agencies that are endorsed by television, radio and newspapers are the ones that are the most recognisable and this credit is eventually passed on to the clients. These agencies have a specific code of conduct to follow and an image to portray, which makes them the most reliable in the industry.

Agency Ranking

An agency that works hard to provide results and easy to approach, is the one to consult. Which is why, it is important to research the current market standing held by the agency? Agencies with a higher ranking are more reliable and provide better returns on investment.

14.18. Advertising Appeal

Advertising appeals aim to influence the way consumers view themselves and how buying certain products can prove to be beneficial for them. The message conveyed through advertising appeals influences the purchasing decisions of consumers. Advertising uses appeals as a way of persuading people to buy certain products. Advertising appeals are designed in a way so as to create a positive image of the individuals who use certain products.

14.19. Classification of Advertising Appeals

The most important types of advertising appeals include emotional and rational appeals. Emotional appeals are often effective for the youth while rational appeals work well for products directed towards the older generation. Here are just some of the various different kinds of advertising appeals seen in the media today.

Emotional

An emotional appeal is related to an individual's psychological and social needs for purchasing certain products and services. Many consumers are emotionally motivated or driven to make certain purchases. Advertisers aim to cash in on the emotional appeal and this works particularly well where there is not much difference between multiple product brands and its offerings. Emotional appeal includes personal and social aspects.

Personal

Some personal emotions that can drive individuals to purchase products include safety, fear, love, humour, joy, happiness, sentiment, stimulation, pride, self esteem, pleasure, comfort, ambition, nostalgia etc.

Social

Social factors cause people to make purchases and include such aspects as recognition, respect, involvement, affiliation, rejection, acceptance, status and approval.

Fear

Fear is also an important factor that can have incredible influence on individuals. Fear is often used to good effect in advertising and marketing campaigns of beauty and health products including insurance. Advertising experts indicate that using moderate levels of fear in advertising can prove to be effective.

Humour

Humour is an element that is used in around 30% of the advertisements. Humour can be an excellent tool to catch the viewer's attention and help in achieving instant recall which can work well for the sale of the product. Humour can be used effectively when it is related to some benefit that the customer can derive without which the joke might overpower the message.

Sex Appeal

Sex and nudity have always sold well. Sexuality, sexual suggestiveness, over sexuality or sensuality raises curiosity of the audience and can result in strong feelings about the advertisement. It can also result in the product appearing interesting. However use of sex in types of advertising appeals can have a boomerang effect if it is not used carefully. It can interfere with the actual message of the advertisement and purpose of the product and can also cause low brand recall. If this is used then it should be an integral part of the product and should not seem vulgar. The shift should be towards sensuality.

Music Appeal

Music can be used as types of advertising appeals as it has a certain intrinsic value and can help in increasing the persuasiveness of the advertisement. It can also help capture attention and increase customer recall.

Scarcity Appeal

Scarcity appeals are based on limited supplies or limited time period for purchase of products and are often used while employing promotional tools including sweepstakes, contests etc.

Rational Appeal

Rational appeals as the name suggests aims to focus on the individual's functional, utilitarian or practical needs for particular products and services. Such appeals emphasize the characteristics and features of the product and the service and how it would be beneficial to own or use the particular brand. Print media is particularly well suited for rational appeals and is often used with good success. It is also suited for business to business advertisers and for products that are complex and that need high degree of attention and involvement.

Masculine Feminine Appeal

Used in cosmetic or beauty products and also clothing. This type of appeal aims at creating the impression of the perfect person. The message is that the product will infuse the perfection or the stated qualities in you.

Brand Appeal

This appeal is directed towards people who are brand conscious and wish to choose particular products to make a brand statement.

Snob Appeal

This appeal is directed towards creating feeling of desire or envy for products that are termed top of the line or that have considerable qualities of luxury, elegance associated with them.

Adventure Appeal

This appeal is directed towards giving the impression that purchasing a product will change the individual's life radically and fill it with fun, adventure and action.

Less than Perfect Appeal

Advertisements often try to influence people to make certain purchases by pointing out their inadequacies or making them feel less perfect and more dissatisfied with their present condition. These types of advertising appeals are used in cosmetic and health industries.

Romance Appeal

These advertisements display the attraction between the sexes. The appeal is used to signify that buying certain products will have a positive impact on the opposite sex and improve your romantic or love life. Fragrances, automobiles and other products use these types of advertising appeals.

Emotional Words/Sensitivity Appeal

These advertisements are used to drive at and influence the sensitivities of consumers.

Youth Appeal

Advertisements that reflect youth giving aspects or ingredients of products use these types of appeals. Cosmetic products in particular make use of these appeals.

Endorsement

Celebrities and well known personalities often endorse certain products and their pitching can help drive the sales.

Play on Words

Advertisements also make effective use of catch phrases to convey the message. Such appeals help in brand recognition and recall and can be quite popular with the youth in particular.

Statistics

Advertisements also use statistics and figures to display aspects of the product and its popularity in particular.

Plain Appeal

These advertisements use every day aspects of life and appeal to ordinary people regarding the use of a product or service.

Bandwagon Appeal

This type of advertising appeal is meant to signify that since everybody is doing something you should be a part of the crowd as well. It appeals towards the popularity aspect or coolness aspect of a person using a particular product or service

14.20. Advertising Copy

An advertisement copy is the text used in the advertisement, be it print, radio, television or other form of advertisement. The text so used can be in the form of dialogs, some catchy phrase, a company's motto or slogan or any word.

14.21. Essentials of a Good Advertising Copy

The advertisement is technically known as **advertising copy.** It consists of the written or spoken message. According to Sohrab R. Davar, an effective advertising copy should contain the following qualities.

(i) Attention Value: The first essential of a good advertisement is that it must be so designed as to attract the attention of those whom it is addressed. Most of the people are very busy and have a very cursory or hurried look at advertisements. Unless the advertisement can draw their attention, it will go waste. The following techniques may be used to build attention or display value in advertising copy:

(a) By using catchy but short headlines. The headlines may be a slogan or reference to the quality of the product.

(b) By using pictures or drawings of the product being advertised. .

(c) By putting a question, e.g.; 'Is your premium due this month?' by LIC

(d) By quoting price where the price is comparatively low and is likely to attract the attention of the customers,

(e) By inserting reply coupons for gifts or free literature.

(f) By using artistic borders, blank spaces, bold types, bright colors, etc., which bring the message into sharp focus by separating it out from the rest of the material? Use of right page or space and underlining of key words also help to attract attention to the advertising copy.

(ii) ***Memorizing Value:*** The design and layout of the advertising copy should be such that it has a lasting Expression on the minds of the people. Repeated use of brand names and trademarks helps to make the advertisement memorable. A picture depicting the use of the product for a specific need is useful. Association of the product with a symbol or sketch also helps to create a long term impact on mind. For instance, the smiling baby has become associated with Murphy radios.

(iii) ***Suggestive Value:*** The advertising copy should suggest the advantages and uses of the product. Emphasis on the superiority of the product and its necessity helps to create customers' interest. People take interest in a product only when they feel it will solve their needs and give them good satisfaction.

'Amul builds healthy bodies', 'where there is Lifebuoy, there is health', 'Smoke Panama, they are good to the last puff, 'Fanta Orange so good one feels to be thirsty' are a few examples of suggestive value.

(iv) ***Educational Value:*** A good advertising copy should educate the people by providing knowledge relating to the mode of using the product, precautions required in its use, sources where fee product is available, services available with the product and new uses of the product.

14.22. Types of Advertising Copy

The different types pertaining to advertising copy are discussed in the following.

(i) Institutional Copy

Institutional Copy neither sells nor the products neither the service but the name of the business house. The aim is to build the sound edifice of reputation for the selling house. It seeks to build goodwill through its philosophy, objectives, and policies towards public so that the prospects remember it.

(ii) Reason Why Copy

Reason Why Copy offers reasons as to why the customer is expected to buy a product or service of the advertiser. It appeals straight to the intellect or the judgment of an individual than emotion or impulses. It attempts to prove the product superiority by means of evidences in the forms of performance test, records, testimonials, guarantees and the like.

(iii) Human Interest Copy

Human Interest Copy appeals to the emotional and the senses than intellect and the judgment, sympathy, affection, love, fear, humour, curiosity and other emotional appeals are used to the sense of sight, touch, taste, smell and hearing.It tells about the product in relation to the people instead of conforming to the facts about the products. It takes several forms of which four are very significant namely, 'fear', 'humorous', 'story' and 'predicament' copy.

(iv) Suggestive Copy

Suggestive Copy tries to suggest or pinpoint or convey the message of the advertiser directly or indirectly to the readers. Much is left to the reader to infer the ad message. Like a poem, suggestive language is freely used where the hidden meaning is to be picked by the readers. Such copy can be 'direct' or 'indirect' suggestive copy. The first tells directly about the products or services of the company while the latter does indirectly.

(v) Expository Copy

Expository Copy is open copy that exposes unlike suggestive copy. It is so open that the facts are given in very simple and clear way so that there is no need for interpretation. The information given is so clear and concise that hardly it taxes the reader's brain. It makes possible effortless grasp and act.

14.23. Structure of Advertising Copy

The structure of advertising copy is described below.

- Headline
- Subhead line
- Body Copy
- Tag line
- Logo

Headlines

- Headlines usually have the largest font size. It is usually 5 to 8 words in length. Use simple, easy to understand words.
- Appeal to the self Interest of the audience.

The Headline has several functions

- Gives news
- Reinforces the brand
- Attracts attention
- Attracts target market

- Increases curiosity
- Arouses emotions
- Calls to action

Subhead Line

- This optional device often occurs right below the headline.
- The subhead line uses a few words that clarify, reinforces or explains the headline.
- The goal is to provide a smooth transition into the body copy.

Body Copy

- This is the text in the advertisement that provides support and details about the product or the current offer.
- Often the body copy will use present tense, singular.
- Use Active verbs.
- Vary the sentence length.
- Involve the audience.

Many types of Body Copy are possible.

- Benefits of the product
- Testimonial from customers
- Expert opinion
- Narrative about the product or a customer
- Examples
- Options
- Rhetorical questions
- Statistics about the product
- Positioning information

Tagline

- Often this is the brand slogan that has been used for years

Logo

- Brand symbol and/or words

14.24. Copy Testing

It is a specialized field of marketing research that determines an advertisement's effectiveness based on consumer responses, feedback, and behavior. Also known as pre-testing, it might address all media channels including television, print, radio, outdoor signage, internet, and social media. Types of copy testing measurements.

(i) Recall

The predominant copy testing measure of the 1950s and 1960s, Burke's Day-After Recall (DAR) was interpreted to measure an ad's ability to "break through" into the mind of the consumer and register a message from the brand in long-term memory (Honomichl). Once this measure was adopted by Procter and Gamble, it became a research staple (Honomichl).

(ii) Link between Recall Scores and Actual Sales

In the 70s, 80s, and 90s, validation efforts found no link between recall scores and actual sales (Adams & Blair; Blair; Blair & Kuse; Blair & Rabuck; Jones; Jones & Blair; MASB; Mondello; Stewart). For example, Procter and Gamble reviewed 10 year's worth of split-cable tests (100 total) and found no significant relationship between recall scores and sales (Young, pp. 3–30). In addition, Wharton University's Leonard Lodish conducted an even more extensive review of test market results and also failed to find a relationship between recall and sales (Lodish pp. 125-139).

(iii) *Breakthrough Measure*

The 1970s also saw a re-examination of the "breakthrough" measure. As a result, an important distinction was made between the attention-getting power of the creative execution and how well "branded" the ad was. Thus, the separate measures of attention and branding were born (Young, p. 12).

14.25. Types of Copy Editing

The different types of copy editing are discussed in the following.

(i) Persuasion: In the 1970s and 1980s, after DAR was determined to be a poor predictor of sales, the research industry began to depend on a measure of persuasion as an accurate predictor of sales. This shift was led, in part, by researcher Horace Schwerin who pointed out, "the obvious truth is that a claim can be well remembered but completely unimportant to the prospective buyer of the product the solution the marketer offers is addressed to the wrong need" (Honomichl). As

with DAR, it was Procter and Gamble's acceptance of the ARS Persuasion measure (also known as brand preference) that made it an industry standard. Recall scores were still provided in copy testing reports with the understanding that persuasion was the measure that mattered (Honomichl). Harold Ross of Mapes & Ross found that persuasion was a better predictor of sales than recall (Ross), and the predictive validity of ARS Persuasion to sales has been reported in several refereed publications (Adams & Blair; Jones & Blair; MASB; Mondello).

(ii)Diagnostic: The main purpose of diagnostic measures is optimization. Understanding diagnostic measures can help advertisers identify creative opportunities to improve executions.

(iii) Non-Verbal: Non-verbal measures were developed in response to the belief that much of a commercial's effects – e.g. the emotional impact may be difficult for respondents to put into words or scale on verbal rating statements. In fact, many believe the commercial's effects may be operating below the level of consciousness (Young, p. 7). According to researcher Chuck Young, "There is something in the lovely sounds of our favorite music that we cannot verbalize and it moves us in ways we cannot express" (Young, p. 22). In the 1970s, researchers sought to measure these non-verbal measures biologically by tracking brain wave activities as respondents watched commercials (Krugman). Others experimented with galvanic skin response, voice pitch analysis, and eye-tracking (Young, p. 22). These efforts were not popularly adopted, in part because of the limitations of the technology as well as the poor cost-effectiveness of what was widely perceived as academic, not actionable research. In the early 1980s the shift in analytical perspective from thinking of a commercial as the fundamental unit of measurement to be rated in its entirety, to thinking of it as a structured flow of experience, gave rise to experimentation with moment-by-moment systems. The most popular of these was the dial-a-meter response which required respondents to turn a meter, in degrees, toward one end of a scale or another to reflect their opinion of what was on screen at that moment. More recently, research companies have started to use psychological tests, such as the Stroop effect, to measure the emotional impact of copy. These techniques exploit the notion that viewers do not know why they react to a product, image, or ad in a certain way (or that they reacted at all) because such reactions occur outside of awareness, through changes in networks of thoughts, ideas, and images.

14.26. Sales Promotion – Meaning and Definition

Sales promotions are the set of marketing activities undertaken to boost sales of the product or service. Description: There are two basic types of sales promotions: trade and consumer sales promotions.

14.27. Advertising Effectiveness

Advertising effectiveness pertains to how well a company's advertising accomplishes the intended. Small companies use many different statistics or metrics to measure their advertising effectiveness.

14.28. Methods to Measure Advertising Effectiveness

There may be two types of methods to measure advertising effectiveness which are:

- Direct measures
- Indirect measures

In the following a brief discussion is made about the above measures.

Direct Measures of Advertising Effectiveness

Under direct measures, a relationship between advertising and sales is established. A comparison of sales of two periods or two periods or two markets may be done and the corresponding changes may be noted. The following are some of the methods that are generally used in measuring that advertising effects.

(i) Historical Sales Method

Some insights into the effectiveness of past advertising may be obtained by measuring the relationship between the advertising expenditure and the total sales of the product. A multiple regression analysis of advertising expenditure and sales over several time periods may be calculated. It would show how the changes in advertising expenditure have corresponding changes in sales volume. This technique estimates the contribution that advertising has made to explaining in a co relational manner rather than a casual sales, the variation in sales over the time periods covered in the study

(ii) Experimental Control Method

The other measure of advertising effectiveness is the method of experimental control where a casual relationship between advertising and sales is established. This method is quite expensive when related to other advertising effectiveness measuresyet it is possible to isolate advertising contribution to sales. Moreover this can be done as a pre-test to aid advertising in choosing between alternative creative designs. Media schedules expenditure levels or some combination of these advertising decision areas. One experimental approach to measuring the sales effectiveness of advertising is test marketing.

Before-after with Control Group Design: This classic design uses several test and control cities in this design two types of cities are selected. Cities in which advertising campaigns are affected may be named as test cities and other cities may be called central cities. First of all, the normal sales level is calculated for both type of cities prior to advertising campaign, and then the advertising campaign is presented to the test cities and not the central cities. The effect of advertising campaign, can then, be measured by subtracting the amount of post campaign figure of sale from the pre campaign sale figures in test cities

Multivariable Experimental Designs: While the experimental design discussed above yields a reasonably accurate estimate of the effects of the advertising on sales, it is not successful in explaining the success or failure of the campaign itself. Multivariable designs produce these explanations and are, therefore used by some very large firm because of their diagnostic value.The power of this multivariable factorial design is explained by G.H.Brown, former Fords Director of Marketing Research. For any single medium, eight possible geographic areas have been exposed and eight have not been exposed. Thus, in this experimental model it is possible to evaluate how each individual medium behaves alone and in all possible combinations with other media.

(iii) Indirect Measures of Advertising Effectiveness

As it is very difficult to measure the direct effect of advertising on company's profits or sales, most firms rely heavily on indirect measures. These measures do not evaluate the effects of advertisements directing on sales or profits but all other factors such as customer awareness or attitude or customer recall of advertising message affect the sales or profits or goals of the business indirectly. Despite the uncertainties about the relationship between the intermediate effects of advertising and the ultimate results, there is no other alternative but to use indirect measures. The most commonly used measures are:

Exposure to Advertisement: In order to be effective, the advertisement must gain exposure. The management is concerned about the number of target audiences who see or hear the organization message set in the advertisement. Without exposure, advertisement is bound to failure. Marketers or advertisers may obtain an idea of exposure generated by the medium by examining its circulation or audience data which reveal the number of copies of the magazine, newspaper or journal sold the number of persons passing the billboards or riding in transit facilities, or the number of persons living in the televiewing or radio listening area, and the number of persons switching on their T.V. and radio sets at various points of time. This number can be estimated by interviewing the numbers of the audience for different media.

Attention or Recall of Advertising Message Content: This is one of the widely used measures of advertising results. Under this measure, a recall of the message content among a specified group or groups or prospective customers is measured within 24 hours of the exposure of the advertisement. Attention value is the chief quality of the advertising copy the advertisements cannot be said to be effective unless they attract the attention of the target consumers. There are two methods for evaluating the attention getting value of the advertisements. One is pre-test and the other is post-test. In a pre-test evaluation, the consumers are asked to indicate the extent to which they recognize or recall the advertisement, they have already seen. This test is conducted in the laboratory setting. Here consumers read, hear or listen to the advertisement and then researchers ask question regarding the advertisement just to test the recall and then evaluate it. In post-test method, the consumers are asked questions about the indication of recognition or recall after the advertisement has been run. These measures assume that customers can recall or recognize what they have viewed or listened to. Various mechanical devices are being used in the western countries which provide indices of attention such as eye-camera etc.

Brand Awareness: The marketers who rely heavily on advertising often appraise its effectiveness by measuring the customer's awareness about the particular product or brand. The assumption of this type of measure is that there is a direct relationship between the advertisements and the awareness. This type of measure is also subject to the same criticisms as is applicable to direct measures of effectiveness (sales measures because awareness is also not the direct result of the advertisements. It is also affected by many other factors. But, for new products, changes in awareness can often be attributed to the influence of advertising.

Comprehension: Consumers generally use advertisements as a means of obtaining information about the product, brand or the manufacturer. They cannot be informed unless they comprehend the message (grasp the message mentally and understand it fully). Various tests for valuating comprehension are available. One is recall tests – an indicator of comprehension because it is evident that consumers recall what they comprehend. Another measure of the variable is to ask questions about subjects how much they have comprehended a message they have recently heard or seen. One may employ somewhat imprecise test of the comprehension of a newspaper and radio advertisement. One may ask typical target consumers from time to time such questions like 'what did you think of our new commercial?' and 'Did it get the message across'? The answers of these questions will provide sufficient insight into advertising decision making.

Attitude Change: Since advertising is considered to be one way of influencing the state of the mind of the audience towards a product, service or organisation, the results are very often measured in terms of attitudes among groups exposed to advertising communication. Several measures are used ranging from asking the questions about willingness to buy the likelihood of buying to the measurement of the extent to which specific attributes (such as modern or new) are associated with a product.

Action: One objective of advertisement may be assumed to be to stimulate action or behaviour. The action or intention to take an action may be measured on the intention to buy measuring instrument. Under this type of measure, consumers are asked to respond why they are interested in purchasing the product or brand. One type of action that advertisers attempt to induce is buying behaviour. The assumption is that if an increase in sales follows a decrease in advertising expenditure, the change in sales levels are good indicators of the effectiveness of advertising. Logic suggests that measurement of sales is preferable to other measurements. Thus, these above measures (direct or indirect) are used to evaluate the effectiveness of advertisements.

It seems from the analysis of the above methods of measuring advertising effectiveness that directly or indirectly changes in sales or profits are taken as the measuring rod of the effectiveness of the advertising. Acquire enhanced volumes of sales of products & services.

- Generate awareness about offerings.
- Induce trial of a new product & service.
- Motivate & impress trade channels.
- Change perception & create reassurance.
- Acquire enhanced volumes of sales of products & services.
- Generate awareness about offerings.
- Induce trial of a new product & service.
- Motivate & impress trade channels.
- Change perception & create reassurance.
- Acquire enhanced volumes of sales of products & services.
- Generate awareness about offerings.
- Induce trial of a new product & service.
- Motivate & impress trade channels.
- Change perception & create reassurance